METAL FABRICATION:
A Practical Guide

Robert L. O'Con
Richard H. Carr

Board of Cooperative Educational Services
of Suffolk County, New York

METAL FABRICATION:
A Practical Guide

PRENTICE-HALL, INC., Englewood Cliffs, New Jersey 07632

Library of Congress Cataloging in Publication Data

O'CON, ROBERT L. (date)
   Metal fabrication.

   Bibliography: p.
   Includes index.
   1. Metal-work. I. Carr, Richard H. II. Title.
TS205.026 1985   671.3   84-13322
ISBN 0-13-577685-6

Editorial/production supervision: *Theresa A. Soler*
Interior design: *Shari Ingerman*
Manufacturing buyer: *Anthony Caruso*

Printed in the United States of America
10 9 8 7 6 5 4 3 2 1

ISBN 0-13-577685-6 01

PRENTICE-HALL INTERNATIONAL, INC., *London*
PRENTICE-HALL OF AUSTRALIA PTY. LIMITED, *Sydney*
EDITORA PRENTICE-HALL DO BRASIL, LTDA., *Rio de Janeiro*
PRENTICE-HALL CANADA INC., *Toronto*
PRENTICE-HALL OF INDIA PRIVATE LIMITED, *New Delhi*
PRENTICE-HALL OF JAPAN, INC., *Tokyo*
PRENTICE-HALL OF SOUTHEAST ASIA PTE. LTD., *Singapore*
WHITEHALL BOOKS LIMITED, *Wellington, New Zealand*

CONTENTS

SECTION I
BASIC SHOP COMPETENCIES

SECTION II
STRUCTURAL STEEL AND PLATE FABRICATION

SECTION III
PRECISION SHEET METAL FABRICATION

17   PRECISION LAYOUT 220

18   JOINING AND FINISHING OPERATIONS 251

SECTION IV
ORNAMENTAL IRON WORK AND BLACKSMITHING

19   TOOLS AND EQUIPMENT USED 263

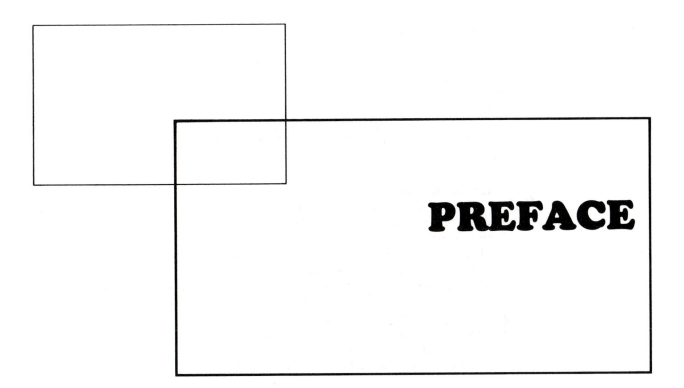

PREFACE

The student observer, when watching the experienced and skilled crafts-person performing a task, has for the most part focused attention on the obvious manipulative skills needed to produce any particular item. Thus the student of welding watches the way the instructor holds and manipulates the rod and torch. The apprentice machinist zeros in on the method of aligning the cutting tool in the tool post holder. The sheet metal mechanic, too, is observing the accurate forming of a precision chassis component in the press brake. Similarly, in drafting classes and engineering labs, theories and principles are being learned that ultimately take shape in the production shop.

That such specialization of skills has served our industrial system well needs no elaboration here. However, what is to be considered is the changeable nature of industrial systems and how such change can affect those specialists who work within the system as well as those students who have elected to follow a career path in metal fabrication.

The motivation to create this metal fabrication text stems from three concluding observations made after years of classroom and shop teaching, as well as years spent working as metal fabricators. The first observation relates to the need to differentiate between "training" and "education." A student can be trained to operate a wide variety of machines or to perform either a singular or a sequential operation. In highly methodized and repetitive manufacturing, this is not only desirable but relatively easy to accomplish. "Education," on the other hand, implies something more abstract, more elusive, and ultimately more valuable. By knowing, understanding, and intelligently applying specific training, the fabricator cannot only deal with subtle variations in the manufacturing process, but can also improve, sophisticate, and expand that process to make the work even more productive and personally rewarding. Specifically, it is the aim of this text not only to show how tools and machines are used in certain ways, but to explain and demonstrate the reasons why.

The second observation has to do with the fact that basic knowledge and skills always seem to be taught separate and apart from the realities of the shop. Mathematics and the associated computational skills, for instance, which may have been only exercises in chalk dust, take on new and critically important meaning to the student faced with the task of learning a marketable skill. The areas of general science also take on new dimensions when viewed in the light of practical applications so common in metal work. Here, too, the text will not only show how to work with materials using specific tools and methods, but also instruct and reinforce knowledge in those basic sciences that are an intrinsic component to modern and not-so-modern industrial processes.

The final purpose and aim of this text is to shorten what the philosopher John Lachs called "psychic distance." In his reference to the separation between thought and action, we draw on the analogy of the designer engineer contemplating a fabricated structure with no thought of the actual physical and mechanical requirements needed to make the part, and the shop fabricator who must execute the design autonomously and even robotically, each hoping and tenaciously betting that the other person knows what he or she is doing. Similarly, it is the purpose here to attempt to shorten the distance between the engineer, the designer, the draftsperson, the fabricator, and the student by treating each as an equal recipient of those basic competencies and skills common to all metalworking disciplines.

Robert L. O'Con
Richard H. Carr

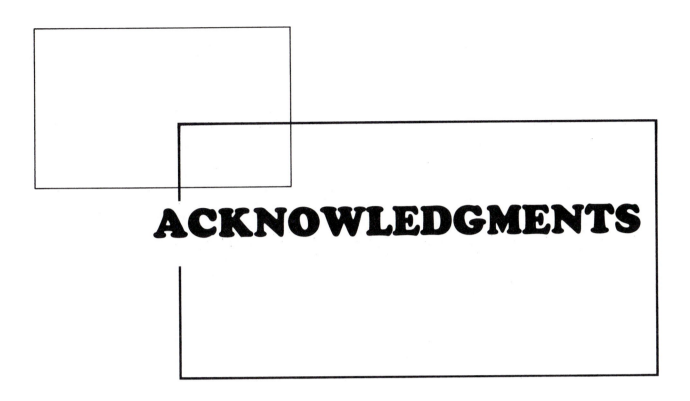

ACKNOWLEDGMENTS

A work of this nature is never accomplished without the help and encouragement of persons other than the authors. The following list of businessmen were very gracious in their permission to allow us to come into their shops and make the photographic record of their operations which accompany this text.

Mr. Vincent Leo, President
Vin-Mar Products Inc.
Bay Shore, New York

Mr. Daniel Michel, President
Michel Fabricators Inc.
Bohemia, New York

Additionally, the following firms provided certain charts, illustrations, and tables which appear throughout the book.

Joseph T. Ryerson and Sons
Jersey City, New Jersey

Norton Abrasives Company
Worcester, Massachusetts

The Office of Training and Education
OSHA (United States government)

Black and Decker Manufacturing Co.
Towson, Maryland

L.S. Starrett Company
Athol, Massachusetts

Buffalo Forge Company
Buffalo, New York

United Abrasives, Inc.
Mount Vernon, New York

Emerson Electric Company
Special Products Division
Hazelwood, Missouri

The Rawlplug Company
New Rochelle, New York

ESAB Heath Gas Cutting Division
Fort Collins, Colorado

Comeq, Incorporated
Baltimore, Maryland

Milwaukee Tool Corporation
Brookfield, Wisconsin

U.S. Amada, Ltd.
Buena Park, California

METAL FABRICATION:
A Practical Guide

"Go ahead, touch it"... "Feel any pulse?"... "Is there any heartbeat or body temperature?"... "There's no conscience either"... "This thing will rip off your fingers and grind up the stub of your hand without losing a minute of sleep that same night"....

Chapter 1

FABRICATING SAFETY

That lecture, given by a hard-faced but grandfatherly looking old foreman years ago, may seem a little melodramatic by today's standards. As movies and television give us our daily dose of make-believe and not so make-believe blood and gore, the safety lecture becomes something to think about for the moment but mostly just something to be endured until the real work and the real learning begins.

True enough, the safety lecture does come at the beginning and a good curriculum will continue to include it in specific instances as it progresses. Then, on the job, the safety posters and slogans are dutifully hung, and although many of the larger companies have active safety programs and campaigns, we sometimes forget the lecture that came so early in our training.

Then one day it happens. Over the thump of the heavy presses and the whine of high-speed automatic equipment, a scream ricochets off the walls of the shop. Little by little the sounds of pumps and motors die out and a spinning flywheel, like a carnival wheel of fortune, creeps to a stop. Everyone looks, craning their necks, as co-workers walk the unlucky one out of the shop. On the floor are spots of blood that dripped from the rag that was quickly wrapped around the mangled hand. That day you will look at the machine and remember the safety lecture—for a moment, anyway.

This chapter describes the various hazards of mechanical motion. On particular machines and during certain process situations, the specific danger will be explained in the appropriate chapter as the text progresses. The three basic danger areas of moving parts are:

1. The point of operation—where the tool actually touches the work
2. Power transmission—at the flywheel, the pulley, various cranks, levers, spindles, and gears
3. Auxiliary mechanisms—the reciprocating, rotating, and transverse moving parts that are part of feed mechanisms and accessory devices

All these items represent motions and actions that are potentially hazardous to the operator. They are typical of nearly all machines and power tools; therefore, recognizing them is the first step in protecting yourself. The basic motions and actions are:

    Rotating
    Reciprocating
    Transverse
    Cutting
    Punching
    Shearing
    Bending

Each of these will be discussed briefly.

ROTATING HAZARDS

Rotating either fast or slowly, collars, couplings, cams, clutches, flywheels, shaft ends, spindles, and horizontal or vertical shafting can be the cause of many accidents in the shop.

Loose-fitting clothing, unbuttoned cuffs, exposed shirttails, and longer-styled hair can be gripped by these turning parts. The hazard is increased when setscrews, bolt heads, and locking keys are exposed and are turning with the shaft or spindle (see Fig. 1-1). Of particular danger with rotating equipment is the "pinch" or "nip point." This is where either two rotating parts or one turning and one stationary part come in contact or very close to each other. Figure 1-2 shows some of these hazards that are found in every shop.

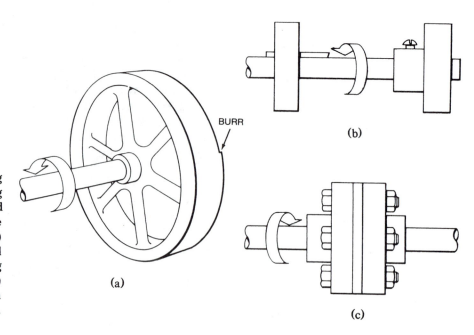

BURR

(b)

(a)

(c)

Figure 1-1 Rotating hazards: (a) rotating pulley with spokes and a projecting burr on the face of the pulley; (b) rotating shaft and pulleys with projecting key and set screw; (c) rotating coupling with projecting bolt heads.

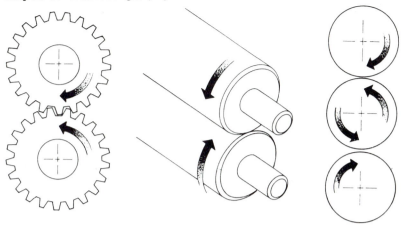

Figure 1-2 Nip points of close-fitting rotating parts.

RECIPROCATING HAZARDS These dangers occur when machinery beds, toolholders, or auxiliary components move either back and forth or up and down. The worker may be struck by the moving part or be caught between it and a stationary part of the machine. Figure 1-3 depicts situations where these hazards are common.

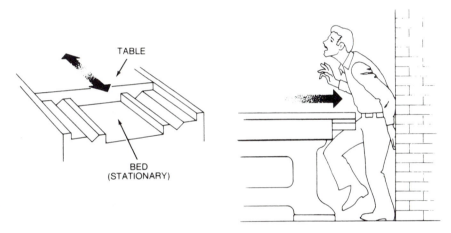

Figure 1-3 Reciprocating hazard.

TRANSVERSE MOTIONS These are motions traveling in a long, continuous straight line. Usually horizontal, the distances traveled are such that the danger of the motion tends to appear to be minimal. Long continuous grinding and sanding belts and chain drives with projecting connection links can grab hands or clothing and drag them along to "running-in" nip points, as shown in Figure 1-4.

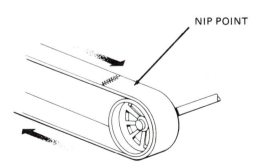

TRANSVERSE MOTION OF BELT

Figure 1-4 Transverse motion hazards.

POINT-OF-OPERATION ACTIONS

Cutting, shearing, punching, and bending become hazardous when either the hands or fingers come in direct line with the movement of the tool or when capacities are exceeded, and a structural failure occurs on the equipment.

The specific hazard is in the insertion, holding, and removal of stock between machine cycles. There is also danger when, due to the action of the machine on the stock, material flies into the face of the operator or those standing nearby (see Fig. 1-5).

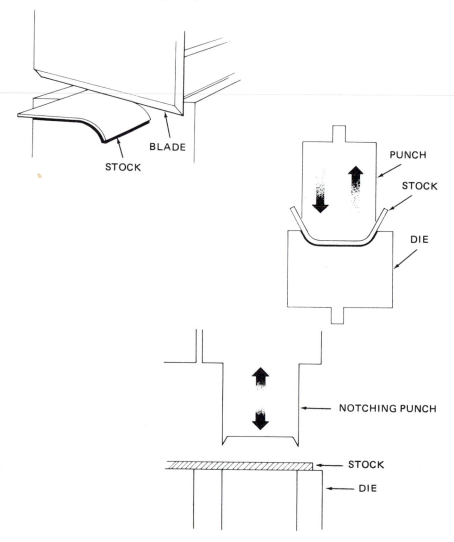

Figure 1-5 Point-of-action hazards.

NONMECHANICAL HAZARDS

A safety concern, sometimes neglected, involves those aspects of shop operation which, although secondary to production, can be just as dangerous as the machinery.

Electrical power in a shop is widely distributed through wall-hung bus ducts and hanging drop cords. Input power can be 110, 220, 440 or even 600 volts. These distribution lines are therefore extremely dangerous. Even a shock from a 110-volt line can kill under the "right" conditions. Areas to be checked include not only conduit condition and connection, but also machine grounding. Another danger is in the fact that many machines are wired for three-phase electrical input, which means that component rotation is affected by the electrical hookup. Usually, strategically placed arrows will indicate the rotational direction of the equipment.

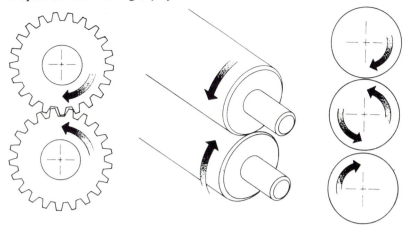

Figure 1-2 Nip points of close-fitting rotating parts.

RECIPROCATING HAZARDS These dangers occur when machinery beds, toolholders, or auxiliary components move either back and forth or up and down. The worker may be struck by the moving part or be caught between it and a stationary part of the machine. Figure 1-3 depicts situations where these hazards are common.

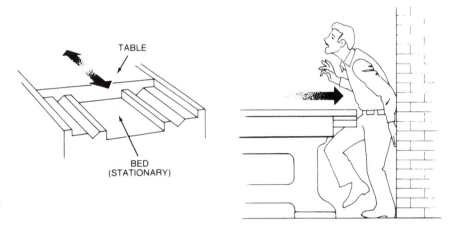

TABLE

BED
(STATIONARY)

Figure 1-3 Reciprocating hazard.

TRANSVERSE MOTIONS These are motions traveling in a long, continuous straight line. Usually horizontal, the distances traveled are such that the danger of the motion tends to appear to be minimal. Long continuous grinding and sanding belts and chain drives with projecting connection links can grab hands or clothing and drag them along to "running-in" nip points, as shown in Figure 1-4.

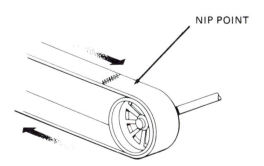

NIP POINT

Figure 1-4 Transverse motion hazards.

TRANSVERSE MOTION OF BELT

POINT-OF-OPERATION ACTIONS

Cutting, shearing, punching, and bending become hazardous when either the hands or fingers come in direct line with the movement of the tool or when capacities are exceeded, and a structural failure occurs on the equipment.

The specific hazard is in the insertion, holding, and removal of stock between machine cycles. There is also danger when, due to the action of the machine on the stock, material flies into the face of the operator or those standing nearby (see Fig. 1-5).

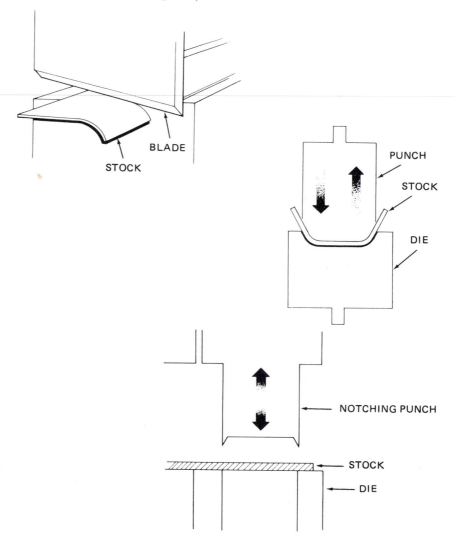

Figure 1-5 Point-of-action hazards.

NONMECHANICAL HAZARDS

A safety concern, sometimes neglected, involves those aspects of shop operation which, although secondary to production, can be just as dangerous as the machinery.

Electrical power in a shop is widely distributed through wall-hung bus ducts and hanging drop cords. Input power can be 110, 220, 440 or even 600 volts. These distribution lines are therefore extremely dangerous. Even a shock from a 110-volt line can kill under the "right" conditions. Areas to be checked include not only conduit condition and connection, but also machine grounding. Another danger is in the fact that many machines are wired for three-phase electrical input, which means that component rotation is affected by the electrical hookup. Usually, strategically placed arrows will indicate the rotational direction of the equipment.

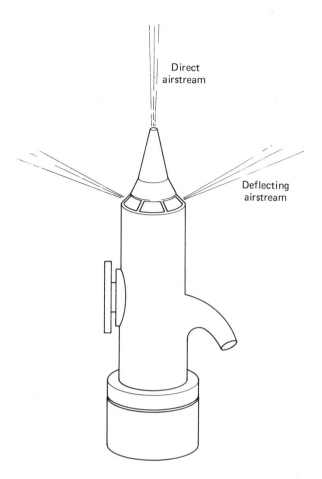

Direct
airstream

Deflecting
airstream

Figure 1-6 Air nozzle
with a deflecting
shield.

Compressed air is used in shops for powering pneumatic machinery, spraying, automatic piece ejection in stamping operations, and in hand tools such as drills and riveting guns. Chip removal and general cleanup operations are all accomplished with air hoses and various nozzle types.

Shop personnel should never underestimate the force of compressed air. One has only to recall the childhood prank of partially obstructing the faucet of a drinking fountain and seeing how far the water will squirt as the pressure builds up behind it. So it is with compressed air, as it is distributed in small-diameter lines, with even smaller orifice guns and nozzles, with usually 80 to 100 pounds of pressure behind it. Such a blast of air can cause permanent damage to the unprotected eyeball. A relatively small laceration can be ripped open while using compressed air to dry hands and arms. Small chips and debris can be blown with unbelievable velocity into the face and eyes.

Figure 1-6 shows an air nozzle approved by the Occupational Safety and Health Administration (OSHA). The side jets allow the pressure at the orifice to be reduced for adequate but safer pressure while providing a shield so that debris forced back toward the operator is deflected. Pressure to hoses and fittings should always be turned off or bled down before being connected or disconnected.

USE OF
HAND TOOLS

Elsewhere in the text, the proper use of various hand tools is discussed. But in general, the smaller hand tools are not often addressed directly. Both powered and hand-operated, such tools still present hazards in much larger proportions to their actual size.

The list of hand tool safety tips that follows will bring several basic points into focus.

1. Use the right tool for the job. Do not try to do heavy-duty work with light-duty tools.
2. Never try to force a tool to work beyond its safe rated limit.
3. Always keep tools properly oiled, sharpened, and in perfect working condition.
4. Use all safety guards and devices supplied with power tools.
5. Never carry power tools by the cord or yank the cord to disconnect a plug. Check cords periodically for cuts or cracks in the insulated covering.
6. Always unplug tools before servicing.
7. Avoid accidental starts. Never carry a power tool with your finger on the trigger.
8. Make sure that all tightening keys and adjusting wrenches are removed prior to operating.
9. Always secure work with clamps or a vise, not with your hand.
10. Remove all loose-fitting clothing or jewelry that might be caught by moving parts.
11. Keep the work area floor clear of debris.
12. Never work in an awkward position. Maintain sound footing and balance at all times.
13. Always use proper eye protection.
14. Never use power tools in damp or wet areas.

THE SAFE WORKER   All the safety posters, rules, and campaigns cannot overcome a negative and careless attitude on the part of the individual shop person. There is no end to the variety of safeguards that can be built into or added onto machines or tools. Yet if the mechanic does not bring to bear a sense of self-preservation and even just a modicum of intellect when using tools and machinery, it will only be a matter of time before an injury of some sort will occur.

Foremost in any kind of shop work is the wearing of eye protection and, if conditions warrant, the protection of the entire facial area. The use of safety eyeglasses is often mandated by either law or strict company policy, but the dictates of common sense should be enough to encourage their constant use (Fig. 1-7).

Figure 1-7 Eye safety is paramount in shop operations.

Next in importance is the use of proper foot gear. The most obvious precaution would be the use of steel-tipped shoes to protect the toes if a heavy object is dropped. Although this may not be necessary in every shop, certainly the selection of nonskid soles and an upper shoe construction that can resist tears and to some degree penetration is required. Additionally, shoes with a low heel height are absolutely necessary for balance and firm support when lifting and reaching. Once again the dictates of common sense must take precedence over the dictates of fashion.

In that same vein, a comment on clothing is called for. Most clothing classified as "work clothes" is of a cotton–polyester blend. Select those garments that contain a greater percentage of cotton rather than of the man-made fibers. These will prove to be the longest wearing and more important, are less flammable, less reactive to chemical and solvent spills, and less likely to shred or tear. Unfortunately, the pure cotton work outfit, which was always the longest wearing, has all but disappeared, except, of course, for denim jeans.

RESPONSIBILITIES OF THE INDUSTRIAL WORKER AND THE SHOP PERSON

Both novice and experienced shop people have a responsibility to each other and to the organization for which they work. The novice must recognize that a lack of experience results in the questionable value of their judgment in any particular situation. The course must then be to seek out the counsel and advice of the senior members of the group. Older workers, too, must realize that by reaching out to help the inexperienced novice, they protect not only their own safety but also their own vested interest in the business. Finally, management must foster and encourage an atmosphere in which such cooperation can take place.

Chapter 2

SHOP MATHEMATICS

The purpose of this chapter is not to discuss mathematics in depth, but to offer a review and reinforcement of basic computations and to offer a guide to the solutions of the type of math problems that the metal fabricator is faced with in the day-to-day shop situation.

Current students or those recently graduated will no doubt be proficient in math. However, for those who have been out of school for several years, the section on review of fraction and decimal manipulation may prove to be quite helpful. If a more extensive review is necessary, see the readings in Appendix 2.

BASIC RULES OF FRACTIONS

The skilled fabricator must have the ability to work quickly and accurately with fractional dimensions. The manipulation of these dimensions is all-important if the job is to be completed satisfactorily. The following rules and examples can be used as a guide and review.

Addition and Subtraction

Rule: *Fractions that are to be added or subtracted must have the same denominator. Before the addition and subtraction can be done, each fraction must be expressed in terms of a common denominator.*

EXAMPLE: Add $\frac{1}{4} + \frac{3}{8} + \frac{3}{16}$.

$$\frac{1}{4} = \frac{4}{16}$$
$$\frac{3}{8} = \frac{6}{16}$$
$$+\frac{3}{16} = \frac{3}{16}$$
$$\frac{13}{16}$$

EXAMPLE: Subtract $^{13}\!/_{32}$ from $\frac{7}{8}$.

$$\frac{7}{8} = \frac{28}{32}$$
$$-\frac{13}{32} = \frac{13}{32}$$
$$\overline{\qquad\quad \frac{15}{32}}$$

When adding or subtracting mixed numbers, the same rule applies.

EXAMPLE: Add $1\frac{7}{16}$ and $3\frac{1}{8}$.

$$1\frac{7}{16} = 1\frac{7}{16}$$
$$+\;3\frac{1}{8} = 3\frac{2}{16}$$
$$\overline{\qquad\quad 4\frac{9}{16}}$$

EXAMPLE: Add $13\frac{7}{8}$ and $6\frac{9}{16}$.

$$13\frac{7}{8} = 13\frac{14}{16}$$
$$+6\frac{9}{16} = \;6\frac{9}{16}$$
$$\overline{\qquad 19\frac{23}{16} = 20\frac{7}{16}}$$

Multiplication of Fractions

Rule: When fractions are multiplied, the product of all the numerators is placed over the product of all denominators.

EXAMPLE: Multiply $\frac{1}{2} \times \frac{3}{8} \times \frac{1}{4}$.

$$\frac{1}{2} \times \frac{3}{8} \times \frac{1}{4} = \frac{3}{64}$$

EXAMPLE: Multiply $5 \times \frac{3}{8}$.

$$5 \times \frac{3}{8} = \frac{5}{1} \times \frac{3}{8} = \frac{15}{8} = 1\frac{7}{8}$$

Division of Fractions

Rule: Invert the second fraction and multiply.

EXAMPLE: Divide $\frac{5}{8}$ by $\frac{7}{16}$.

$$\frac{5}{8} \div \frac{7}{16} = \frac{5}{8} \times \frac{16}{7} = \frac{5}{\overset{}{8}_1} \times \frac{\overset{2}{16}}{7} = \frac{10}{7} = 1\frac{3}{7}$$

Multiplication and Division of Mixed Numbers

Rule: Convert the mixed numbers to improper fractions and apply the rules of multiplication and division.

EXAMPLE: Multiply $3\frac{1}{8} \times 2\frac{1}{2}$.

$$3\frac{1}{8} \times 2\frac{1}{2} = \frac{25}{8} \times \frac{5}{2} = \frac{125}{16} = 7\frac{13}{16}$$

EXAMPLE: Divide $4\frac{1}{8}$ by $3\frac{1}{2}$.

$$4\frac{1}{8} \div 3\frac{1}{2} = \frac{33}{8} \div \frac{7}{2} = \frac{33}{\overset{}{\underset{4}{8}}} \times \frac{\overset{1}{2}}{7} = \frac{33}{28} = 1\frac{5}{28}$$

Note: Mixed numbers are converted to improper fractions by multiplying the whole-number part by the denominator, adding the product to the numerator, and placing this sum over the original denominator.

FRACTION-TO-DECIMAL CONVERSION

Common fractions are easily converted to decimals by dividing the numerator by the denominator.

EXAMPLE: The decimal equivalent of ¼ is 0.250.

$$
\begin{array}{r}
.250 \\
4\overline{)1.000} \\
\underline{8} \\
20 \\
\underline{20} \\
000
\end{array}
$$

EXAMPLE: The decimal equivalent of ⅝ is 0.625.

$$
\begin{array}{r}
.625 \\
8\overline{)5.000} \\
\underline{4\,8} \\
20 \\
\underline{16} \\
40 \\
\underline{40} \\
00
\end{array}
$$

DECIMAL-TO-FRACTION CONVERSION

To convert a decimal to a fraction, multiply it by 64. The resulting number will be the numerator of the fraction. The denominator will be 64. Remember to reduce the fraction to its lowest terms.

EXAMPLE: The fractional equivalent of .4375 is 7/16.

$$.4375 \times 64 = 28$$
$$.4375 = \frac{28}{64} = \frac{7}{16}$$

EXAMPLE: The fractional equivalent of .610 is $\frac{39}{64}$.

$$.610 \times 64 = 39.04 \quad \text{(Round off to nearest 64th)}$$
$$.610 = \frac{39}{64}$$

The ultimate goal of fabricators who frequently deal with fraction-decimal conversions is to memorize the commonly used equivalents and manipulate them without having to refer constantly to the conversion chart.

Start by memorizing the simple conversions.

EXAMPLE: 1 inch = 1.000
½ inch = 0.500
¼ inch = 0.250
⅛ inch = 0.125
1/16 inch = 0.062

$$\tfrac{1}{32} \text{ inch} = 0.031$$
$$\tfrac{1}{64} \text{ inch} = 0.015$$

Once this step is taken, manipulation of fraction–decimal conversions becomes a simple mental exercise.

EXAMPLE: Find the decimal equivalent of $\tfrac{5}{32}$.

$$\tfrac{4}{32} = \tfrac{1}{8} = 0.125$$
$$\tfrac{1}{32} \quad\;\; = 0.031$$

Therefore,

$$\tfrac{5}{32} = 0.156$$

EXAMPLE: Find the decimal equivalent of $\tfrac{9}{64}$.

$$\tfrac{8}{64} = \tfrac{1}{8} = 0.125$$
$$\tfrac{1}{64} \quad\;\; = 0.015$$

Therefore,

$$\tfrac{9}{64} = 0.140$$

SQUARE ROOT A square root is a factor of a number which, when multiplied by itself, will produce the original number. Of all the basic math computations, the manual calculation of square roots is probably the most confusing. Many fabrication shops will have charts or manuals containing square- and cube-root tables (see Appendix 3). Unfortunately, there will be times when these tables are not available and square roots will have to be hand calculated in order to solve many of the commonly used geometric and trigonometric formulas.

Calculation of Square Roots

EXAMPLE: Find the square root of 119,025.

Step 1: Break the number down into groups of two digits starting from the right.

$$\sqrt{11\,90\,25}$$

Step 2: Determine a perfect square which is nearest to but not greater than the first group. In this case the nearest perfect square to 11 is 9 (3 × 3). Place the 9 under the first group and subtract. Place its square root (3) in the answer.

$$\begin{array}{r} 3 \quad\;\; \\ \sqrt{11\,90\,25} \\ \underline{9 \quad\quad\quad} \\ 2 \quad\quad\quad \end{array}$$

Step 3: Bring down the next group and place it next to the remainder, 2.

$$\begin{array}{r} 3 \quad\;\; \\ \sqrt{11\,90\,25} \\ \underline{9 \quad\quad\quad} \\ 290 \quad\quad \end{array}$$

Step 4: Double the number in the answer and place it to the left of 290.

$$\begin{array}{r} 3 \quad\;\; \\ \sqrt{11\,90\,25} \\ \underline{9 \quad\quad\quad} \\ 6 \quad 290 \quad\quad \end{array}$$

Step 5: Divide the 6 into the first two digits of the 290. Place that number in the answer and next to the 6.

$$
\begin{array}{r}
3\ 4 \\
\sqrt{119025} \\
9 \\
\hline
\end{array}
$$

64 | 290

Step 6: Multiply 64 by 4. Subtract this from 290 and bring the next group down to the remainder.

$$
\begin{array}{r}
3\ 4 \\
\sqrt{119025} \\
9
\end{array}
$$

64 | 290
256
3425

Step 7: Double the existing answer and place it to the left of 3425.

$$
\begin{array}{r}
3\ 4 \\
\sqrt{119025} \\
9
\end{array}
$$

64 | 290
256
68 | 3425

Step 8: Divide 68 into the first three digits of 3425. Place this number in the answer and next to the 68.

$$
\begin{array}{r}
3\ 4\ 5 \\
\sqrt{119025} \\
9
\end{array}
$$

64 | 290
256
685 | 3425

Step 9: Multiply 685 by 5 and subtract the answer from 3425.

$$
\begin{array}{r}
3\ 4\ 5 \\
\sqrt{119025} \\
9
\end{array}
$$

64 | 290
256
685 | 3425
3425
0000

Check the answer by multiplying it by itself: $345 \times 345 = 119{,}025$.

REVIEW OF BASIC RULES OF ALGEBRA

Addition

When combining numbers with like signs, add the numbers together and give the sum the same sign.

EXAMPLES: $6 + 4 = 10$

$-6 - 4 = -10$

When combining numbers with unlike signs, subtract the smaller from the larger and give the answer the sign of the larger number.

EXAMPLES: $10 - 12 = -2$

$-8 + 4 = -4$

$14 - 10 = 4$

Multiplication and Division

When multiplying or dividing numbers with like signs, the answer is always positive.

EXAMPLES: $3(3) = 9$

$(-3)(-3) = 9$

$\dfrac{-3}{-3} = 1$

When multiplying or dividing numbers with unlike signs, the answer is always negative.

EXAMPLES: $(3)(-3) = -9$

$\dfrac{3}{-3} = -1$

Algebraic Notations

Notation	Meaning
π	The Greek letter pi is a constant equal to 3.1416 (close approximation)
xy	x times y
$(x)(y)$	x times y
$14y$	14 times y
$3(x + y)$	$3x$ plus $3y$
$\dfrac{x}{y}$	x divided by y
x^2	x times x
x^3	x times x times x
x^{-2}	$\dfrac{1}{x^2}$
$x^2 x^3$	$x^{2+3} = x^5$
$\dfrac{x^4}{x^2}$	$x^{4-2} = x^2$
y^0	When the exponent is 0, the number is equal to 1

Transposing

The following rules of transposition must be followed when manipulating equations.

1. Whatever is added or subtracted from one side of the equation must be added or subtracted from the other side.
2. If one side of the equation is multiplied or divided by a number, the same operation must be done to the other side.

EXAMPLES: Solve for x.

(1)
$$x + 10 = 12$$
$$x + 10 - 10 = 12 - 10$$
$$x = 2$$

(2)
$$x + y = a$$
$$x + y - y = a - y$$
$$x = a - y$$

(3)
$$3x = 18$$
$$\frac{{}^{1}\cancel{3}x}{\cancel{3}_{1}} = \frac{\cancel{18}^{6}}{\cancel{3}_{1}}$$
$$x = 6$$

(4)
$$\frac{x}{2} = 9$$
$$\frac{x}{\cancel{2}_{1}}(\overset{1}{\cancel{2}}) = 9(2)$$
$$x = 18$$

(5)
$$8x + 3 = 19$$
$$8x + 3 - 3 = 19 - 3$$
$$8x = 16$$
$$\frac{{}^{1}\cancel{8}x}{\cancel{8}_{1}} = \frac{\cancel{16}^{2}}{\cancel{8}_{1}}$$
$$x = 2$$

These basic examples can be applied to solving geometric equations. For example, if you have a piece of thin steel flat stock 38 inches long and you need to calculate the diameter of the circle that can be formed with this material, you will have to transpose the equation for circumference.

EXAMPLE:

$$c = \pi d \qquad\qquad c = 38 \text{ inches}$$
$$\pi = 3.1416$$

$$\pi d = c \qquad\qquad \text{Equation sides can be exchanged}$$
$$\text{without changing the value.}$$

$$\frac{\pi d}{\pi} = \frac{c}{\pi}$$

$$d = \frac{c}{\pi}$$

$$d = \frac{38}{3.1416}$$

$$d = 12.7 \text{ inches}$$

Parentheses

If a portion of the equation is enclosed within parentheses, the operations inside the parentheses must be done first.

EXAMPLES: $(8 + 10)(2 + 3) =$

$$(18)(5) = 90$$

$$86 - (8 + 2 + 6) =$$

$$86 - 16 = 70$$

Terms

Those portions of an equation separated by either plus (+) or minus (−) signs are called terms. In the equation $18 + 8 - 2(6)$, 18, 8, and −2(6) are the terms. Any multiplication or division operation within a term must be done before terms can be combined.

EXAMPLE: $18 + 8 - 2(6) =$

$$18 + 8 - 12 = 14$$

GEOMETRIC AND TRIGONOMETRIC FORMULAS

The following geometric equations and trigonometric functions will help you determine several important factors. Anything that is fabricated, whether it is a small precision sheet metal part or a large structural assembly, will conform to one or more of the basic geometric shapes. Aside from the obvious use of geometry and trigonometry to derive indirect measurements, the fabricator must use these formulas to determine material requirements. Calculating the amount of material needed will also allow you to determine material weight and cost.

Properties of Geometric Shapes

THE CIRCLE (Fig. 2-1)

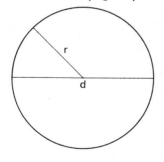

Figure 2-1   Circle.

$$C = \pi d \text{ or } 2\pi r$$

$$A = \pi r^2$$

$$d = \frac{C}{\pi}$$

$$r = \frac{C}{2\pi}$$

where C = circumference
A = area
r = radius
d = diameter
π = 3.1416

THE HOLLOW CIRCLE (Fig. 2-2)

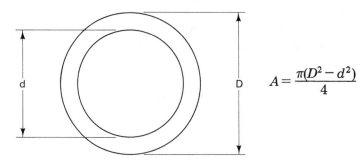

Figure 2-2   Hollow
circle.

$$A = \frac{\pi(D^2 - d^2)}{4}$$

SEGMENTS OF A CIRCLE   (finding the radius given only chord and segment height); Fig. 2-3)

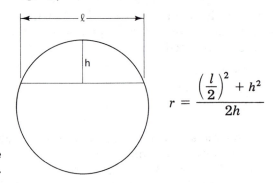

Figure 2-3   Circle
segments.

$$r = \frac{\left(\dfrac{l}{2}\right)^2 + h^2}{2h}$$

where l = length of chord
h = height of segment

RECTANGLE (Fig. 2-4)

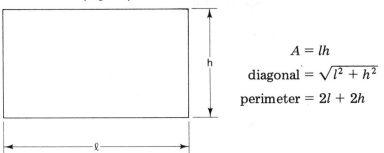

Figure 2-4   Rectangle.

$$A = lh$$
$$\text{diagonal} = \sqrt{l^2 + h^2}$$
$$\text{perimeter} = 2l + 2h$$

SECTOR OF A CIRCLE (Fig. 2-5)

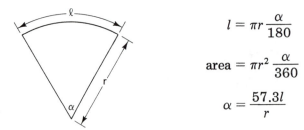

Figure 2-5   Sector of a
circle.

$$l = \pi r \frac{\alpha}{180}$$
$$\text{area} = \pi r^2 \frac{\alpha}{360}$$
$$\alpha = \frac{57.3l}{r}$$

CIRCULAR CONE (Fig. 2-6)

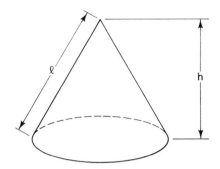

Figure 2-6   Circular cone.

lateral surface area $= \pi r l$

$$\text{volume} = \frac{\pi r^2 h}{3}$$

where r denotes the base radius.

FRUSTRUM OF CONE (Fig. 2-7)

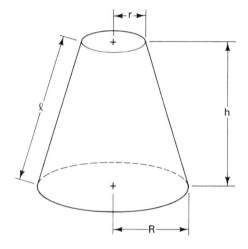

Figure 2-7   Frustrum of a cone.

lateral surface area $= \pi l (R + r)$

$$\text{volume} = \frac{\pi h}{3}(R^2 + Rr + r^2)$$

where r = upper base radius
R = lower base radius

CYLINDERS (Fig. 2-8)

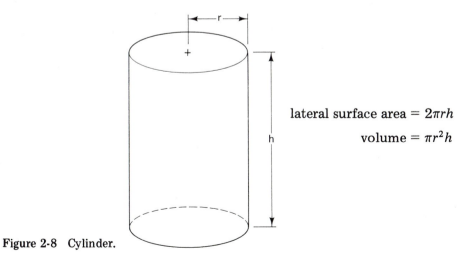

Figure 2-8   Cylinder.

lateral surface area $= 2\pi r h$

$$\text{volume} = \pi r^2 h$$

CUBES (Fig. 2-9)

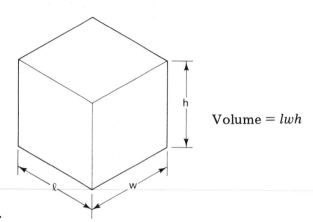

$$\text{Volume} = lwh$$

Figure 2-9   Cube.

SPHERES (Fig. 2-10)

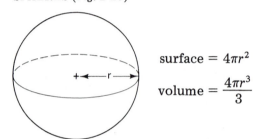

$$\text{surface} = 4\pi r^2$$

$$\text{volume} = \frac{4\pi r^3}{3}$$

Figure 2-10   Sphere.

TRAPEZOIDS (Fig. 2-11)

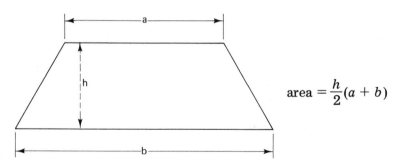

$$\text{area} = \frac{h}{2}(a + b)$$

Figure 2-11   Trapezoid.

CAPACITY OF HORIZONTAL CYLINDRICAL TANKS (close approximation; Fig. 2-12)

$$\text{capacity} = lh\sqrt{0.017d + 1.7dh - h^2}$$

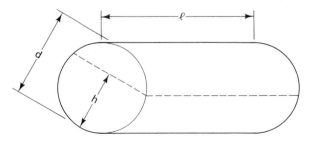

Figure 2-12   Horizontal cylindrical tank.

CALCULATIONS FOR TANK CAPACITY (Fig. 2-13). Calculating the capacity of a cylindrical tank is done by using the formula for cylinder volume and applying the following conversions:

231 cubic inches will hold 1 gallon.
1 cubic foot will hold 7½ gallons.
1728 cubic inches = 1 cubic foot.
31½ gallons = 1 barrel.

$$\text{volume} = \pi r^2 h$$

or

$$\text{volume} = 0.7854 d^2 h$$

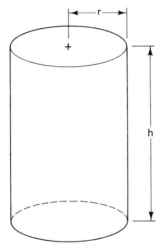

Figure 2-13 Cylinder.

For example, how many gallons will a tank 10 inches in inside diameter and 30 inches long hold?

$$\text{volume} = \pi r^2 h$$
$$= 3.14(5^2)(30)$$
$$= 3.14(25)(30)$$
$$= 2355 \text{ cubic inches}$$
$$\text{Capacity in gallons} = \frac{2355}{231} = 10.19 \text{ gallons}$$

The following variations of this formula can be used to determine a cylinder size needed to hold a specified volume.

$$(1)\ \ h = \frac{\text{volume}}{\pi r^2} \qquad (2)\ \ r = \sqrt{\frac{\text{volume}}{\pi h}}$$

EXAMPLE: Construct a tank no greater than 30 inches in length to hold 50 gallons.

Because volume and desired height are given, use the following procedure:

$$r = \sqrt{\frac{\text{volume}}{\pi h}} \qquad \text{volume for 50 gallons} = (231)(50)$$
$$\text{volume} = 11,550 \text{ cubic inches}$$

$$= \sqrt{\frac{11{,}550}{3.14(30)}}$$
$$= \sqrt{122.6}$$
$$= 11.08$$
$$d = 2r = 22.16 \text{ inches}$$

The cylinder would need an inside diameter of 22.16 inches.
Formula (1) would be used if the diameter had to be a predetermined size.

RIGHT TRIANGLES
(Fig. 2-14)

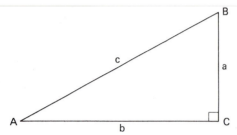

Figure 2-14   Right triangle.

Trigonometric function	Example
Sine of an angle $= \dfrac{\text{opposite side}}{\text{hypotenuse}}$	$\sin A = \dfrac{\text{side } a}{\text{side } c}$
Cosine of an angle $= \dfrac{\text{adjacent side}}{\text{hypotenuse}}$	$\cos A = \dfrac{\text{side } b}{\text{side } c}$
Tangent of an angle $= \dfrac{\text{opposite side}}{\text{adjacent side}}$	$\tan A = \dfrac{\text{side } a}{\text{side } b}$
Cotangent of an angle $= \dfrac{\text{adjacent side}}{\text{opposite side}}$	$\cot A = \dfrac{\text{side } b}{\text{side } a}$

Solutions of Right Triangles

$$\text{area} = \frac{ab}{2}$$

$$c = \sqrt{a^2 + b^2} \qquad \sin A = \frac{a}{c} \qquad \sin B = \frac{b}{c}$$
$$b = \sqrt{c^2 - a^2}$$
$$a = \sqrt{c^2 - b^2} \qquad \cos A = \frac{b}{c} \qquad \cos B = \frac{a}{c}$$

$$\tan A = \frac{a}{b} \qquad \tan B = \frac{b}{a}$$

$$\cot A = \frac{b}{a} \qquad \cot B = \frac{a}{b}$$

Formulas for solving right triangles are given in Chart 2-1.

CHART 2-1   Formulas for Solving Right Triangles

Measurements given	Measurement to find				
	a	b	c	A	B
a, b			$a^2 + b^2$	$\tan A = \dfrac{a}{b}$	$\tan B = \dfrac{b}{a}$
a, c		$c^2 - a^2$		$\sin A = \dfrac{a}{c}$	$\cos B = \dfrac{a}{c}$
b, c	$c^2 - b^2$			$\cos A = \dfrac{b}{c}$	$\sin B = \dfrac{b}{c}$
A, a		$a \cot A$	$\dfrac{a}{\sin A}$		$90 - A$
A, b	$b \tan A$		$\dfrac{b}{\cos A}$		$90 - A$
A, c	$c \sin A$	$c \cos A$			$90 - A$
B, a		$a \tan B$	$\dfrac{a}{\cos B}$	$90 - B$	
B, b	$b \cot B$		$\dfrac{b}{\sin B}$	$90 - B$	
B, c	$c \cos B$	$c \sin B$		$90 - B$	

OBLIQUE TRIANGLES (Fig. 2-15)

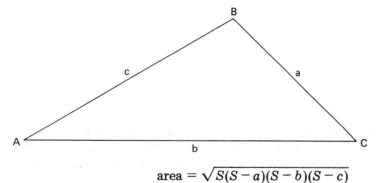

Figure 2-15 Oblique triangle.

$$\text{area} = \sqrt{S(S - a)(S - b)(S - c)}$$

The value for S is calculated as follows:

$$S = \frac{a + b + c}{2}$$

Solutions for Oblique Triangles When Two Sides and an Included Angle Are Known

$$a^2 = b^2 + c^2 - 2bc \cos A$$
$$b^2 = a^2 + c^2 - 2ac \cos B$$
$$c^2 = a^2 + b^2 - 2ab \cos C$$

**Oblique Triangle Solutions When Two Sides
and an Opposing Angle Are Known**

$$\boxed{\frac{a}{\sin A} = \frac{b}{\sin B} = \frac{c}{\sin C}}$$

Therefore,

$$\sin A = \frac{a \sin B}{b} \qquad \text{or} \qquad \sin A = \frac{a \sin C}{c}$$

$$\sin B = \frac{b \sin A}{a} \qquad \text{or} \qquad \sin B = \frac{b \sin C}{c}$$

$$\sin C = \frac{c \sin B}{b} \qquad \text{or} \qquad \sin C = \frac{c \sin A}{a}$$

**Oblique Triangle Solutions When Two Angles
and One Side Are Known**

$$a = \frac{b \sin A}{\sin B} \qquad b = \frac{a \sin B}{\sin A} \qquad c = \frac{b \sin C}{\sin B}$$

$$a = \frac{c \sin A}{\sin C} \qquad b = \frac{c \sin B}{\sin C} \qquad c = \frac{a \sin C}{\sin A}$$

Oblique Triangle Solutions When Three Sides Are Known

$$\cos A = \frac{b^2 + c^2 - a^2}{2bc}$$

$$\cos B = \frac{a^2 + c^2 - b^2}{2ac}$$

$$\cos C = \frac{a^2 + b^2 - c^2}{2ab}$$

METRIC SYSTEM   The metric linear measurement system is based on powers of 10, with the meter being the fundamental unit. The system is easy to work with because all units are related. The greatest advantage of the metric system is the elimination of fractions.

The basic linear measurement units are as follows:

Millimeter (mm) =	0.001	Slightly more than $\frac{1}{32}$ inch
Centimeter (cm) =	0.010	
Decimeter (dm) =	0.100	
Meter (m) (base unit) =	1.00	Equivalent to 39.37 inches
Dekameter (dkm) =	10.0	
Hectometer (hm) =	100.0	
Kilometer (km) =	1000.0	Approximately $\frac{5}{8}$ mile

One metric measurement can be easily converted to another by simply manipulating the decimal point.

EXAMPLE: 15 m = 150 dm − 1500 cm = 15,000 mm

15 m = 1.5 dkm = 0.15 hm = 0.015 km

Rarely will the fabricator be faced with a job using a combination of standard and metric measurements. If such a situation arises, refer to the conversion chart in Appendix 3 or the following conversion factors:

1 inch = 25.4 millimeters or 2.54 centimeters

1 foot = 204.8 millimeters or 30.48 centimeters

1 millimeter = 0.03937 inch

Chapter 3

MEASUREMENTS and MEASURING DEVICES

The metal fabricator must be competent in all forms of computational mathematics so that the continuous task of mensuration in the shop can be done quickly and accurately.

A variety of measuring tools can be used in any one kind of shop with highly specialized devices being used by shops dealing with very close tolerances and intricate work. The measuring devices described in this chapter have a commonality to all kinds of fabrication, including work done to commercial and precision specifications.

Before going into the individual aspects of the various instruments, it would be well to discuss measurements in general. Readings are either taken from or applied to an object. The mechanic must, in the final analysis and regardless of the simplicity or sophistication of the measuring tool, make a mental connection between what the device reads and what "is" or "must be." The general desire for speed, and the particular desire to hurry things up as readings get finer and more exacting, both tend to make the scale read what you would like it to read rather than what the object actually measures.

STEEL RULES (Fig. 3-1) Unlike the typical notebook ruler, the steel rule is a precision measuring instrument. Available in either rigid or flexible form, its accuracy is due to both the precise spacing of the graduations and the fineness of the graduating lines.

Steel rules are available in 6-, 12-, 18-, 24-, 36-, and 48-inch lengths. The four available measuring edges are graduated in $\frac{1}{8}$ths, $\frac{1}{16}$ths, $\frac{1}{32}$nds, and $\frac{1}{64}$ths. As the $\frac{1}{8}$-inch scale is not often appropriate for more precise metalworking measurements, many rules incorporate a $\frac{1}{100}$th scale in its place. Read with a jeweler's loupe (see Fig. 3-2), very accurate readings of fractional dimensions are possible.

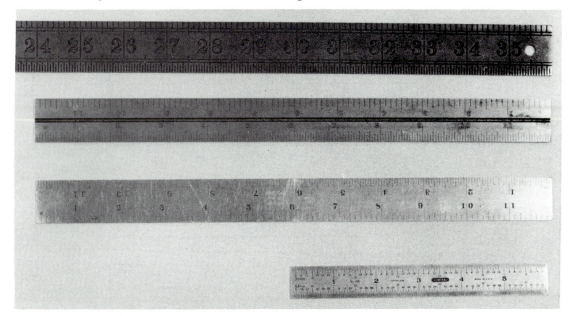

Figure 3-1   Steel rules.

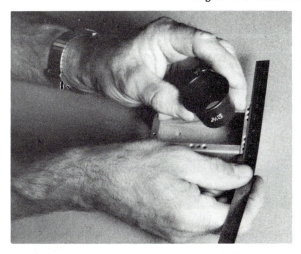

Figure 3-2   Close reading of a scale using a jeweler's loupe.

Using the Steel Rule

Generally, the rule is read from the zero end with the appropriate scale facing the reader. It is important that the rule be parallel to the intended line of measurement (see Fig. 3-3) and read by looking directly at the graduating lines rather than by looking obliquely. Many mechanics prefer to make their measurements from the first whole-inch graduation. In this way a rule with the zero edge worn away or the problem of accurately aligning the zero edge with the edge of the item being measured is eliminated (see Fig. 3-4). But in so doing the mechanic must remember to deduct 1 inch from the reading at the other end.

Reading the Steel Rule

The reader must avoid the obvious method of measuring, that is, by counting the graduation lines. By counting lines one can simply lose count, not to mention the time involved. The proper reading of a scale involves the visual

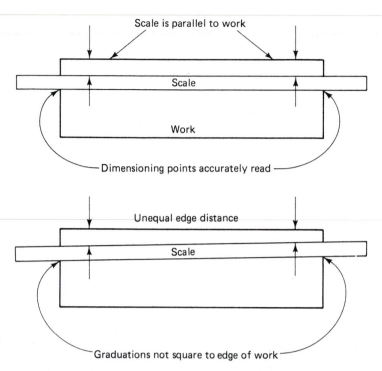

Figure 3-3 Holding a scale parallel to the work.

Figure 3-4 Reading a scale from the 1-inch mark rather than beginning from zero.

pinpointing of a logical reference point, followed by the translating of that reference point to the language of the scale being read, with the addition or subtraction of the appropriate number of graduations. For example, in reading the scale shown in Figure 3-5, the logical reference point is ¾ of an inch.

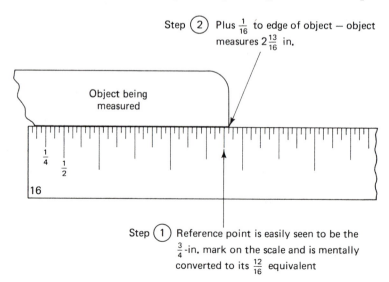

Figure 3-5 Reading a scale graduated in 16ths.

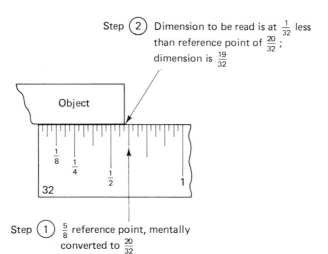

Step ② Dimension to be read is at $\frac{1}{32}$ less than reference point of $\frac{20}{32}$; dimension is $\frac{19}{32}$

Object

$\frac{1}{8}$ $\frac{1}{4}$ $\frac{1}{2}$ 1

32

Figure 3-6 Reading a scale graduated in 32nds.

Step ① $\frac{5}{8}$ reference point, mentally converted to $\frac{20}{32}$

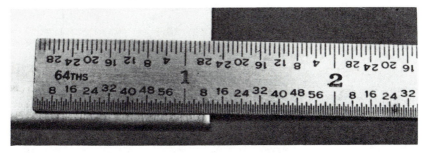

Figure 3-7 Reading a scale graduated in 64ths.

On a $\frac{1}{16}$th scale this translates to $\frac{12}{16}$ths plus 1 more graduation. Thus the reading is $\frac{13}{16}$ths.

In Figure 3-6 the logical reference point is $\frac{5}{8}$ of an inch. On the $\frac{1}{32}$ scale, this should be read as $\frac{20}{32}$, less 1 graduation, or $\frac{19}{32}$.

In Figure 3-7 the closest reference point is $\frac{1}{8}$. As this is the $\frac{1}{64}$ scale, $\frac{1}{8}$ must be read as $\frac{8}{64}$. Adding 3 more graduations indicates a measurement of $\frac{11}{64}$. Used also as a straightedge guide, the steel rule becomes the most commonly used measuring tool.

STEEL TAPES Flexible steel tapes are available in 6-, 8-, 10-, 12-, and 25-foot lengths and can be used to make fast, accurate measurements in much the same manner as steel rules. Usually, the first 24 inches are graduated in $\frac{1}{32}$nds with the balance of the tape in $\frac{1}{16}$ths. Many tapes sold today have centimeter scales on the opposite edge as a step toward universal metrification (see Fig. 3-8).

The steel tape is particularly useful in making long measurements without the help of another person. The rigid steel flange or hook at the end of

Figure 3-8 Steel tape with dual scale.

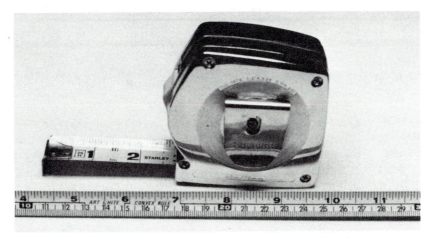

the tape is the "zero point." "Inside" and "outside" measurements can be made with a fair amount of accuracy because the hook is riveted through slotted holes at the beginning of the tape. The length of movement permitted in the slots corresponds to the thickness of the hook, which slides back and forth as the tape is used for either outside or inside dimensions.

As with steel rules, the mechanic will often begin reading with the first 1-inch marking if the hook slots are elongated through use or the hook has been bent to other than a right angle, as shown in Figure 3-9. This guarantees a reasonably accurate reading with the tape.

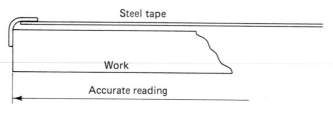

Figure 3-9 Source of errors in using steel measuring tapes.

The steel tape can also be used to measure the length of an arc as found on outside or inside radii. An example of this application is shown in Figure 3-10. Although not as accurate as with indirect measurements which involve an appropriate formula, this method provides a quick solution to many layout problems.

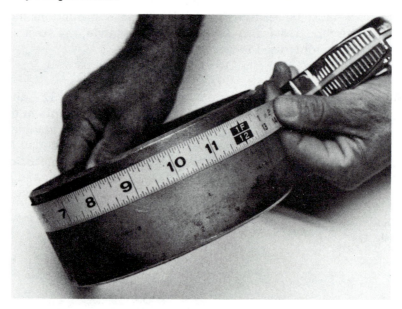

Figure 3-10 Measuring the length of an arc with the steel tape.

COMBINATION SQUARE, PRECISION SQUARE, AND FRAMING SQUARE

The terms "square," "squaring," and "squared" are used consistently in all types of metal fabrication. Either as verbs or adjectives, the implication in the use of the term is the creation of one or more 90-degree angles. Keeping in mind that a straight line is actually an angle of 180 degrees, a line rising at a right angle to that line forms two 90-degree angles, as shown in Figure 3-11.

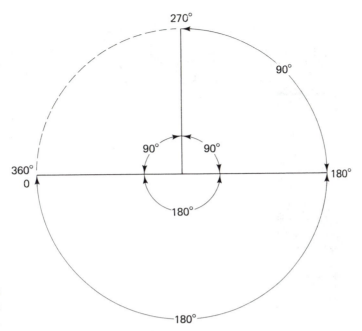

Figure 3-11 Angles contained within a circle.

Thus any geometric arrangement of two or more components that form any number of 90-degree angles is said to be "square."

THE COMBINATION SQUARE (Fig. 3-12). The primary use of this device is in the setting or measuring of recurring 90-degree and 45-degree angles. However, as a measuring tool, it enables very accurate dimensioning from the outside edges of an object. Inside measurements can also be made as long as the movable blade can be extended (see Fig. 3-12).

The combination square is most commonly used with a 12-inch grooved blade that slides through the frame of the square. This type of square may also be used with an 18-inch or even a 24-inch blade, but with a greater chance of angular error, as the frame leg is only 4 inches long.

(a)

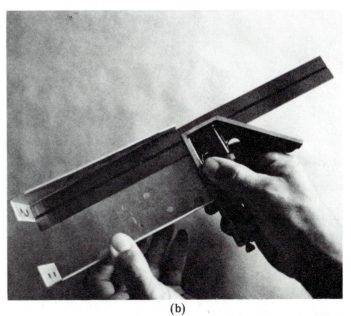

(b)

Figure 3-12 Using the combination square: (a) checking an outside dimension; (b) checking an inside dimension.

Figure 3-13 Precision
square.

THE PRECISION SQUARE (Fig. 3-13). The precision square has a fixed blade not more than 12 inches long, with a 6-inch model being most common. This square's primary function is the setting and checking of 90-degree angles and assembly squaring.

THE MACHINIST SQUARE (Fig. 3-14). This type of square is similar to the carpenter's framing square. The basic application is in the layout or construction of right angles and in the determination of the length of a hypotenuse through the Pythagorean theorem, stated as: $(altitude)^2 + (base)^2 = (hypotenuse)^2$. This rule is more commonly known as a "3–4–5 rule" (see Fig. 3-15).

Figure 3-14 Machinist's
square.

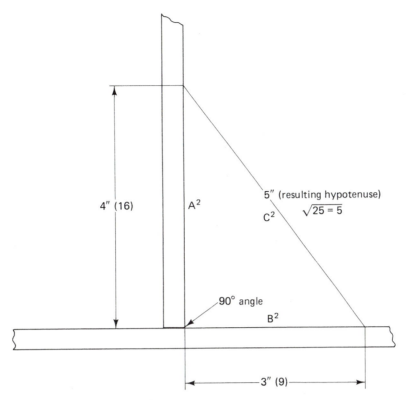

4" (16) A^2

5" (resulting hypotenuse)
$\sqrt{25} = 5$

C^2

90° angle B^2

3" (9)

Figure 3-15 Use of the 3-4-5 rule to set up a right angle.

Using a Square

As with other measuring devices, the square is most effective when used correctly and in respect to the design of the square. All squares have legs that are unequal in both length and mass, with the shorter leg being the wider and often the thicker of the two. The most accurate use of the square is obtained when this leg is placed first against the surface or edge of the material and then slid into the position required for the other leg of the square to be utilized (see Fig. 3-16).

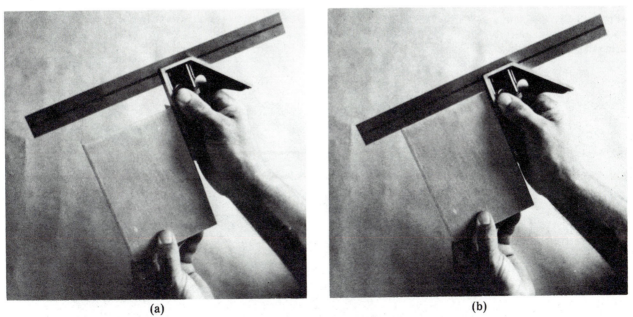

(a)   (b)

Figure 3-16 (a) Heavier leg of a square is placed against the right side of an object, (b) then moved downward until the blade makes contact with the edge being checked.

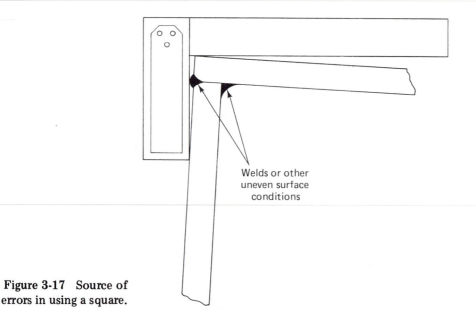

Welds or other
uneven surface
conditions

**Figure 3-17   Source of
errors in using a square.**

The surface or edge must be flat, straight, and regular for accurate use.
Figure 3-17 shows how such deviations can affect accurate squaring. Also,
the larger the item being squared, the more error can accumulate from these
deviations.

In determining the squareness of such large structures as shown in
Figure 3-18, the mechanic can again utilize the Pythagorean theorem. If a
welded frame can be measured diagonally from opposite corners, and these
measured hypotenuses are found to be equal, then the angles at each corner
must be 90 degrees. If the measured hypotenuses are not equal, the angle
(or angles) are not a perfect 90 degrees, or one or more of the sides of the
frame are not the proper length.

**Figure 3-18   Checking
a frame for squareness
using diagonal measure-
ment.**

Figure 3-19 Measuring the diameter of a section of pipe with a centering head.

THE CENTERING HEAD (Fig. 3-19).   The centering head is usually part of the combination square set. Placed on the blade as shown, it enables the determination of the diameter centerline and the center point of a round object of any size.

PROTRACTORS The protractor is used for both the direct measurement of angles and the indirect determination of angles through consideration of the following:

1. A *right angle* contains 90 degrees.
2. A *straight angle* contains 180 degrees.
3. An *acute angle* contains less than 90 degrees.
4. An *obtuse angle* contains more than 90 degrees but less than 180 degrees.
5. Angles are *complementary* if they total 90 degrees.
6. Angles are *supplementary* if they total 180 degrees.
7. An *included angle* is one equally divided by the center line or central axis of the workpiece (see Fig. 3-20).

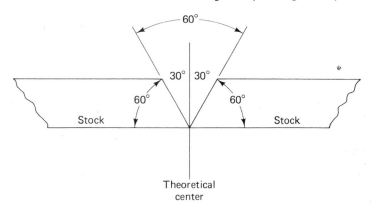

Figure 3-20 Arriving at a specified "included angle" of 60°.

The protractor ordinarily measures no closer than 1 degree. Vernier protractors are capable of measuring as fine as $\frac{1}{60}$ of a degree, or 1 minute. Figure 3-21 illustrates various protractor types.

In practical shop fabrication, the use of the protractor is limited to

Figure 3-21 Protractors.

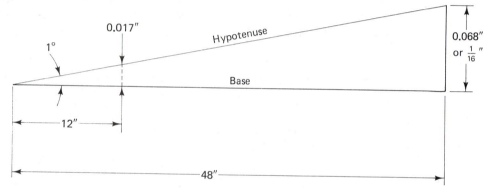

Figure 3-22 Effect of 1 degree of angular error upon the length of the side opposite the angle.

relatively few measurements on parts of limited size. Linear dimensions that would be the result of angular measurements are more easily and accurately determined by triangulation or "full-size" layout. The point to remember in angular measurement using a protractor is the magnification of error as the work gets larger. As illustrated in Figure 3-22, an error of only 1 degree 48 inches out from the angle can result in a deviation of more than $\frac{1}{16}$ inch in the length of the side opposite the angle.

VERNIER GAUGES The need for precision measurements in both sheet metal and plate fabrication results in the use of three basic instruments; the micrometer, the caliper, and the height gauge. These devices are used to determine dimensions down to one thousandth of an inch (0.001). The vernier scale is based on the fact that although the human eye cannot accurately discern the distance between two parallel lines, it can distinguish two opposing lines that line up with one another as in Figure 3-23.

Figure 3-24 shows typical types of vernier micrometer, caliper, and a height gauge. The common elements to all three are the beam or fixed scale and the sliding or movable scale. On a caliper, the beam scale is graduated in inches up to the capacity of the instrument (6 inches, 8 inches, 24 inches, etc.). The beam scale is further divided in hundreds of thousandths as indicated by the numbers 1 through 9 between the inch graduations (see Fig.

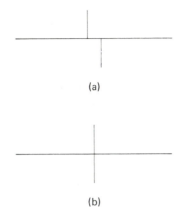

(a)

(b)

Figure 3-23 Principle involved in reading a vernier scale: (a) distance between opposing lines must be estimated; (b) even a slight misalignment could be seen.

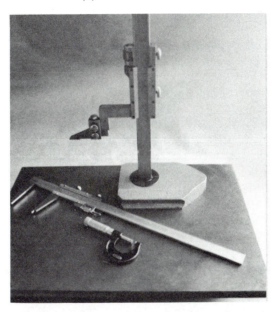

Figure 3-24 Typical vernier measuring tools.

Figure 3-25 Vernier caliper beamscale: (a) in increments of 25 thousandths; (b) in increments of 50 thousandths.

3-25). The beam scale is further divided into either 50-thousandth or 25-thousandth increments. The micrometer is always divided into 25 thousandth, as they come in sets, with each one having an adjustment of only 1000 thousandths or 1 inch. The individual 50- or 25-thousandth graduations are next found on the sliding or movable scales, as shown in **Figure 3-26**.

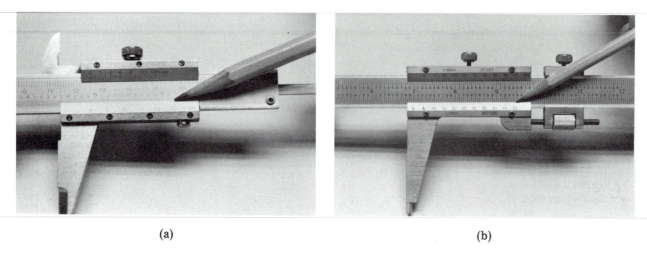

(a)   (b)

Figure 3-26 Sliding or movable scales for counting either (a) 25 or (b) 50 individual thousandths.

Reading the Vernier Caliper

In Figure 3-27 the decimal reading of the scale is 3.687. Read as "three inches, six-hundred eighty-seven thousandths," the position of the zero on the sliding scale is seen in relation to the zero on the beam scale. The distance between the jaws is 3 inches plus a certain amount, as the sliding scale zero is past or to the right of the 3 on the beam scale. The zero on the sliding scale is also to the right of the 6, indicating a reading of at least three and six-hundred thousandths. The sliding scale zero is also to the right of the 50-thousandth graduation of the beam scale, giving a reading of three and six-hundred-fifty thousandths plus a certain amount, as the sliding scale zero is even farther to the right of the 50-thousandth mark. Attention is now directed to the 50 individual thousandth graduations on the sliding scale.

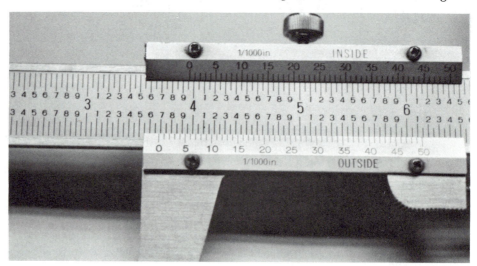

Figure 3-27 Vernier caliper reading of 3.687.

Of all those individual graduations, only one is perfectly aligned with any one line on the beam scale. That one is 37, showing that the zero on the sliding scale is thirty-seven thousandths past the three inches and six-hundred-fifty thousandths already indicated on the beam scale. Thus, as 50 and 37 equal 87, the reading is 3.687. Figure 3-28 shows a graphic sequence of the interpretation.

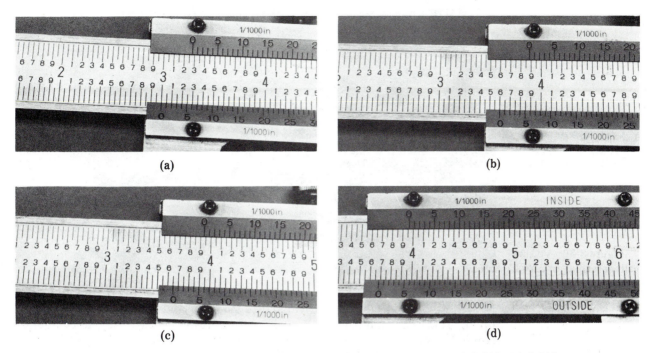

(a)

(b)

(c)

(d)

Figure 3-28 Steps leading up to a final reading (in inches) of 3.687: (a) 3.000; (b) 3.600; (c) 3.650; (d) 3.650 + .037 = 3.687.

In Figure 3-29, the reading of the scale is 2.218, or two inches and two-hundred-eighteen thousandths. The difference between this example and the previous one is the division of the beam scale into 25 thousandths of an inch rather than 50 thousandths. Thus there are four spaces between the two-hundred and three-hundred marks rather than two. The zero on the sliding scale is seen to be past or to the right of the 2-inch mark and the two-hundred-thousandths mark, indicating a reading of at least 2.200 (two inches, two-hundred thousandths). The sliding scale on this model vernier consists of graduations from 0 to 25 thousandths and close observation reveals that only the eighteenth graduation is perfectly aligned with any one mark on the beam. Thus the reading is 2.218. If the zero on the sliding scale was to the right of the first 25-thousandth mark, and the only graduation which was perfectly aligned was still 18, the reading would be 2.225 plus 18 thousandths, or two and two-hundred forty-three thousandths (2.243) (see Fig. 3-30).

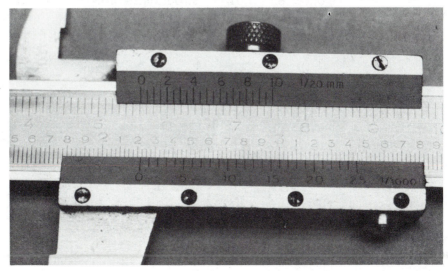

Figure 3-29 Vernier caliper reading of 2.218.

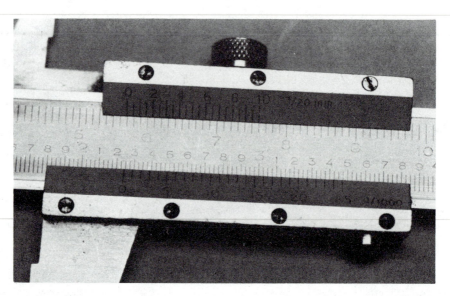

Figure 3-30 Vernier caliper reading of 2.243.

This example can also serve to demonstrate the reading of the micrometer, whose beam scale is also divided into 25-thousandth increments from zero up to 1000 thousandths, or 1 inch. As mentioned previously, micrometers come in sets, with each being adjustable from zero to 1 inch, 1 inch to 2 inches, 2 inches to 3 inches, and so on. In Figure 3-31 a 2-inch micrometer is selected to use in interpreting the same 2.218 dimension. As shown in the figure, the movable scale is laid out in increments from 0 to 25 on the beveled shoulder of the rotating barrel. The barrel has been rotated counterclockwise to open the jaws to just over 2 inches plus two-hundred thousandths, as indicated by the shaft or beam scale, which has just a little more than eight of its 25-thousandth divisions revealed (8 × 0.025 = 0.200). Again, directing attention to the graduations on the movable scale shows that the eighteenth increment is aligned with the longitudinal center line of the fixed scale. The reading is thus 2.218, or 2 inches plus two-hundred thousandths, plus 18 thousandths.

To obtain the 2.243 dimension as in the previous example, Figure 3-32 shows the barrel scale rotated counterclockwise still further, until an additional 25-thousandth graduation is revealed on the shaft scale. The opening is now two-hundred twenty-five thousandths (0.225) and if the eighteenth graduation is again aligned with the longitudinal center line, the reading will be 0.225 plus 0.018 or two-hundred forty-three thousandths (0.243).

The accurate reading of a vernier requires not only the ability to decipher the scale itself but also the employment of certain techniques in han-

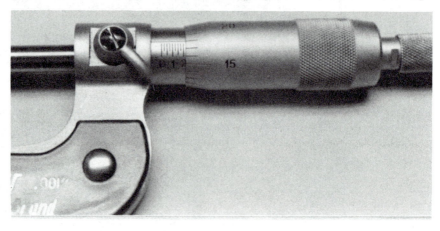

Figure 3-31 Micrometer reading of 2.218.

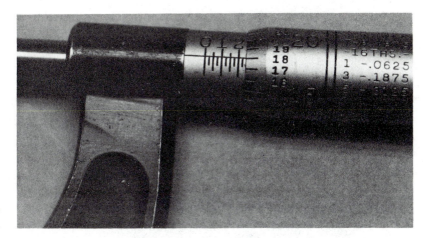

Figure 3-32 Micrometer reading of 2.243.

dling the device so as to guarantee that the reading observed on the scale is indeed the actual dimension between the fixed and movable parts of the device as they contact the surfaces of the object being measured.

Using the Vernier Caliper

Figure 3-33 shows the proper application in measuring a formed sheet metal part. The fixed jaw or blade of the beam scale is laid and held firmly against the edge of the flange. The movable part (attached to the sliding scale) is pushed by the thumb until it makes contact with the object. Care must be

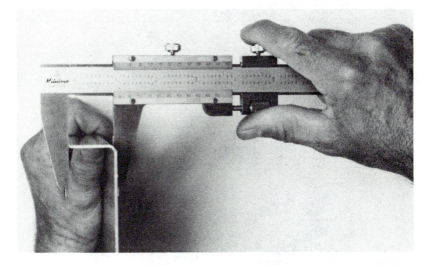

Figure 3-33 Proper holding and use of a caliper in measuring a bent flange.

taken to avoid excess pressure as the caliper is closed on the part. This can cause either the caliper or the part being measured to "give" or deform in some way as to give an inaccurate reading.

Using the Vernier Height Gauge

The height gauge is used in conjunction with a surface plate and an angle block (see Fig. 3-34). The plate and the block are themselves precision devices.

The surface plate may be either cast iron with a precision-ground flat top or a high-quality marble plate, again with a top surface precision ground flat to a very close dimension. It is necessary to keep these surfaces both

Figure 3-34 Height gauge, surface plate, and angle block.

clean and lubricated. Light machine oil may be used on the metal type, and the marble surface plates require either talcum powder or liquid soap.

The angle block is often of cast iron with precision-ground surfaces so as to form a perfect 90-degree angle with the plate surface (see Fig. 3-35). The piece to be laid out or measured is stood up on an appropriate edge and braced against the angle block.

Figure 3-35 90° angle formed by angle block and plate surface.

The reading of the height gauge is exactly like that of the vernier caliper, with the sliding scale being divided in either 25 or 50 graduations of 0.001 each.

When first using the gauge, be sure that it has been "zeroed." This means two things. First, it means that the scriber has been carefully ground to a fine edge, as shown in Figure 3-36. This edge is usually a piece of tool steel brazed onto the scriber body. Second, it means that when the assembled scriber is brought flat down on the surface plate, the reading of the height gauge is "zero" (Fig. 3-37).

Figure 3-36 Accurately ground scriber point.

Figure 3-37 Height gauge reading 0 with a ground scriber flat on the plat surface.

In setting the height gauge to scribe a dimension on a plate, the gauge is best laid on its side, as shown in Figure 3-38. Notice that the thumb is on the knurled adjustment knob of the sliding scale. Assuming a required dimension of five inches and six-hundred fifty-six thousandths, the sliding scale assembly is moved along the beam until its zero is past the 5-inch mark and up to the 650-thousandths graduation on the beam scale. Then, after tightening the main lockscrew, the knurled knob is slowly turned until the 0.006 mark is properly lined up with the appropriate graduation on the beam scale. The other lockscrew is now gently tightened so that there is no movement of the scriber as the gauge is brought upright again.

When scribing the line, use only enough pressure to mark the surface, which will usually have been covered with blue layout dye. Avoid deep layout lines on the actual piece as (1) subsequently, they may have to be removed, and (2) so doing avoids unnecessary wear on the scriber point. If the line to be scribed runs across the entire plate as shown in Figure 3-39, care

Figure 3-38 Method of holding a height gauge while setting the dimension.

Figure 3-39 Scribing a line across the plate.

Figure 3-40 Checking a flange height.

42

must be used to avoid running off the plate onto the angle block. These blocks are often case hardened and thus will damage the scriber point.

In using the height gauge to check the dimension of a finished part as in Figure 3-40, again, lay the part against the angle block so that, as in the photo, the flange to be measured is exactly parallel to the top of the surface plate.

Set the scriber at a dimension slightly higher than what you know to be correct. Once the gauge is positioned over the part, slowly rotate the knurled nut until the bottom of the scriber causes a slight drag on the surface of the part as the base of the height gauge is moved back and forth.

A careful mechanic can determine a dimension within 0.010 inch or even 0.005 inch. If greater accuracy is required, a dial indicator of the type used in machine shop work can be used (see Fig. 3-41).

Figure 3-41 Checking the flange height with a dial indicator attached to the height gauge.

Using the Micrometer

The micrometer is used most often to measure or verify stock thicknesses and diameters. Properly used, it is more accurate than the vernier caliper, especially on smaller dimensions. Typically, as shown in Figure 3-42a, the micrometer is used to determine the difference between 0.040 and 0.050 inch of aluminum sheet. Also, as shown in Figure 3-42b, the 0.006-inch difference between a No. 30 and No. 29 drill can be determined.

In measuring, the micrometer is held as shown, with thumb and fore-

(a)   (b)

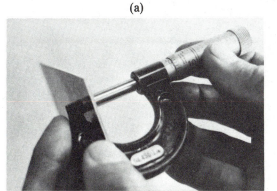
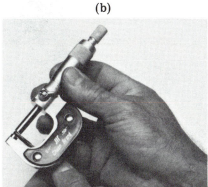

Figure 3-42 Using a micrometer to measure (a) stock thickness and (b) drill diameter.

finger. Rotate the knurled thimble clockwise to extend the spindle until it makes contact with the stock. The fine-adjustment ratchet knob can now be turned in a clockwise direction. Generally, it is turned until two or three "clicks" are heard. This fine adjustment guarantees that the spindle is firmly against the stock being measured without springing the frame of the micrometer open.

DIVIDERS AND TRAMMEL POINTS

As shown in Figure 3-43, dividers and trammel points are used to mark and lay out circles and arcs as well as scribe both inside and outside radii. The divider is similar to the pencil or chalk-holding compass except that both legs are ground to a fine point for greater accuracy. A compass with a clamp for holding a piece of soapstone is very often used in steel plate layout work, while more precise layout work is scribed with the point of the divider, leaving a mark on a dye-covered surface.

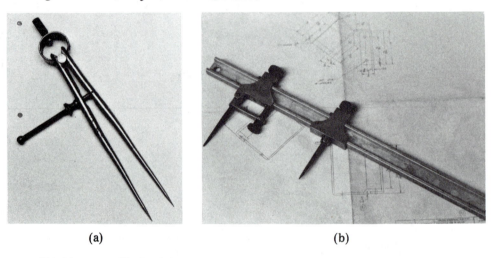

(a)   (b)

Figure 3-43 (a) Dividers and (b) trammel points.

    Dividers are limited in the size of circle they are able to scribe without becoming inaccurate and unwieldly to use. Figure 3-44 shows the divider being set to a 3-inch radius using a steel scale. The finely ground points are placed in the equally fine grooves of the 3-inch and 6-inch graduations. The resulting 6-inch circle will be very accurate both in dimension and in concentricity. A carefully pricked center-punch mark is used as the pivot point for the center of the circle or arc to be scribed.

    When the dimension to which the divider must be set becomes larger, the increasing angle of the divider's legs becomes a hinderance to its use.

Figure 3-44 Setting the divider to the dimension using a steel scale.

Figure 3-45 Using trammel points to scribe a large-diameter circle.

As shown in Figure 3-45, using trammel points overcomes this problem. The center point and the circumference scribe remain perpendicular to the layout surfaces. Although there may be a practical limit to the length of the radius bar, very large circles and arcs may be laid out.

Commercial trammel point sets have a variety of attachments for centering and marking. Many shops will often ingeniously design their own devices to fit their specific needs.

FILLET AND RADIUS GAUGES

Figure 3-46 illustrates the various uses of a radius gauge. Mostly used in machine shop work, the radius gauge provides a very accurate way of checking these difficult dimensions. Radius gauges are usually made of stainless material and are available in complete sets from $\frac{1}{16}$ to 1 inch in increments of $\frac{1}{64}$ inch.

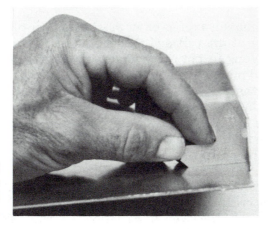

Figure 3-46 Checking a radius with a gauge from a typical assortment.

Chapter 4

BLUEPRINT READING and SKETCHING

Blueprint reading is the systematic and methodical interpretation of various lines, symbols, views, dimensions, written notes, and specifications. The first glance at a complex drawing often causes an inexperienced fabricator to say "I can never make that," while in actuality the part may very well be quite simple from a manufacturing standpoint.

The key here, either in a simple drawing of a two-hole bracket or a print of an involved assembly, is to consider each of the items on the print separately and at the appropriate time. As a guide to this concept, consider the print as a two-dimensional representation of the shape and size of a three-dimensional part.

BASIC VIEWS All prints will contain a series of views, the number of which is dependent on the complexity of the part and the amount of information needed for fabrication. Attempting to put every dimension of every detail on a single pictorial view would produce an almost indecipherable drawing. The orthographic projection of the part in Figure 4-1 clearly shows the advantage of making blueprints in this fashion. Every possible dimension and detail can be accurately represented. Although all six sides can be depicted in six separate views, only those views that are actually needed have to be included. An example of this can be seen in Figure 4-2. The part in drawing (a) is represented by top, front, and right-side views, whereas the part in drawing (b) is detailed in a front, left-side, and bottom view.

The most critical interpretation in blueprint reading is in the orientation of the actual part to the given views. Using the pictorial drawing in Figure 4-3 as an example, each individual view represents how the part appears as viewed from that direction. Usually, the view that gives the best representation of the appearance of the part will be designated as the front view. This does not have to be the actual functional front of the completed part. It is through this careful interpretation that the error of making a "mirror image" of the print is avoided.

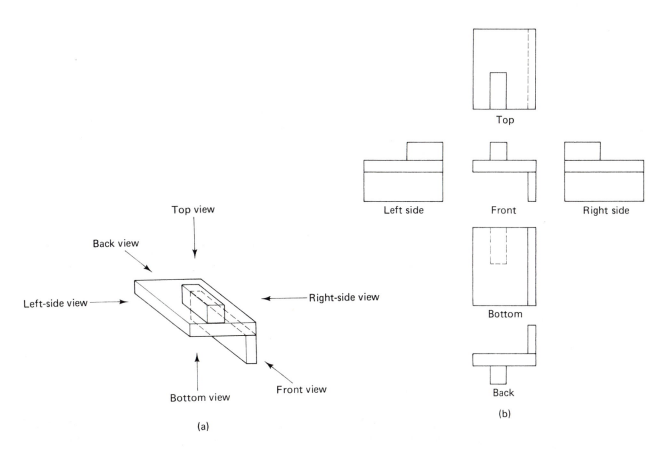

Figure 4-1 (a) Pictorial representation: (b) orthographic projection.

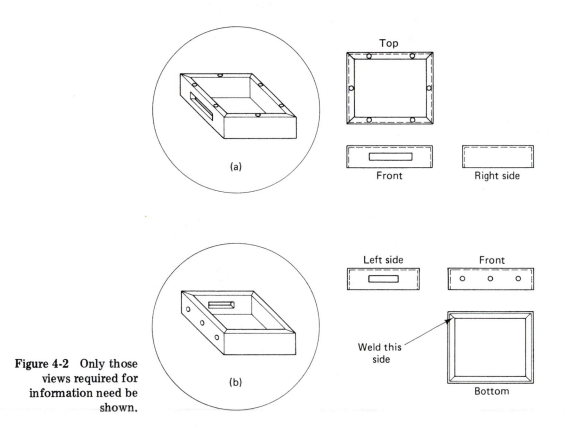

Figure 4-2 Only those views required for information need be shown.

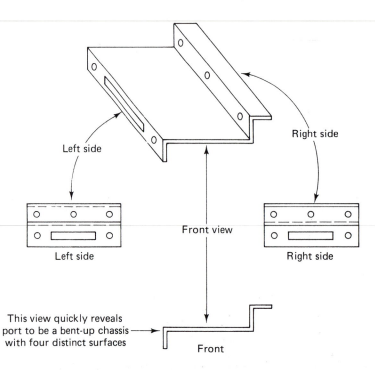

Left side

Right side

Front view

Left side

Right side

Figure 4-3 Front view determination for an orthographic projection.

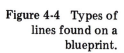

This view quickly reveals port to be a bent-up chassis with four distinct surfaces

Front

LINES

Figure 4-4 illustrates an example of the basic types of lines used on blueprints. Of all the lines shown, those that appear to be the darkest and heaviest are object lines. They are used to represent the shape of the part. Even on the most complex drawings, after a few minutes study, these lines will begin to stand out and the fabricator will be able to visualize the overall part outline.

The hidden lines, which are short dashes of medium thickness, are used to represent edges of surfaces not visible in that particular view. For example, the flange that is visible in the right-side view of Figure 4-5 is not visible in the top view and is therefore represented by a dashed line.

Figure 4-4 Types of lines found on a blueprint.

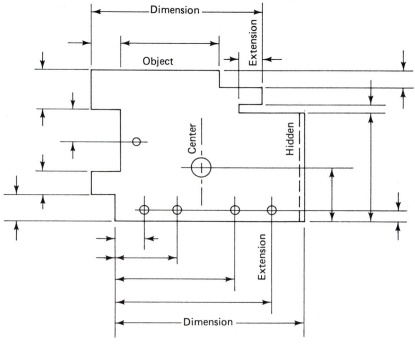

Dimension

Extension

Object

Center

Hidden

Extension

Extension

Dimension

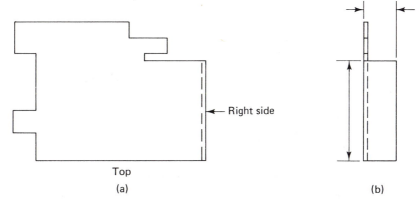

Figure 4-5 How a
hidden line depicts
material not visible
in a particular view:
(a) front view; (b)
right-side view.

(a) (b)

Centerlines are thinner and lighter than hidden lines. They are made up of long and short dashes and used to indicate the center of an object, hole, radius, circle, or curve.

Extension and dimension lines are used together to indicate the exact distance referred to by a dimension. The extension lines are thin, light, solid lines which extend off the object lines and specify the boundaries of a dimension. The dimension line is drawn between the extension lines and has arrowheads at each end. It is on this line that the actual dimension is placed.

METHODS OF DIMENSIONING

Dimensions supply two basic pieces of information. They denote part size and location for placement or machining of details such as holes or cutouts. The two types of dimensioning are the conventional and baseline methods.

Conventional dimensioning is the most commonly used method in metal fabrication. Parts are dimensioned as illustrated in Figure 4-6. Note that both partial and overall measurements are given.

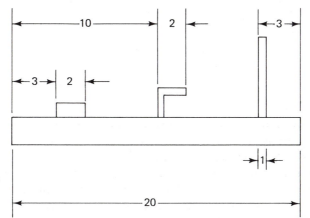

Figure 4-6 Example of
conventional
dimensioning.

When close-tolerance precision work is required, the baseline (datum) method will be used. In this method, all of the dimensions are taken from a base or datum line. This reference line will usually be a machined surface or centerline (see Fig. 4-7). This technique will eliminate any cumulative dimension errors. Baseline dimensioning is also the method most used in precision sheet metal fabrication and is further explained in Chapter 17.

A numerical dimension may be followed by the letters Ref (or REF) which stand for "reference." A reference dimension is not one to be used in construction but rather results from one or two other operations or settings. For example, in the drawing in Figure 4-8, the vertical leg of the

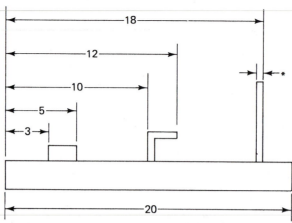

Figure 4-7   Example of baseline   dimensioning.

*Certain stock thicknesses are usually called out elsewhere on the print.

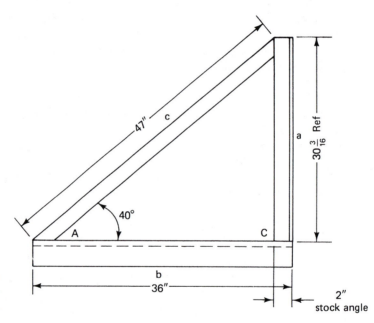

Figure 4-8   Print item giving a reference dimension.

triangular frame is given as a reference dimension and results from the specified trigonometric function of the angle and length of the inclined section that forms the hypotenuse. The intent here is for the fabricator to cut part C to within the tolerance allowed on the print and weld it to part B at an angle also within the tolerance of the print. If the fabricator cuts and fits part A using the reference dimension, it may not be possible for the specified tolerances to be maintained.

When a dimension is followed by the letters Typ (or TYP), it means that this dimension is typical or used in more than one place. The holes in Figure 4-9 are all the same size and located in the same spot in relation to each corner. To keep the drawing uncluttered, the draftsperson will dimension only one of the holes and designate it as typical. This type of dimensioning is also used on parts having identical hole patterns on opposing sides (see Fig. 4-10).

Not all linear dimensions will include indications of being either feet or inches. In an effort to limit unnecessary clutter on the field of the print, that information may be found elsewhere on the drawing.

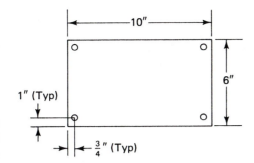

Figure 4-9 How the designation "Typ" is used.

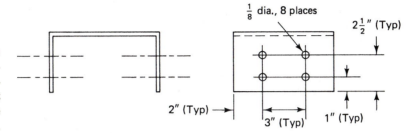

Figure 4-10 Using the term "Typ" to indicate the same dimensions in a view not included on the blueprint.

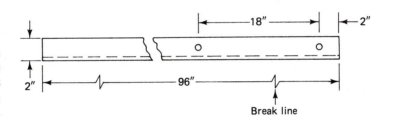

Figure 4-11 How a dimension can be labeled to show that it is not in scale with others on the print.

The dimensions given on a print may be further detailed by the addition of a short curved line under the number (see Fig. 4-11). This indicates that the dimension is not in scale with the other dimensions given. Depending on the style of the draftsperson, the same thing may be said by altering the dimension line as shown in the figure.

SECTIONAL VIEWS Often, the interior portion of a part cannot be clearly represented with a conventional view because it will appear only as dotted lines. In order to show these portions accurately, the draftsperson may use what is called a full section (see Fig. 4-12). When this appears on the drawing, the draftsperson is saying: "If you were to cut the part along the section line and look at it in the direction indicated by the arrows, it would look like the section AA view." The crosshatch marks indicate where the imaginary cut took place.

Depending on the shape of the part, it may be more clearly represented by a half section (see Fig. 4-13). In this view the imaginary cutting plane exposes only half of the cross section. This is adequate because the part is symmetrical.

AUXILIARY VIEWS If the part being drawn has an inclined surface, this surface cannot be accurately detailed without using an auxiliary view. A standard view would make the surface details appear distorted (Fig. 4-14). The auxiliary view will show only the inclined surface, not the entire part. This technique allows the

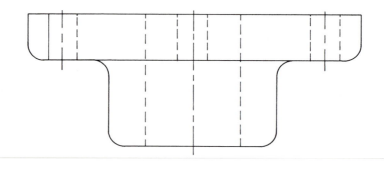

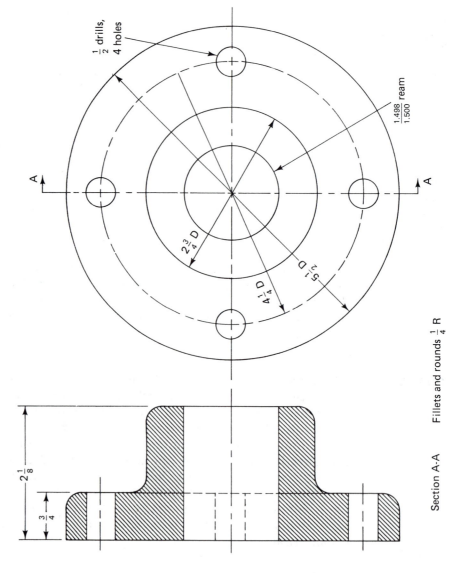

$\frac{1}{2}$ drills, 4 holes

$\frac{1.498}{1.500}$ ream

$2\frac{3}{4}$ D

$4\frac{1}{4}$ D

$5\frac{1}{2}$ D

$2\frac{1}{8}$

$\frac{3}{4}$

Section A-A   Fillets and rounds $\frac{1}{4}$ R

Figure 4-12   Full-section view.

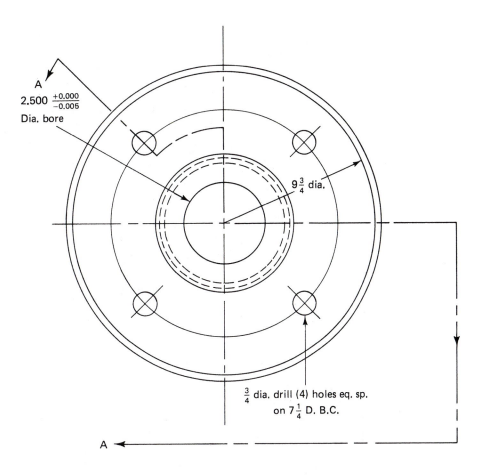

A

2.500 $^{+0.000}_{-0.005}$
Dia. bore

$9\frac{3}{4}$ dia.

$\frac{3}{4}$ dia. drill (4) holes eq. sp.
on $7\frac{1}{4}$ D. B.C.

A

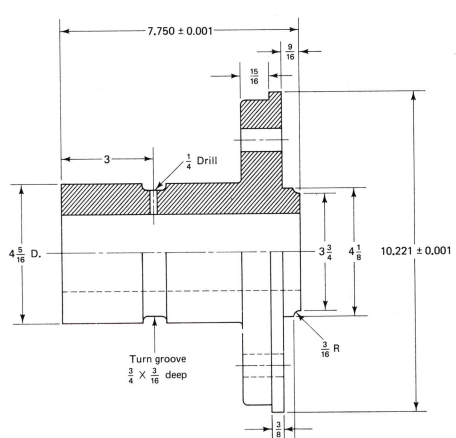

7.750 ± 0.001

$\frac{9}{16}$

$\frac{15}{16}$

3

$\frac{1}{4}$ Drill

$4\frac{5}{16}$ D.

$3\frac{3}{4}$

$4\frac{1}{8}$

10.221 ± 0.001

$\frac{3}{16}$ R

Turn groove
$\frac{3}{4} \times \frac{3}{16}$ deep

$\frac{3}{8}$

$\frac{3}{8}$

Figure 4-13 Half-
section view.

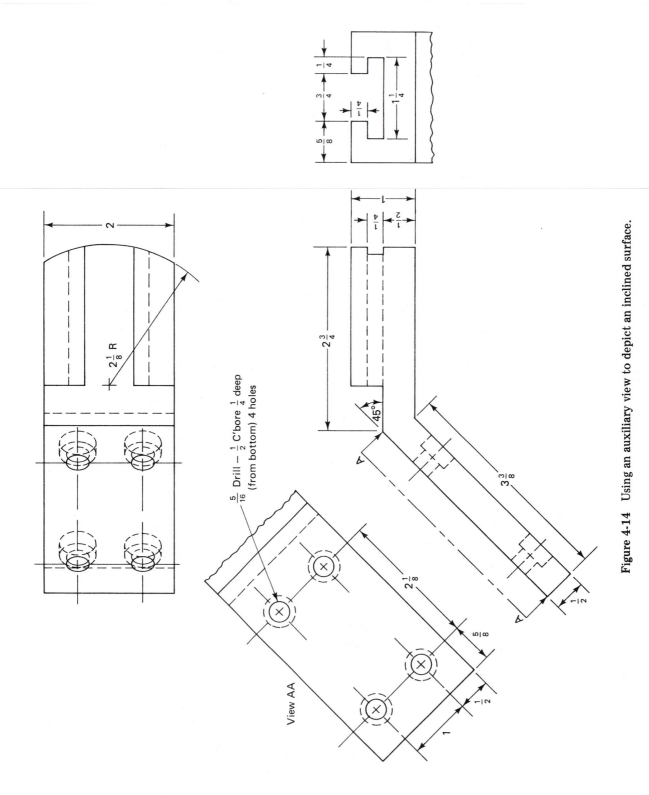

Figure 4-14 Using an auxiliary view to depict an inclined surface.

draftsperson to represent and dimension a surface accurately and detail that which would otherwise be obscure.

NOTES AND SPECIFICATIONS

Notes may be found anywhere on a drawing or in a numbered column off to one side. The note is merely a written instruction that cannot be explained through dimensions or symbols. Typical would be: "Radius this edge to ⅛ inch as shown" or "Countersink 100 degrees to 0.155-inch diameter."

Specifications are, just as the term implies, specific requirements for material, hardware, and a variety of manufacturing processes. Specifications are usually grouped in a bill of materials or "find" list. A detail would be labeled with a teardrop-shaped device which contains a "find" number, which is subsequently found on the list (see Fig. 4-15). This list is most often found on the lower right side of the blueprint just above the title box.

4	MS 20426 AD 3-3	RIVET				11
2	M 24066/2-118	CLIP				16
2		STUD			990214-1	15
2	SE079B01	TERMINAL STUD				14
2	MS 20426AD2-7	RIVET				13
1		SPACER	¼ sq BAR AL AL/2024·T4 PER Q QA·268		398661.8	12
		MARKING		4 5	980024·1	11
AR		ENAMEL EPOXY		4 5	985952·1	10
		CHEMICAL FILM		3	981605·3	9
		WIELDING FUSION		1	981811	8
8	MS 20470 AD -3	RIVET				7
10	MS 20426 AD 2-3	RIVET				6
2		NUT			136145·1	5
4		NUT			990293.31	4
4		RETAINER. BD MTG			334386·1	3
1		SUPPORT	.050 THK AL ALY 5052 H 32 PER QQ-A .250/8		398661.7	2
1		BRACKET	.050 THK AL ALY 5052 H 32 PER QQ-A-250/8		398661.6	

Figure 4-15 Typical specification list, often referred to as a "find list."

TITLE BOX

This area contains a wealth of information that is used in the initial stages of manufacture. Included are:

1. The name of the part
2. The part and/or print number
3. The company or agency using the part
4. The scale of the print
5. The number of prints (sheets) that make up the whole drawing
6. The people connected with making the print
7. The material (if not indicated elsewhere)
8. The finish
9. The application of the part
10. The tolerances required
11. The revision letter

Figure 4-16 shows a typical blueprint title box.

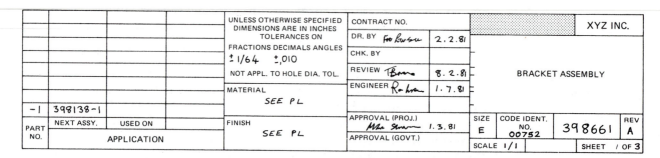

Figure 4-16 Blueprint title box.

REVISION BOX   The upper right corner of the print may contain an area that notes if and where changes have been made in the drawing. Figure 4-17 illustrates a typical box with a list of several revisions which should coincide with the revision letter in the title box. The revision concept is used where minor dimensional and informational changes can be called out without redrawing the entire print.

REVISIONS				
ZONE	LTR	DESCRIPTION	DATE	APPROVAL
	—	ISSUED		
	A	REV PER ECN C60809		
	B	REV PER ECN C69360		
	C	REV PER ECN C74950		
	D	REV PER ECN C77452		

Figure 4-17 Revision box. ECN, engineering change notice.

HOLE LEGEND   Many parts that contain a large number of various-size holes would be difficult to detail on a drawing. In these cases the holes are simply labeled with sequential letters: A, B, C, D, and so on. The hole legend is a list of descriptions for the lettered holes and is shown in Figure 4-18.

It is important to study the print for a period of time in order to get an idea of just what is required and to plan a logical sequence of steps and operations. It soon becomes apparent that more than just a few of these initial decisions are not practical and must be discarded or revised to meet developing situations as the reading of the print proceeds.

Both seasoned and novice fabricators often find it profitable to redraw, in sketch form, many of the print details in order to gain a clearer idea of what is needed to make the part and prepare a material size list.

4 | 3

Hole Legend		
Ltr	Hole Size	Qty
A	See section A-A	28
B	See section B-B	142
C	See detail C	4
D	265 + 0.007 dia.	9
E	0.098 + 0.005 dia.	18
F	0.135 + 0.006 dia.	19
G	0.220 + 0.005 dia.	2

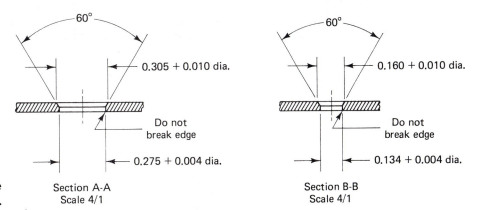

60°
0.305 + 0.010 dia.
Do not break edge
0.275 + 0.004 dia.
Section A-A
Scale 4/1

60°
0.160 + 0.010 dia.
Do not break edge
0.134 + 0.004 dia.
Section B-B
Scale 4/1

Figure 4-18 Hole legend.

SKETCHING   As stated in Chapter 2, almost everything fabricated will be comprised of one or more of the basic geometric shapes. When developing shop sketches, try to visualize the part as just that. The first example used in Figure 4-19 is a welded stainless steel assembly. As each component is examined, you can see that the part consisted of a cylindrical tube, two rectangles, and a square. The number of views required to show all of the detail accurately must now be determined. For this particular example, two will suffice. Remember that

Figure 4-19 Assembly to be sketched.

the goal is not to draw a precise blueprint of exact scale but a readable working drawing. The only items that must be precise are the dimensions. Check all of the dimensions twice for accuracy.

A few simple drafting tools such as a 12-inch ruler, 45-degree triangle, 30–60-degree triangle, and a circle template will be helpful in sketch development.

Start the sketch with the front view. Lightly draw a rectangle to establish the overall size of the view (see Fig. 4-20). Next, sketch in the lines representing the base cross section, cylinder, and side plates (see Fig. 4-21). With the front view roughed out, extend the construction lines up to start forming the top view (see Fig. 4-22). Draw in the horizontal lines representing the base plate and side plates and the circular lines of the cylinder cross section (see Fig. 4-23). A circle template can be used for greater neatness and accuracy.

As the sketch is being developed, draw all of the lines very lightly. This will make the job of erasing mistakes very easy. When the sketch is completed, check for reasonable size proportion of each component and trace over all of the object lines. These lines should be bold and dark. Erase all construction lines.

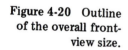

Figure 4-20 Outline of the overall front-view size.

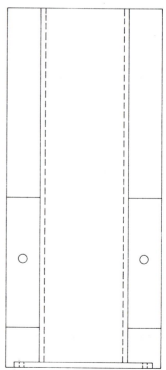

Figure 4-21 Roughed-out front view.

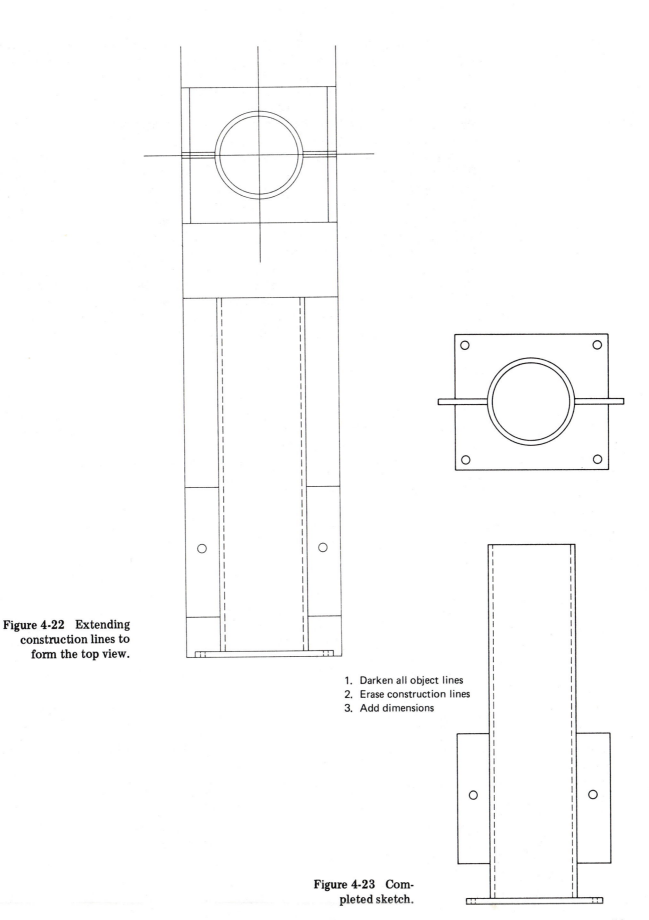

Figure 4-22 Extending construction lines to form the top view.

1. Darken all object lines
2. Erase construction lines
3. Add dimensions

Figure 4-23 Completed sketch.

A pictorial sketch is one that shows the length, width, and height of a part all in one view. Being able to make a reasonable sketch of this type can be a great help in visualizing a piece and determining fabrication methods. As an example, a pictorial sketch will be made of the part represented by the drawing in Figure 4-23. Although these sketches are usually drawn freehand, component parts should be of reasonable proportion to those of the actual piece.

The first step is to sketch the front view of the base plate and a 45-degree reference line from one corner (see Fig. 4-24a). A 45-degree triangle can be used to strike the reference line. Draw the remaining base plate lines (see Fig. 4-24b). All lines representing front and back surfaces will be horizontal, whereas the lines representing left- and right-side surfaces will be at a 45-degree angle. All corner lines are perpendicular. Next, sketch the lines for the base and corners of the upright section and the lines for its top surface (see Fig. 4-24c). Finally, check for reasonable size proportion, erase all unnecessary construction lines, and darken all object lines (see Fig. 4-24d).

As a final note on blueprints, remember that a print is meant to be taken literally. Do not read into it that which is not there and avoid the temptation to second-guess the draftsperson or designer if the print is incomplete. The print is then in error and the fabricator's obligation to build the part ceases until the correction is made by the people responsible. In this respect, never "scale the print." This means that because a dimension is missing, the fabricator might lay a scale on the drawing and take a measurement right off the print. Even taking into account a 1:1, 2:1, or any proportional ratio, this is a poor practice. Many drawings are photographically reproduced and for many reasons may be so enlarged or reduced in overall size. This would explain why a dimension, which, for example, was called out as being 1 inch on a print with a 1:1 scale may actually measure 1½ inches.

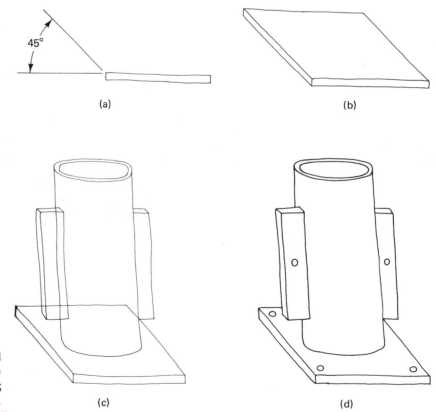

Figure 4-24 Freehand pictorial sketch: (a) step 1; (b) step 2; (c) step 3; (d) step 4.

(a)   (b)   (c)   (d)

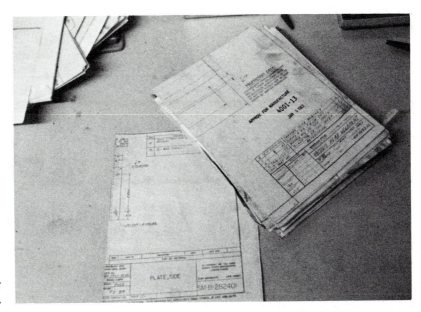

Figure 4-25 Properly folded blueprints.

Avoid writing or doing any computations on the drawing itself. Although it may at times be convenient to write in a clarifying dimension, it should be done judiciously. Figure 4-25 shows the proper method of folding a blueprint for filing when the work is complete. Notice how the part name and print number are easily seen.

Chapter 5

APPLIED METALLURGY

The selection of a particular metal alloy type to be used in fabrication is the result of extensive engineering and design thought which reduces all end-use considerations to the following criteria:

1. Availability and cost
2. Strength-to-weight ratios
3. Corrosion resistance
4. Electrical conductivity
5. Finishing required
6. Workability

It is the last consideration, workability, that can be broken down into each of the shop processes that have been discussed in this text. Workability can be thought of as those factors which make an alloy feasible to use in a product. Broadly speaking, the metal must first exhibit some measure of strength in the way it will be used. Second, as a salable product, it must be of appropriate appearance. Third, the metal selected must be economical to fabricate.

Without delving deeply into the field of metallurgy, the intent here is to acquaint the mechanic with the properties of the alloys commonly fabricated in the shop. Outlined will be those particular characteristics that affect bending and forming, punching and drilling, welding, and finishing requirements. Machining qualities will also be included, but only in the most general way. As a trade, machining is more comprehensively covered in texts devoted exclusively to that subject.

STEEL ALLOYS   The SAE (Society of Automotive Engineers) system of steel classification uses a four- or five-digit number to identify types of steel alloys. The first digit identifies the primary alloying element(s).

1. Plain carbon steels
2. Nickel steels
3. Nickel–chromium steels
4. Molybdenum steels
5. Chromium steels
6. Chromium–vanadium steels
7. Tungsten steels
8. Nickel–chromium–vanadium
9. Silicon–manganese

This numbering system is explained further in Chapter 6. From the standpoint of workability it would be well to detail the effect of these alloying elements as they pertain to the various manufacturing processes. Chart 5-1 provides a summary.

CHART 5-1 Effects of Alloying Elements

Element	Effect
Carbon	Increases in carbon cause greater hardness, greater tensile strength, and more responsiveness to heat treatment; with amounts over 1.7%, steel loses much of its workability and takes on the characteristics of cast iron
Nickel	Increases ultimate strength and toughness without significantly affecting hardenability; generally, additions of 1 to 4% are useful; however, additions of up to 35% are used in steels that have high impact resistance at very low temperatures
Chromium	Increases responsiveness to heat treatment and the depth of hardness penetration when added in amounts of 0.50 to 1.50%; in combination with nickel and in amounts up to 25%, there is high resistance to corrosion and oxidation
Molybdenum	Increases toughness and helps to resist softening at elevated temperatures; used in quantities of 0.10 to 0.40%
Vanadium	In quantities of 0.15 to 0.20%, vanadium retards grain growth after periods of extended heating and imparts significant shock and impact resistance
Tungsten	Used in very small amounts, tungsten produces a very fine grain steel which can maintain the sharp cutting edge so necessary in tools; in larger amounts of 17 to 20%, it permits steel to maintain its strength at extremely high operating temperatures
Silicon	Used mostly during manufacture as an oxidizer; in amounts up to 2.5% in finished steel, it improves strength and hardenability; certain steels may have even higher amounts of silicon to improve electrical characteristics

CHART 5-1   Effects of Alloying Elements (continued)

Element	Effect
Manganese	Second only to carbon in importance; present in all steels in amounts of 0.5 to 2%, acting as a deoxidizer and imparting strength and responsiveness to heat treatment; when manganese is used in larger amounts (10 to 15%), steel exhibits very high resistance to impact and penetration
Lead	In small amounts of 0.15 to 0.35%, lead improves machinability
Sulfur	In amounts of 0.06 to 0.30%, sulfur improves machinability but interferes with welding
Copper	May be added in amounts of 0.15 to 0.25% to improve resistance to atmospheric corrosion and to increase tensile and yield strengths while causing only a slight loss in ductility

In the aforementioned, several terms have been introduced which have a direct bearing on the mechanical aspects of fabricating parts with the typical machinery that has been described in the appropriate sections of the text. The exact meaning of terms such as toughness, hardness, and other descriptive terms in metallurgy can be found in the glossary in Appendix 1.

Applications

Most fabricated products, if made of steel, are of the low-carbon variety. Thus they would typically bear the numbers 1018 through 1024. Even those items considered structural would be fabricated of such low-carbon or mild steel. Rolled steel shapes such as angles, channels, and beams fall into this category. Although in the construction industry there has been an increase in the use of high-strength, low-alloy steels in recent years, most of the fabricated tonnage of steel produced is of the low-carbon non-alloy-bearing type. These steels pose no particular problems in fabrication. Most machinery capacity ratings are based on the use of steels in the tensile strength range, 50,000 to 60,000 psi. Thus, punching operations, as well as bending and forming, can be carried out with standard tooling and with minimum wear and tear on equipment. Because of the limited carbon content, 0.25% or less, both welding and flame cutting can be done without the danger of induced hardness or tempering. The need for pre- and postheat treatment is almost entirely eliminated, and the more commonly available and less expensive welding filler rods can be used.

As steels with higher-carbon contents and with additional alloys added are selected, allowances must be made for their higher strength during the manufacturing process. Capacities of machines must often be reduced by up to one-half to accommodate these stronger and tougher materials. Yet, in machine shop processes such as turning and milling, the metallurgical characteristics of such higher-strength steels are actually an improvement. More stable and accurate dimensioning as well as improved surface finishing is possible with the addition of the various alloying elements. Of course, as strength and hardness increase in a steel alloy, machining can become difficult and expensive.

Hot-Rolled and Cold-Rolled Steel

Within the low-carbon, mild-steel groups there is the option of choosing either the hot-rolled or cold-rolled variety. Although stainless steel and some high-alloy steels are cold rolled, the term "cold rolled" is most often applied to plain, low-carbon, mild steel.

As its name implies, cold-rolled steel has been rolled several times while cold to give a bright, smooth finish and distinct one-way grain orientation. This rolling imparts a degree of hardening that is designated as No. 1 (hard) through No. 6 (soft). This type exhibits close dimensional tolerance and uniform stock sizing and is supplied with an oily coating to preserve the surface.

Hot-rolled steel, which is heated bright red when rolled to its finished size, has a coating of burned oxides as a residue of the rolling operation. Thus this type is not as dimensionally stable and the edge condition differs from the cold-rolled variety, as shown in Figure 5-1.

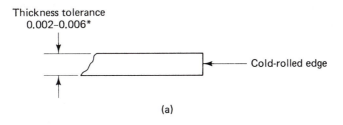

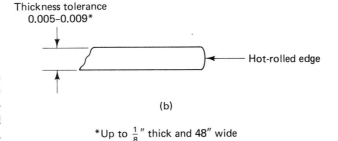

Figure 5-1 Thickness tolerance and edge condition of (a) cold- and (b) hot-rolled steel.

*Up to $\frac{1}{8}$" thick and 48" wide

Hot-rolled steel is generally more ductile and is more easily formed. However, the oxide flakes that continually break off have a tendency to load up on die and cutting surfaces.

The type of final product finishing is usually the determining factor in selection. Although both can be painted, the hot-rolled material requires less preparation and holds both primer and paint very well. Cold-rolled steel requires baking for good adherence and is more suitable for plated finishes.

ALUMINUM Aluminum is alloyed with a variety of elements in order to meet specific commercial requirements. The demands include corrosion resistance, electrical conductivity, strength, and appearance as well as good workability in various manufacturing processes.

The aluminum sheets, plates, and shapes commonly fabricated are approximately 96% pure, with the balance being the alloying elements needed for a particular application. The series designations for these basic types, together with the primary alloying elements, are:

1. 1000 series—commercially pure (99%)
2. 2000 series—copper
3. 3000 series—manganese
4. 4000 series—silicon
5. 5000 series—magnesium
6. 6000 series—silicon and magnesium
7. 7000 series—zinc

Within these series designations are approximately 150 separate alloy types which meet a variety of end-use demands and workability criteria. The following paragraphs describe the characteristics and workability of those alloys most commonly fabricated in the metal shop. In addition to the basic numerical designation, there is often a letter suffix which denotes degree of hardness which has been induced by either cold working (H) or heat treatment (T). The letter O indicates the softest type within an alloy group. Melting temperatures vary with alloy content but average approximately 1100°F.

Alloy 2024-T3

This is a strong, hard alloy with a tensile strength of 70,000 psi (at 75°F). Its greatest use is in machined structural components. Bending and forming are difficult. Internal bend radii must be at least three to five times the material thickness up to 1/16 inch and six to nine times thickness for 1/4 inch. The alloy punches well, leaving a clean, straight-walled hole with minimum burr.

Figure 5-2 Heat-affected zone (HAZ) of a weldment. The size of the HAZ (shaded area) is determined by the amount of heat applied and the relative cross section of the work.

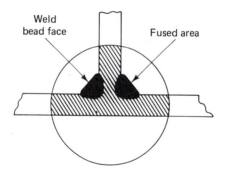

Weld bead face

Fused area

Fusion welding is not recommended. The heat-affected zone becomes extremely brittle (see Fig. 5-2). Resistance spot welding is applicable; however, design allowances should be made for this crack-sensitive hardness. Brazing should not be attempted, which leaves riveting as the most satisfactory fabrication method. The alloy will also hold a good thread if of appropriate thickness.

Alloy 3003-0

This alloy is extremely malleable and with a tensile strength of 16,000 psi is one of the lowest-strength alloys commonly fabricated. Because of its softness it is often either deep-drawn or spun into intricate shapes such as seamless containers and tanks. Thicknesses up to 3/8 inch can be bent with a zero internal-bend radius. Such cold working will, however, increase its hardness and tensile strength appreciably. Punching and drilling must be done carefully with minimum die clearances and sharp "high-spiral" drills due to its almost gummy softness. Fabrication by machining should be avoided.

This alloy can be purchased in a strain-hardened condition with a tensile strength of 22,000 psi, which allows for better fabricating qualities.

The alloy is highly weldable, both by fusion and resistance spot. This type also brazes well. The 3000 series aluminum will not respond to any kind of heat treatment, including that of welding, and with the use of the proper filler rod the entire weldment will remain soft and ductile.

Alloy 5052-H-32

This alloy, cold worked and thus strain hardened to a ¼-hard condition as indicated by the suffix H-32, is widely used in all forms of fabricated sheet metal products. As a magnesium-based alloy, it is one of the most corrosive-resistant aluminums. Grades 5083 and 5086, which have an even higher alloy content, are referred to as "marine grades."

This is a medium-strength alloy with an average tensile strength of 34,000 psi. However, it is prudent to take into account its yield point of 27,000 psi. This results in a relatively low percent of elongation compared to other grades discussed here. Although this rigidity and hardness may allow for dimensionally stable and sturdy sheet metal structures, intelligent design and careful fabrication methods must be used to overcome its crack sensitivity. This aluminum bends and forms very well with zero internal-bend radii possible up to ⅛-inch thickness. Even ¼-inch material may be bent with no radius if carefully done. Punching and drilling can be accomplished easily and with adequate dimensional stability. The material is hard enough to take a thread, but thinner cross sections usually require the installation of the various types of hardware described elsewhere in the text.

This type is also highly weldable as long as the proper filler rod is used. Spot-welding qualities are excellent; however, brazing is difficult. Machining is good but the increased hardness of higher H designations should be considered. This trade-off, however, may be unacceptable with the lower ductility needed for bending and forming.

Alloy 6063-T5

This type of aluminum is found and used mostly in the form of extruded shapes (see Fig. 5-3). After some heat treatment, the final hardness is achieved as the material is drawn through the dies to give it particular shape. Known as "architectural grade," its uniform shape and dimensions, as well as its characteristically bright and smooth finish, make it ideal for fascia trim and for use in metal furniture and cabinetry. The tensile strength of the alloy is 30,000 psi.

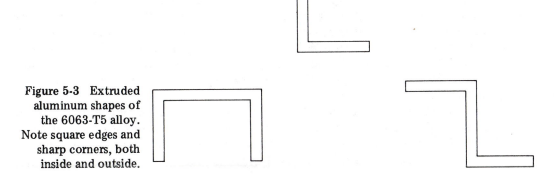

Figure 5-3 Extruded aluminum shapes of the 6063-T5 alloy. Note square edges and sharp corners, both inside and outside.

Series 6063 aluminum contains 0.4% silicon. Silicon additions provide responsiveness to thermal heat treatment. That is, the alloy containing silicon can be hardened or softened by specific heating and cooling conditions. There is also a very small amount of magnesium added, but as a largely "pure" alloy, it exhibits excellent resistance to corrosion—thus its wide use in exterior applications.

Series 6063 aluminum is hard enough to fabricate with ease, and although it is considered highly weldable, there is a loss of strength in the immediate weld area. As a result, design allowances for welded structures must be made. This type can also be brazed with great success.

The alloy has good fabricating qualities; however, machining can only be rated fair. When turning and milling there is a tendency for the cuttings to load up on the tool bit.

It might be prudent at this time to discuss methods of lubricating aluminum when it is being processed in various ways. All aluminum will start to become soft and gummy when approaching 650 to 700°F. This temperature is easily reached during any type of machining operation.

Series 6063 alloy and most other types are generally sawed to size or shape. This is particularly true for rolled or extruded shapes and for plate thicknesses which may be beyond shear capacity. Both radial-arm and table saw blades as well as band saw blades should be loaded with beeswax before beginning to cut. Candle wax is an adequate substitute. Similarly, the wax should be applied to grinding and sanding disks. Without this protective film of wax, cutting teeth and grits become literally plastered with the soft aluminum and are useless. When milling and turning, kerosene is the ideal lubricant. Tapping and drilling calls for a mixture of kerosene and white lead. Automatic tapping particularly requires constant and complete lubrication for which there are several commercial preparations.

Alloy 6061-T6

With a tensile strength of 45,000 psi, this alloy is used for most of the structural applications of aluminum. It is a complex alloy consisting of relatively small amounts of copper, magnesium, chromium, and a full 1% of silicon. This last addition allows the alloy to be heat treated to a suitable hardness and relatively high yield point (40,000 psi). The alloy, because of this hardness, machines and fabricates very well. Forming and bending, however, can be difficult. Minimum-bend radii of three times material thickness up to 1/8-inch thick are required to avoid cracking.

This alloy, purchased in the T6 condition, can partially be annealed at the point of use to allow easier forming. The annealing temperature of aluminum is a little over 600°F. A heat marker such as a Tempstick could be used, but blackening the area to be formed with the carbon from a highly carburizing oxyacetylene torch will do just as well. Manipulating a neutral flame back and forth over the blackened area until the carbon burns away will be a good indicator of annealing temperature. The material is now in the O temper condition if heated through its entire cross section. Even after the material cools, it will remain soft for several hours. The alloy will eventually harden back up to a T3 or T4 condition (natural aging) over a period of 20 to 24 hours.

6061-T6 is purchased both in sheet thicknesses and as plate several inches thick. The structural shapes are similar to those found in hot-rolled steel (see Fig. 5-4). Solid bar stock as well as tubing and pipe of this alloy have good corrosive resistance. Although machining qualities are not as good

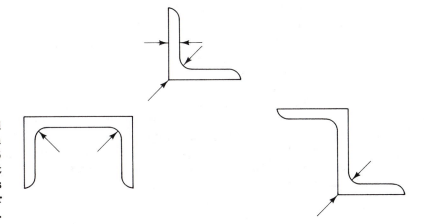

Figure 5-4 Typical structural aluminum shapes of the 6061-T6 alloy. Note the slight taper on stock legs and thicker corner sections.

as those of the harder alloys, when subsequent welding is specified, this is the type of aluminum to use.

Series 6061 can be welded by resistance spot and fusion methods and it brazes very well. As with all aluminum, the inert-gas welding processes provide the most sound and X-ray-quality welds. Fusion welding must employ filler materials high in silicon so that the fused areas respond to heat treatment exactly in the same way as does the parent metal.

Recall that the heat of welding will soften the alloy to the O temper. As shown in Figure 5-5, the weldment will show varying degrees of temper immediately after welding. After 20 to 24 hours of natural aging, while the fused area will regain some hardness, the heat-affected areas will still vary in temper.

To achieve full hardness and strength throughout such weldments, it is required that the full thermal treatment be repeated. This includes, at specified temperatures and time durations, annealing (stress relief), solution heat treatment (quenching), and artificial aging (holding-oven time). If this procedure is not possible or practical, the loss of strength due to welding can be compensated for by increased cross-section dimensions and design factors.

Series 6061 alloy is also used for fabrication and joining by the dip brazing process. Purchased in the O temper, intricate assemblies and shapes can be formed and held together by tack welding or by employing slots and tabs. The joints to be brazed are painted with a flux, then the entire assembly

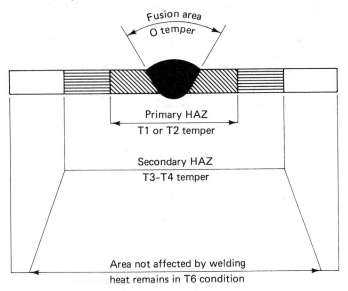

Figure 5-5 Effect of welding heat on temper (6061-T6).

is immersed in a bath of molten braze material. The braze flows through the prepared joints and at the same time the alloy is solution heat treated to the T4 condition.

7000 Series Aluminum

This series contains relatively large amounts of zinc (4 to 6%) as well as significant amounts of copper and magnesium. The result is a very hard, strong alloy that has excellent machining qualities and is often selected as forging material. It is available in both O and up to T6 tempers with over 80,000 psi tensile strength. Although it can be resistance spot welded, its fusion welding and brazing qualities are poor and not recommended.

MAGNESIUM   The mechanic today is most likely to see magnesium in the form of a casting that may require repair or modification. It is the lightest of all structural metals, with aluminum being 1½ times heavier. Thus for a time it was in direct competition with aluminum for use in air frame construction. But as a fabricated metal in either sheet or bar stock, its workability has proven to be too conditional in most modern metalworking applications. Magnesium parts can be welded and brazed by a variety of processes. Fusion welding is best accomplished with the inert-gas processes.

Many magnesium alloys are subject to stress corrosion cracking during and after fabrication. This means that any bending and forming operations must be done with great care. Radii many times the material thickness must be used when bending even the thinnest sheet. The use of induction-heated V dies may reduce the need for such larger radii, but may still require 20 to 30 times material thickness.

Magnesium also presents problems of galvanic action when in close assembled contact with itself, other metals, and even wood. The use of primers, nonmetalic washers, and careful alloy selection is very critical.

Solid magnesium stock will not easily ignite and burn; however, finely divided particles such as grindings, chips, and turnings are a definite fire hazard. Accumulation of such debris must be disposed of promptly and properly.

STAINLESS STEEL   Stainless steel is an alloy which contains significant amounts of chromium. The material is highly corrosion resistant and extremely strong. Depending on alloy type, the average tensile strength will be approximately 85,000 psi.

There are four basic types, bearing the American Iron and Steel Institute (AISI) numerical designations 410, 430, 302, and 202. The primary alloy content of each is as follows:

Type	Content
410	Chromium, 12%
430	Chromium, 17%
302	Chromium, 18%; nickel, 8%
202	Chromium, 18%; nickel, 5%; manganese, 8%

Additional alloy types are derived by adding specific elements in closely controlled amounts. These additions either change or enhance a particular alloy's corrosive resistance, strength, or most important from the fabricator's standpoint, the material's workability. In this respect stainless types are broadly classified as being hardenable by various methods according to their basic grain structure. The austenitic type, which includes both the 200 and 300 series numbers, are hardened only by cold-working operations. The martensitic type, which includes most but not all of the 400 series, are hardenable either by air or furnace cooling or by quenching. The ferritic type includes a group of 400 designations that is not hardenable.

Most stainless types are nonmagnetic, but several alloys in the 400 group are magnetic in all conditions. Additionally, there have been alloys developed with particular properties that enhance high-temperature service. These fall into a 500 series designation or may have special manufacturer's designations.

For sheet metal fabrication, which would include welding and brazing as well as extensive bending and forming, type 304 is recommended. All of the stainless alloys have good welding and machining qualities, but careful review of the manufacturer's specifications will reveal which number is best in each instance. Obviously, in the case of welding, the hardening types will require an additional post-heat-treatment operation.

Careful consideration must also be given to the end-use application. As stainless steel is used in the medical, chemical, and food-processing industries, resistance to particular corrosive environments is an important criterion for alloy selection.

Stainless steel fabrication is very hard on both machinery and tooling. Machine capacities must often be downgraded due to the material's strength and toughness. Downtime for tooling changes can be a significant factor in estimating costs. Also, the surface appearance of stainless often requires special handling during the fabrication process.

The old job-shop rule of thumb for estimating costs when fabricating stainless is to figure the job as mild steel, then triple the hours and dollar amount.

BRASS ALLOYS   Brass is an alloy containing primarily copper and zinc. Lead and silicon are also added to enhance workability. Increases in zinc additions progressively lower the melting temperature of brass. Zinc additions also increase the yellow appearance of the metal. Simple copper–zinc brasses are made in typical degrees of hardness or temper. Annealing is accomplished by quenching in water from about 1000°F.

Many types of brass carry both generic and proprietary names. *Form-brite, Revere Alloy 120*, and *red brass* and *clock brass* are typical. The type known as *naval brass* contains small amounts of tin and arsenic to inhibit the corrosive effects of salt water, while *leaded brass* has improved machining qualities.

Using the manufacturer's literature as a guide will allow intelligent selection of the type that will complement both end use and the fabrication processes involved.

COPPER   Most copper used commercially is in a high-purity state where its characteristic malleability and electrical properties can be used to maximum advantage. Annealed wrought copper has a tensile strength of 32,000 psi and 56% elongation, while cold-drawn (work-hardened) copper has a tensile strength of 56,000 psi but with only 6% elongation.

The addition of various alloying elements, as in brass, enhances both end-use applications and workability. Silver additions will raise the annealing temperatures of copper, while the electrolytic or oxygen-free type is of 99.9% purity and will not work harden even after extensive cold working. Additions of phosphor can increase the strength and resistance to corrosion but will lower the electrical conductivity of copper.

Again, various companies supply types of copper with particular end uses in mind. *Rocan Copper* (Revere Copper and Brass, Inc.) and *Cupaloy* (Westinghouse Electric Corp.) are but two examples. Local distributors that deal exclusively with such products are the best source of manufacturing data.

IDENTIFICATION OF METALS

The mechanic must be able to identify particular alloy types from within the larger group of the same material. As explained in the preceding sections, the particular alloy selected for use was so designated because it exhibited the required characteristics conducive to the desired end use and method of fabrication. When a part of aluminum sheet or steel plate unexpectedly cracks during a forming operation or cannot be properly welded, the shop not only experiences a loss in material cost, but also a loss in the hours of labor that went into the part up to that point.

End-use failure, where the part fails in service, can cause the loss of virtually thousands of dollars in associated equipment as well as the loss of human life. Many agencies and companies require that materials used be certified as to alloy content and analysis. This "certificate of compliance" is part of a documentation procedure that follows a plate or sheet of raw stock from the manufacturer's mill, through the distributor's warehouse, to the fabricator, and right on up to the end-use purchaser.

The fabricating shop will purchase either one or two alloy types or many different metals, depending on their product line and need. Most of the material, but not all, will be delivered with some sort of identifying labels or coding. It depends largely on the source and, to some extent, the type of material. Domestically manufactured material from the better-known mills (Alcoa, U.S. Steel, etc.) usually carry identifying stencils repeated at intervals across the stock. Alloy and tool steels often carry color coding to identify each specific type, but this code is not common to all manufacturers. Thus there is a burden on the shop and its personnel to make sure they are using and processing stock that will perform as expected during both fabrication and as a product.

Identification of Steels

The identification of various steel alloys can be accomplished by several methods. Most common is the spark test. The pattern of sparks thrown off can be used to identify several distinct alloy types as well as types of cast iron by the use of a pedestal grinder. Chart 5-2 depicts these patterns. However, the best use of the grinding wheel is in comparing the unknown material with the spark pattern of a known sample. A magnet can be used to distinguish between stainless and other types of steel; however, this is not conclusive, as not all stainless is nonmagnetic. Of course, the magnet is always used to differentiate between ferrous and nonferrous metals when weight and appearance is not that easily discernible. Fracture and chip examination is also a suitable method but is not always practical.

CHART 5-2 Spark Chart

| White cast iron | Gray cast iron | Wrought iron | Mild steel | High-carbon (tool) steel | Stainless steel |

White cast iron: Short, small spark pattern, red at the start and straw yellow at the end.

Gray cast iron: Short, very small spark pattern, red at the start and straw yellow at the end.

Wrought iron: Long spark pattern, few sparks, straw yellow at the start and white at the end.

Mild steel: Long spark pattern, moderate amount of sparks, white in color.

High-carbon tool steel: Moderate pattern length, many sparks, white in color.

Stainless steel: Moderate pattern length, few sparks, straw yellow at the start and white at the end.

Identiciation of Aluminum Alloy Types

To the experienced eye, the various grades of aluminum are distinguishable from one another. By analyzing the amount of flexability, one can also determine the hardness or softness of the alloy.

The examination of a sheared edge can also identify an alloy group. Figure 5-6 illustrates such an edge condition within a group of alloys.

During the chemical baths used to clean aluminum for either welding or further finishing, certain types of alloys will exhibit distinct chemical reactions. The silicon–magnesium alloys (6061) will show a dark gray film when the chemical etchant acts on its oxide coating. Aluminums in the 5000 series will acquire a distinct light gray film, while the copper-based alloys will turn jet black. This film is removed in subsequent baths. The purer aluminums (1100 series) show no change in appearance during cleaning.

Magnesium

The various alloy types are almost impossible to identify visually. Physical tests that can be employed in the shop are also inconclusive. Often, when the lighter weight of magnesium is not readily apparent when compared with aluminum, these two similar-appearing materials can be identified in the following manner. Catch a small amount of filings in the center of a piece of

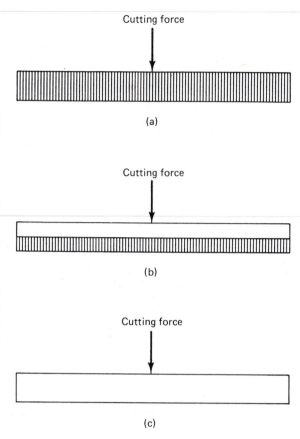

Figure 5-6 Identifying aluminum by sheared edge examination. (a) The sheared edge of harder aluminums (6061T6, 2024T6, 7000) will show distinct vertical break marks caused by cracking of the material when hit by a shear blade. (b) Medium-hard aluminum in the 5000 series will show a partially "knifed" cut edge; then a final "break" will occur. (c) Soft aluminum alloys will exhibit a bright, shiny edge as the shear blade "knifes" through the material.

note paper. The filings should be spread out rather than in a heap. Light the paper with a match. If the filings are magnesium, they will begin to flare brightly as the flame reaches them.

METAL IDENTIFICATION: AN OVERVIEW

When material is delivered to the shop and if it is not already stenciled or labeled in some way, it should be identified immediately and marked as to alloy type and thickness. A well-organized shop will have stock storage facilities that will keep the various materials separated until they are needed. In addition and most important, provisions must be made to identify and store drop-off or leftover random pieces. Many shops have either bins or barrels for this purpose and depend on the careful and conscientious effort of the mechanics to keep these less-than-full-size pieces separated.

The mechanic should make some effort to verify that the material selected is what it is supposed to be. Cutting off a small piece and attempting to bend, punch, or drill it might reveal an error in labeling that could save many dollars in subsequent time and material. The newly hired mechanic in any facility should make an immediate effort to become familiar with the types of material used and how they are cataloged and stored.

Chapter 6

STRUCTURAL SHAPES and SIZES

PLATE Steel plate is available in a wide variety of thicknesses and sizes. To be classified as plate, the steel must be at least $\frac{3}{16}$ inch thick and 9 inches wide. Anything thinner is considered sheet steel and is covered in the sheet metal section. Widths narrower than 9 inches are referred to as flat stock. Because the overwhelming majority of fabrication is done with low-carbon and low-alloy steels, emphasis is on these materials.

When ordering plate, the following information must be given: (1) type of steel, (2) thickness, (3) plate width, and (4) plate length. Steel mills manufacture plate in lengths up to 40 feet and widths to 10 feet but because of the obvious difficulty in handling plates of this size, most steel suppliers will only stock sizes up to 5 feet wide and 20 feet long.

The steel stock list book, which is one of the most important references for fabricators, will list not only steel types and available sizes but also the weight per foot.

EXAMPLE:

Size (in.)		Weight per foot (lb)
Thickness	Width	
½ X	9	15.45
	10	17.17
	12	20.60
	36	61.80
	48	82.40

As discussed in Chapter 2, steel is priced by the pound. Being able to calculate the weight of the steel is all-important for cost estimating. Weight must also be considered for material handling. It is wise to order only sizes that can be handled with the equipment available.

Low-alloy steels, which are sold under such brand names as Hi-Steel and Cor-Ten, are also readily available in stock sizes from most dealers. Although higher in price, they offer greater tensile strength and excellent corrosion resistance and are ideally used when weight reduction or constant exposure to the weather are primary considerations. Cor-Ten is commonly used in steel-hull boat and barge construction.

STRUCTURALS Like plate, structural steel shapes are available in a variety of sizes and weights. Differences in weight for a particular size of structural member are caused by an increase or decrease in cross-sectional thickness and in the case of I beams, flange width. For example, 8-inch I beams all measure 8 inches in height but are available in two web thicknesses.

EXAMPLE:

Depth of beam and weight per foot	Thickness of web (in.)	Width of flange (in.)
8 × 18.4	0.270	4.000
× 23.0	0.441	4.171

Basic structural shapes are dimensioned as follows. This is the information that must be specified when describing or ordering.

I beams (designated as S beam); Fig. 6-1): height and weight (lb/ft)

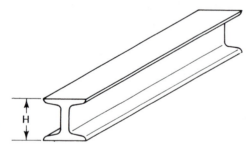

Figure 6-1 S beam (I beam).

Wide-flange beams (Fig. 6-2); height and weight (lb/ft)

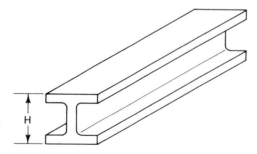

Figure 6-2 Wide-flange (WF) beam.

Channels (Fig. 6-3): width and weight (lb/ft)

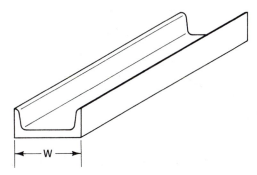

Figure 6-3 Channel.

Angles (Fig. 6-4): length of leg times length of leg times thickness ($L \times L \times T$)

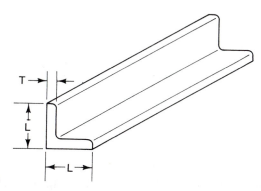

Figure 6-4 Angle.

Rounds (Fig. 6-5): diameter

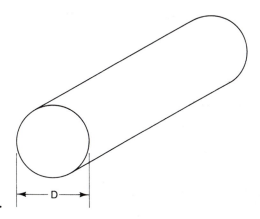

Figure 6-5 Rounds.

Squares (Fig. 6-6): width

Figure 6-6 Squares.

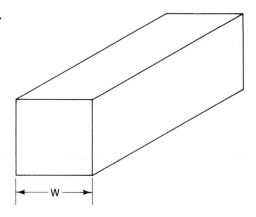

Flats (Fig. 6-7): thickness × width (*T* × *W*)

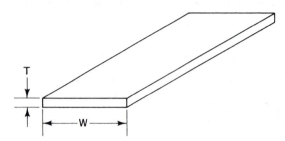

Figure 6-7   Flats.

Square structural tubing (Fig. 6-8): width and wall thickness (*W* × *T*)

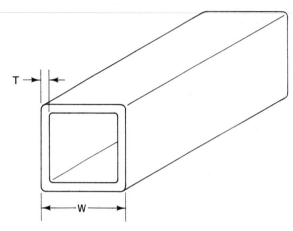

Figure 6-8   Square structural tubing.

Rectangular structural tubing (Fig. 6-9): height, width, and wall thickness (*H* × *W* × *T*)

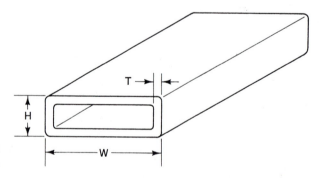

Figure 6-9   Rectangular structural tubing.

Round mechanical tubing (Fig. 6-10): outside diameter and wall thickness (O.D. × *T*)

Figure 6-10   Round mechanical tubing.

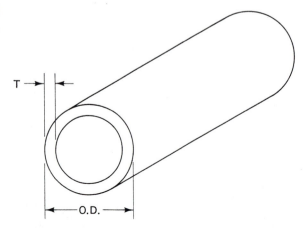

Pipe (Fig. 6-11): under 12 inches—inside diameter; 12 inches and over —outside diameter

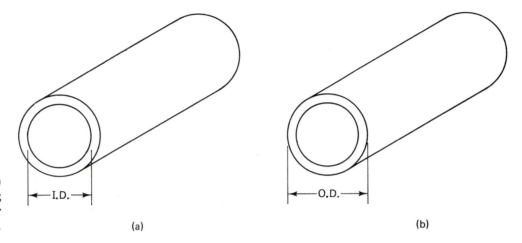

Figure 6-11 Pipe: (a) under 12-inch diameter; (b) 12-inch diameter and over.

(a)   (b)

Pipe will be generally available in three wall thicknesses and is referred to as either standard (schedule 40), heavy (schedule 80), or extra heavy wall (schedule 160).

Commonly stocked available lengths for structural shapes:

Beams	20 ft, 40 ft, 60 ft	Round	20 ft
Channel	20 ft	Square	20 ft
Angle	20 ft	Structural tubing	24 ft
Flat	20 ft	Mechanical tubing	24 ft
		Pipe	21 ft

STEEL CLASSIFICATION

Carbon and alloy steels in sheet, plate, and bar form are most commonly identified and classified by an SAE (Society of Automotive Engineers) and AISI (American Iron and Steel Institute) number designation system.

The SAE-AISI classification (see Chart 6-1) is based on a four-digit number. The first digit indicates the major alloying element. The second digit indicates the approximate percentage of the major alloying element, and the last two digits indicate the midpoint of the carbon range.

EXAMPLE: SAE-AISI number 1020 identifies a carbon steel with a carbon content of 0.18 to 0.23%.

CHART 6-1   SAE–AISI Steel Classification System

Type of steel (alloying elements)	*Number designation*
Carbon steels	1xxx
Plain carbon	10xx
Free cutting (screw stock)	11xx
Free cutting, manganese	X13xx
High-manganese steels	T13xx
Nickel steels	2xxx
0.50% nickel	20xx

CHART 6-1   SAE-AISI Steel Classification System (continued)

Type of steel (Alloying elements)	Number designation
1.50% nickel	21xx
3.50% nickel	23xx
5.00% nickel	25xx
Nickel–chromium steels	3xxx
1.25% nickel, 0.60% chromium	31xx
1.75% nickel, 1.00% chromium	32xx
3.50% nickel, 1.50% chromium	33xx
3.00% nickel, 0.80% chromium	34xx
Corrosion- and heat-resisting steels	30xxx
Molybdenum steels	4xxx
Chromium	41xx
Chromium–nickel	43xx
Nickel	46xx and 48 xx
Chromium steels	5xxx
Low-chromium	51xx
Medium-chromium	52xxx
Corrosion- and heat-resisting	51xxx
Chromium-vanadium steels	6xxx
Tungsten steels	7xxx and 7xxxx
Silicon–manganese steels	9xxx

Structural steel shapes are also identified by the ASTM (American Society for Testing and Materials) designation system. The ASTM classification is most commonly used in steel distributors' stock lists and is prefaced by the letter A. For example, ASTM A36 designates structural-quality carbon steel shapes; ASTM A283 designates structural-quality plate.

Most steel fabrication is done with carbon steel, which is classified into three groups; low, medium, and high carbon. Increasing the carbon content of steel will have two effects; increased hardness and decreased ductility.

Carbon steel is available in two forms: hot rolled (HRS) and cold rolled (CRS). Metallurgically, they are similar but quite different in appearance. HRS has a scaly surface and is slightly oversized from its specified dimensions. CRS is put through an additional rolling process at the mill, is bright in appearance, and accurate to its specified dimensions. CRS is widely used for machining and tool and fixture building where accuracy is of paramount importance.

Low-carbon steel (0.05 to 0.30% carbon) is referred to as mild steel. This material is the most common steel used in fabrication because of its high ductility, ease of welding and machining, and relatively low cost. However, with the exception of case hardening, it cannot be heat treated.

Medium-carbon steel (0.30 to 0.45% carbon) is harder and stronger than mild steel but not as easily worked. This material responds well to heat treatment and is used in parts where toughness is a primary design consideration. Examples of this are automotive parts, such as drive shafts, axles, and engine connecting rods.

High-carbon steel (0.45 to 1.5% carbon) can be heat treated to obtain the highest strength and greatest hardness of all the carbon steels. This quality can also make this material difficult to work with. It must be heated to be formed, and annealed to be machined. Through the use of the various heat-treatment techniques, high-carbon steel can be used for a variety of parts, such as springs, saw and knife blades, files, punches, shear blades, and chisels.

Chapter 19 will discuss the making of tools from high-carbon steel parts that can be found in any junkyard.

Chapter 7

LAYOUT METHODS

MARKING In order for any proper type of fabrication work to be done, layout lines must be carefully and accurately marked. In structural steel fabrication, tolerances are usually within $\frac{1}{16}$ inch; therefore, layout lines can be easily made with soapstone (see Fig. 7-1). Soapstone has the advantage of making a clearly visible line and being fairly heat resistant, which is extremely important if the parts being fabricated have to be flame cut. Soapstone for this purpose is usually purchased in $\frac{1}{4}$-inch square, or $\frac{1}{4}$-inch by $\frac{1}{2}$-inch by 5-inch sticks. They must be properly sharpened in order to make the crisp, clear lines desired (see Fig. 7-2). The easiest way to accomplish this is with the use of a grinder or belt sander. As the point wears down, it should be touched up. This will prevent inaccurate layout due to an excessively wide mark.

Figure 7-1 Soapstone layout lines.

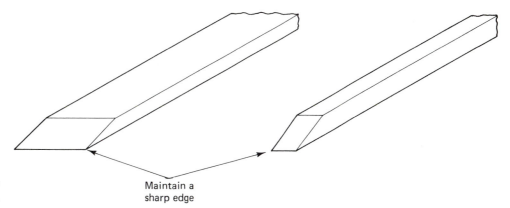

Figure 7-2 Soapstone edge preparation.

Maintain a
sharp edge

If the job requires greater accuracy, layout dye should be used. The layout surface must be thoroughly cleaned and the dye applied by brush or spray. After the dye has dried, precise layout marks can be made with a scribe (see Fig. 7-3). When done properly, this produces a very fine line and is the recommended procedure when close tolerances are specified.

Figure 7-3 Scribed line on layout dye.

LAYOUT TECHNIQUES The skillful fabricator plans the job to take full advantage of stock material sizes and maximum cutting efficiency. This is not that difficult to accomplish. If, for instance, the job requires 12 pieces of ⅜-inch by 4-inch by 12-inch hot-rolled steel (HRS), the first step would be an inventory of material of suitable thickness available in stock. If available, ⅜-inch by 4-inch flat stock would be the logical choice, because only one cut is required to make each piece (see Fig. 7-4). If ⅜-inch material is on hand only in plate sizes, measure the overall plate dimensions to determine the least wasteful cuts. One of the most common plate widths is 48 inches. On a plate of this size the job could be done in two ways with no waste (see Fig. 7-5).

If pieces of varying sizes have to be made, try to group them by a common dimension. For example, a job requires the following pieces (in inches):

(4) ½ by 6 by 12
(4) ½ by 3 by 6
(2) ½ by 12 by 15

All of these parts can be cut from a piece of steel ½ inch by 12 inches by 60 inches (see Fig. 7-6).

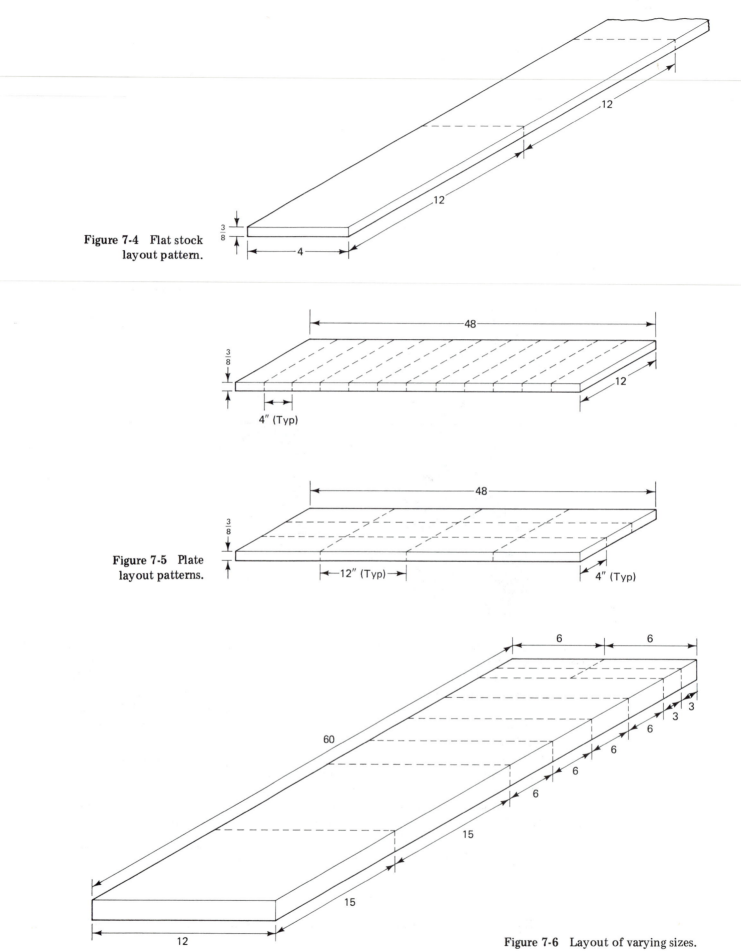

Figure 7-4 Flat stock layout pattern.

Figure 7-5 Plate layout patterns.

Figure 7-6 Layout of varying sizes.

84

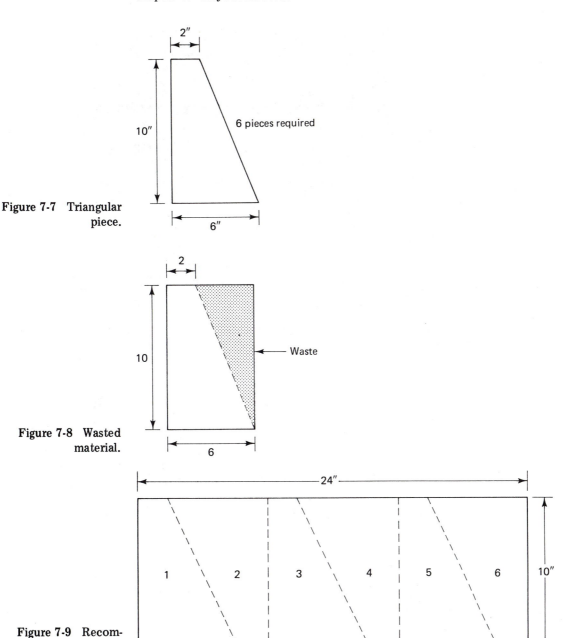

Figure 7-7 Triangular piece.

Figure 7-8 Wasted material.

Figure 7-9 Recommended layout.

Triangular pieces can be the cause of much wasted material and time if poor layout techniques are used. The part shown in Figure 7-7 can serve as an example. If six pieces, 6 inches by 10 inches, were to be cut to make the parts, a piece of steel 10 inches wide and 36 inches long would be required and the material shown in the shaded area would be wasted (see Fig. 7-8). A more efficient layout is shown in Figure 7-9; here the same job is accomplished with one-third less material and fewer cuts.

There will be times when a certain amount of waste is unavoidable, particularly with circular shapes. However, if the job is planned properly, the waste can be kept to a minimum.

SQUARING The tools most commonly used for squaring are the combination and framing squares. The purpose of these tools is to provide an accurate 90-degree reference so that right-angle corners and intersections can be set (see Fig. 7-10).

Figure 7-10 Squaring a
corner with a framing
square.

The combination square is also used to strike perpendicular and 45-degree lines for cutting and assembly. Develop the habit of using the square for this purpose, as it will increase your accuracy and save rework time caused by faulty layout or unsquare cuts.

There are several factors which, if not considered, can render the squaring tools useless:

1. All the members being squared must be straight.
2. Check the edges on which the square is to be set to make sure that there are no burrs or weld spatter. Perfect mating between square and workpiece is imperative.
3. When squaring a rectangular frame, opposing sides must be equal in length.

Combination and framing squares will also become ineffective on very large assemblies. Rarely, if ever, are long lengths of structural steel perfectly straight. Deflections and bends common to these members make it necessary to use diagonal measurement or triangulation to check squareness.

DIAGONAL MEASUREMENT (Fig. 7-11). To check the squareness of a rectangular shape (either plate size or assembly), dimensions *AC* and *BD* must be equal. Remember that opposing sides must also be of equal length.

TRIANGULATION (Fig. 7-12). Setting two members 90 degrees to each other can be done by using any proportional variation of the basic 3-4-5 right triangle. *Note:* If the sides of the assembly being squared are greater than three times the length of the squaring tool, diagonal measurement or triangulation should be used.

Squaring with a Level

In many instances a level can be used as a squaring tool (when working with steel, a magnetic base level is most desirable). They can be extremely useful in setting vertical legs or columns. For a level to be used for this purpose, the

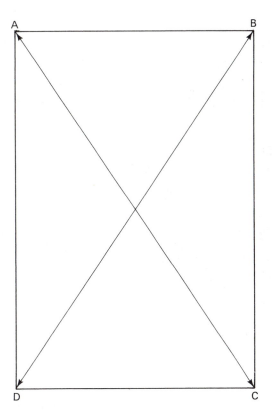

Figure 7-11 Diagonal measurement.

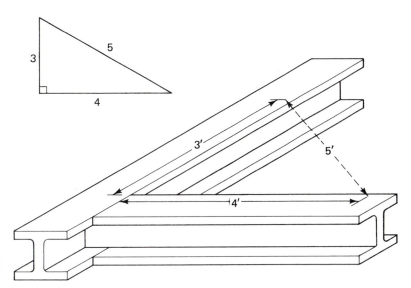

Figure 7-12 Squaring by triangulation.

horizontal surface being worked from must also be level. For this reason most fabrication shops will have layout tables and welding platens set perfectly level. If the horizontal surface you are working from is not level, making it level is the first step. After this is accomplished the vertical members can be set. If practical, place the level at the midpoint of the member (see Fig. 7-13) and set it so that it reads level in all directions. Checking any two sides 90 degrees apart will accomplish this.

Figure 7-13 Squaring
with a level.

CORNERS AND
CROSS MEMBERS*
There are three basic types of corner and cross member tie-in joints for structural steel shapes: square, coped, and mitered (Fig. 7-14). The choice of which type to use is determined by strength and appearance requirements, prefabrication needs for field assembly, or production efficiency.

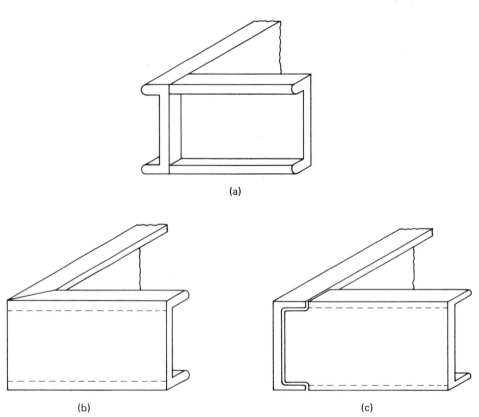

(a)

Figure 7-14 Corner
and cross member
joints: (a) square; (b)
miter; (c) coped.

(b)   (c)

*This section discusses techniques used for general shop fabrication. Beam connection design for use in building and bridge construction is a specialized area having its own specific requirements. For additional information, see the readings in Appendix 2.

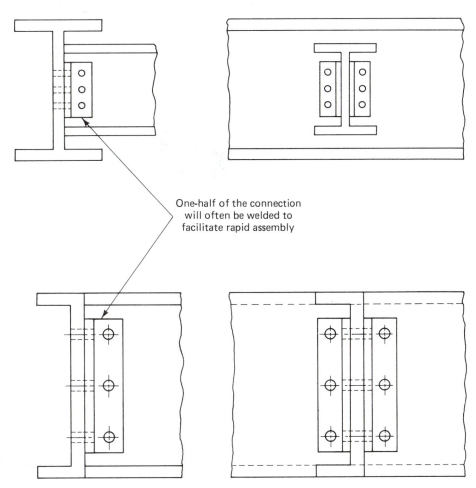

One-half of the connection
will often be welded to
facilitate rapid assembly

Figure 7-15 Variation
of a square joint for
bolted connections.

Square joints are the easiest to fabricate because only one cut is required. This makes this joint the ideal choice when production speed is a primary consideration. Variations of the square joint (see Fig. 7-15) are ideal for bolted connections and parts being prefabricated in the shop for field assembly.

Mitered corner joints are also fairly easy to fabricate. They produce the cleanest finished appearance and are the ideal choice when this is the primary consideration. As with the square joint, only one cut is required. All cuts are made at a 45-degree angle. When laying out these cuts, always use the combination square (see Fig. 7-16). Even if you are using a power hacksaw or band saw that can be set for 45-degree cuts, the line can be used as a check for saw accuracy and proper alignment. Always check twice for proper alignment. Cuts made in the wrong direction are common errors with this type of joint. For example, Figure 7-17 shows one of four pieces being mitered to form a rectangular frame. The miters on each end must be made on the same leg and angled toward each other.

Coped corner joints are the most difficult to fabricate because of the complexity of the cuts. When joined by welding, this joint produces a strong connection without the need for additional weld joint preparations such as edge beveling. The reason for this is the increased amount of contact surface. An example of this can be seen with ¼-inch by 2-inch by 2-inch angle (see Fig. 7-18). The three joints are all made with the same material, but note the differences in mating surface length.

When fabricating a coped joint, all of the cutting is done on one mem-

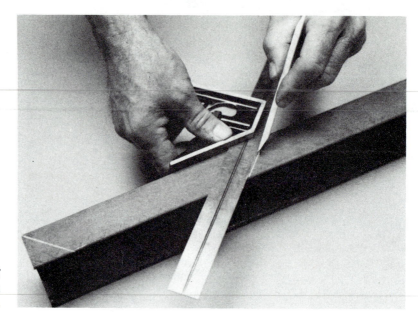

Figure 7-16 Layout of a 45° cut with a combination square.

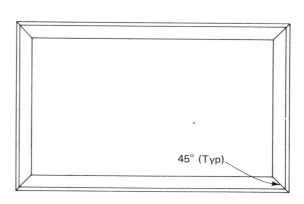

45° (Typ)

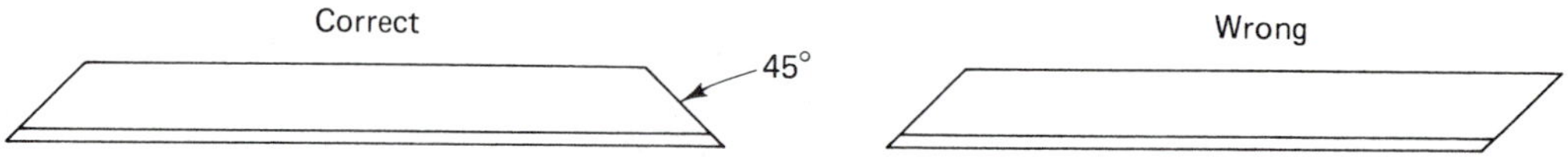

Correct   Wrong

Figure 7-17 45° miter cut.

45°

Figure 7-18 Joint comparison: (a) 4-inch contact; (b) 4.8-inch contact; (c) 5.75-inch contact.

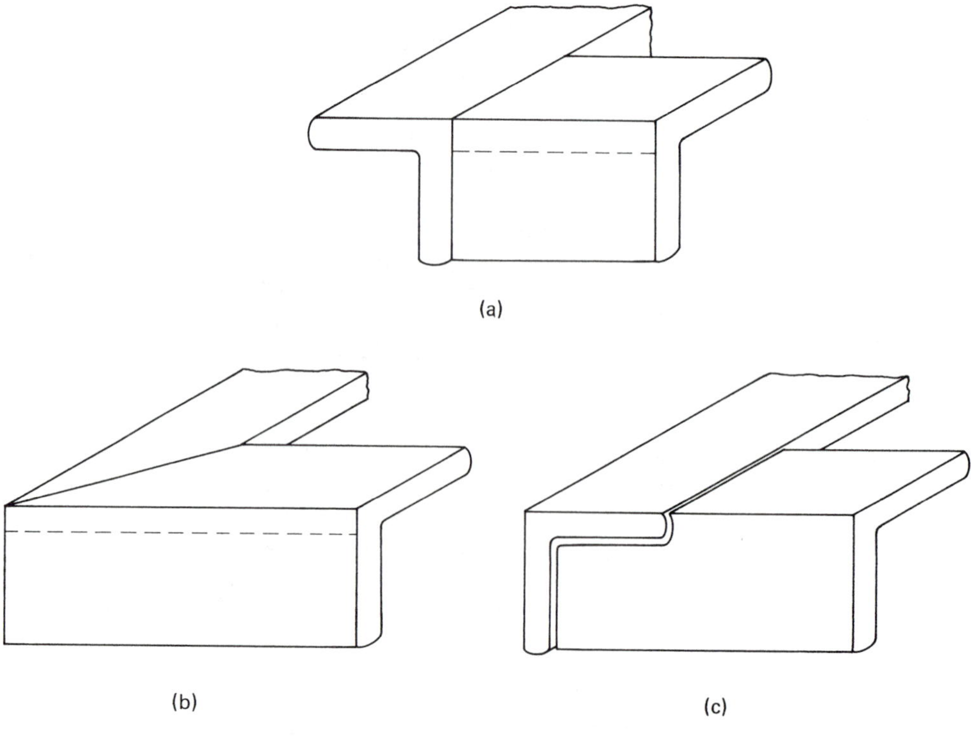

(a)

90

(b)   (c)

Figure 7-19 Layout of a coped joint.

ber. The part being cut must be made to match the inside contour of its mating member. A short piece of the structural shape being coped can be used as a template to lay out the ends to be cut (see Fig. 7-19). After the parts have been carefully marked, the cuts can be made with a band saw or cutting torch. Care must be taken not to overcut, as this will produce a joint with wide gaps.

CURVES The two tools required for layout of curves are dividers and trammels (see Fig. 7-20). Since a curve is always dimensioned by its radius, the first step in layout is to determine the point from which the radius is struck. The following is an example of one of the easiest layouts (see Fig. 7-21a).

To determine the center point for this layout, strike a line 6 inches down from the top of the plate and 6 inches in from the right side (see Fig. 7-21b). The intersection of these lines is the center point. Next, set your dividers for 6 inches and strike the curve.

Figure 7-20 Striking a curve with trammels.

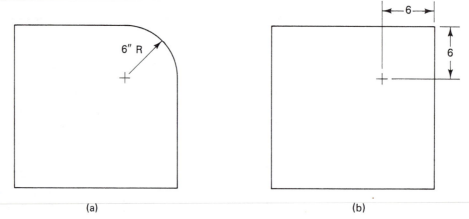

Figure 7-21 Outside radius.

(a)   (b)

This next example is slightly more complicated because the center of the radius is off the plate (see Fig. 7-22a). The first step is to mark the points at which the curve will cut the plate (Fig. 7-22b, points 1 and 2). Next, secure the plate to the worktable. This can be done by clamping or tack welds. From point 1 measure 10 inches to the right and strike a line parallel to the right side of the plate. Measure 10 inches down from point 2 and strike a line parallel to the bottom of the plate. The intersection of these two lines will be the center of the curve. Now you can set your trammels for 10 inches and strike the curve.

Compound curves (curves with more than one radius) are more difficult to layout. The example shown in Figure 7-23 has a curve with two radii. In this situation the first step is to lay out the centerline 8 inches in from the left side (Fig. 7-23b). From the top of the plate measure down the centerline and make marks at 10 and 30 inches. Set your dividers for 10 inches and strike the left portion of the curve. Next set the trammels for 30 inches, set one point on the 30-inch mark, and strike the right portion of the curve.

Most commercially manufactured beam trammels are not made to strike arcs with a radius larger than 35 inches. Often in steel plate fabrication you may be required to lay out curves with a very large radius. For these situations a set of clamp-on trammel points can be utilized. This type of trammel can be clamped to a length of flat stock or wood of appropriate length to do the job.

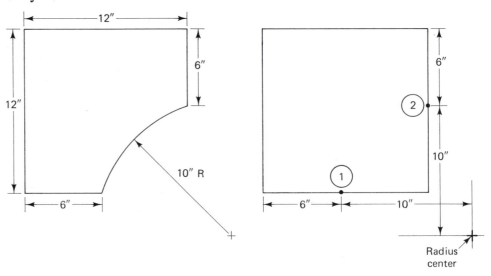

Figure 7-22 Inside radius.

(a)   (b)

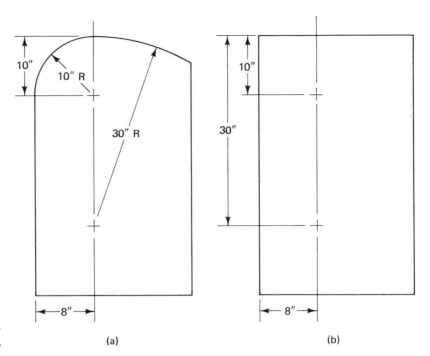

Figure 7-23 Com-
pound curve.

(a)   (b)

ANGULAR LAYOUT   The laying out of angles can usually be done using a protractor and sliding T-bevel or protractor head and combination square. Forty-five-degree angles can easily be derived by direct measurement because each leg of the formed triangle is of equal length (see Fig. 7-24).

In this example you can see that a 45-degree angle will cause distance *CD* (which is known to be 12 inches) and distance *BC* to be equal. Laying out this angle becomes a simple matter of measuring 12 inches from point *C* to locate point *B* and striking a line from *B* to *D*.

In the following example (Fig. 7-25), the 25-degree angle can be set on a T-bevel or protractor head. The set tool is then lined up on point *C* and line *BC* is struck. When laying out angles on large plate, the layout tools will become less accurate (see the earlier section on squaring). In these cases indirect measurement (trigonometry) should be used.

If, for example, the measurements in Figure 7-25 were 8 feet and 24 feet, a standard protractor head would be useless. Layout of line *BC* would then be done as follows. Line *AD* is known to be 8 feet; therefore, distance *BE* is also 8 feet. Angle *C* is given as 25 degrees. Use the trigonometric formula

$$\tan = \frac{\text{opposite}}{\text{adjacent}}$$

Figure 7-24 45° angle
layout.

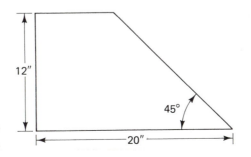

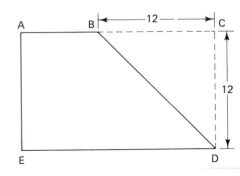

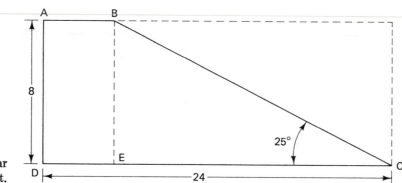

Figure 7-25 Angular
layout.

$$\tan 25° = \frac{8}{x}$$ Let $x =$ the adjacent measurement EC

$$x = \frac{8}{\tan 25°}$$ Equation was transposed (see Chapter 2)

$$x = \frac{8}{0.466}$$ Refer to trigonometric table in Appendix 3
for tangent 25° value (0.466)

$$x = 17.2$$

Therefore, distance $EC = 17.2$ feet.

By subtracting 17.2 from the overall length of 24, distance AB is found
to be 6.8. With point B established, the layout line can now be struck from
corner C to point B, completing the layout.

Chapter 8

CUTTING, SHEARING, and PUNCHING

An infinite variety of cutting and shearing tools are available to the metal fabricator. These can range from a $10 hand hacksaw to a $25,000 plate shear. The tools you can choose to do a particular job will depend on availability, material hardness, budget limitations, and whether or not the job is to be done in the shop or in the field. For field applications the tools most often must be portable. This chapter will list and discuss the proper use of the most commonly used cutting and punching tools. You will discover that most jobs can be accomplished by several methods and the choice of method should be based on which piece of equipment or tool you are most proficient with.

HACKSAW Although the hacksaw is the simplest and most common steel cutting tool, it is also a tool commonly misused. The hacksaw frame is designed to accept blades of two lengths: 10 and 12 inches. The blades are always positioned in the frame so that the teeth point away from the handle (see Fig. 8-1) and are

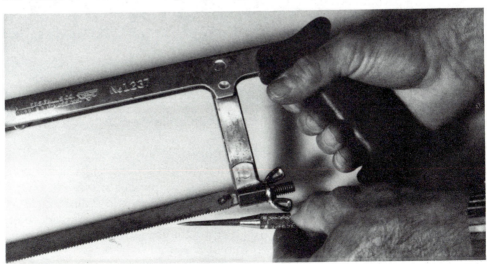

Figure 8-1 Hand hacksaw with the blade correctly mounted.

available with 14, 18, 24, and 32 teeth per inch. Blade selection is based on material thickness and hardness. For example, a 14-tooth blade would be used to cut soft metal, whereas a 24-tooth blade would be the choice for tubing and steels of greater hardness, such as tool steel and drill rod (see Chart 8-1).

CHART 8-1   Hand Hacksaw Blade Selection

Number of teeth per inch	Typical applications
14	Solid mild steel, iron, aluminum, brass, bronze, and copper
18	Structural shapes, pipe, and general metal work
24	Steel tubing, drill rod, tool steel, and stainless steel
32	Light-gauge material and thin-walled tubing

The hacksaw should be held as shown in Figure 8-2. Cutting speed should be between 35 and 45 strokes per minute, with moderate pressure applied on the forward stroke only. Pressure is released on the return stroke. Keeping pressure applied to the blade on both strokes or sawing at an excessive rate of speed will greatly shorten blade life. This can also be the cause of blade breakage and personal injury.

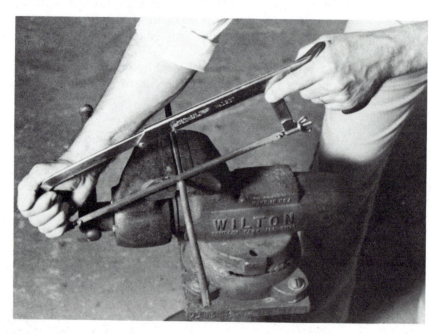

Figure 8-2 Hacksaw properly held.

RECIPROCATING SAW   The hand-held reciprocating saw (see Fig. 8-3) has the obvious advantage of portability but is limited in the size and thickness of steel it is designed to cut. These tools are used primarily on steel ⅛ inch or less in thickness and for pipe and tubing up to 3 inches in diameter. Most saws of this type have two speeds, 1100 and 2200 strokes per minute. Speed ranges may vary slightly with different manufacturers; however, the slowest setting should always be used for cutting steel.

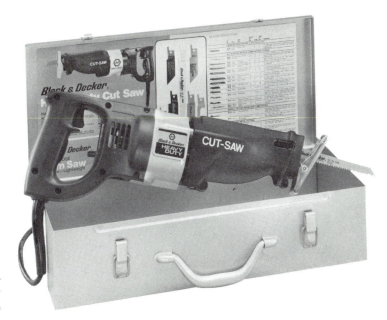

Figure 8-3 Reciprocating saw. (Courtesy of Black and Decker.)

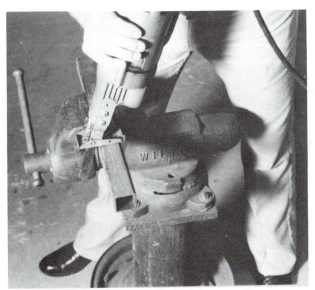

Figure 8-4 Reciprocating saw properly held against the workpiece.

Because of the reciprocating action of the saw blade, the foot of the saw must be held firmly against the work to prevent excessive vibration (see Fig. 8-4). As the blade begins to cut, a moderate downward force should be applied. Safety glasses or face shields should always be worn when using this tool.

ABRASIVE CUTOFF MACHINES

Cutoff machines (see Fig. 8-5) most often used in metal fabrication should be permanently mounted on a workbench or stand. The largest machines of this type use a 26-inch-diameter disk; however, the most common sizes use either a 12- or 14-inch aluminum oxide abrasive disk. These machines have a high production efficiency because of the ability to make very fast, accurate cuts on pipe and structural tubing up to 4 inches in diameter and solid-steel bars to 2½ inches thick.

When using an abrasive cutoff saw, the work must be securely clamped to the bed (see Fig. 8-6). Depending on the manufacturer, the machine will

Figure 8-5 Abrasive cutoff machine. (Courtesy of Black and Decker.)

Figure 8-6 Work secured in a cutoff machine vise.

have either a vise or a clamping dog. Securing the work is absolutely essential. The abrasive wheel is only $\frac{3}{32}$ inch thick and spins at 4000 rpm. Any movement of the work during the cutting operation will cause the wheel to break, creating a serious safety hazard. (A word of caution: Never use a cutoff machine without the blade guards and full face protection.)

After the work is properly secured, the cuts are made using a gradual, steady pressure. Although the quality of the cut is excellent, these machines tend to leave a large burr on the bottom side of the cut edge. These burrs are very sharp and should always be filed or ground off.

Hand-held cutoff machines (see Fig. 8-7) can be efficiently utilized for on-the-job cuts. The abrasive wheel used is 12 inches in diameter and spins at 5000 rpm; however, the recommended cutting capacity is substantially less than the bench models. Typical applications would be tubing and pipe up to $\frac{1}{8}$ inch in wall thickness and bar stock up to $\frac{3}{4}$ inch in diameter. This machine must be held very steady and cuts made with a straight, smooth motion.

An important point to remember is the amount of material lost in the cutting operation (approximately $\frac{3}{32}$ inch). When setting the cutoff disk to the work, always line up on the scrap side of the cut (see Fig. 8-8) to ensure accuracy. Cutoff disk recommendations are given in Chart 8-2.

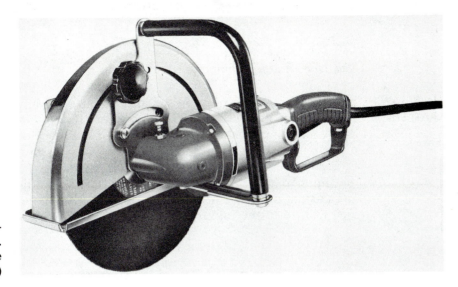

Figure 8-7 Hand-held cutoff saw. (Courtesy of Milwaukee Tool Corp.)

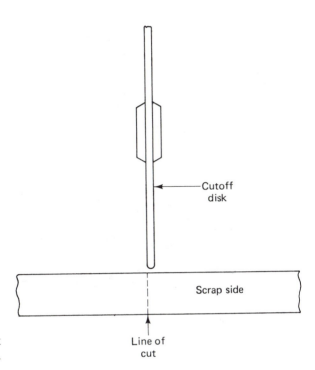

Cutoff disk

Scrap side

Line of cut

Figure 8-8 Cutoff disk alignment.

CHART 8-2 Abrasive Cutoff Disk Recommendations
(Aluminum Oxide)

Material being cut	Disk grit size (dry cut)[a]	Disk grit size (wet cut)
Mild-steel bar stock and structural shapes	24–30	46–54
Hardened steel	30–46	46–54
Stainless steel	46–54	46–54
Steel tubing	54–60	60
Nonferrous material[b]	24	46

[a]*Caution:* Never use a dry abrasive cutoff on magnesium.

[b]A silicon carbide disk will also give good results on nonferrous materials.

**POWER HACKSAWS
AND BAND SAWS**

Power hacksaws of the type shown in Figure 8-9 have the advantage of not requiring constant attention during the cutting operation. Most power saws have an automatic shutoff switch. This, coupled with the ability to gang-cut many pieces of material simultaneously, gives the fabricator the opportunity to perform other tasks while the saw is operating. Power hacksaws are easy machines to use because they require only two adjustments: stroke speed and cutting pressure. A coarse-tooth blade with between 6 and 10 teeth per inch will work well for cutting structural shapes. (see Chart 8-3).

CHART 8-3   Power Hacksaw Blade Selection

Teeth per inch	Material thickness (in.)
6	Over 1
8	⅜ to ¾
10	Under ⅜

Blade speed and cutting pressure are determined by analyzing the cutting chips. Cutting pressure should be increased until the chips are well defined and curled. If the chips have a burned-blue look, the blade speed and cutting pressure is too high. If the chips have a powdery appearance, the cutting pressure is too light. Using a water-soluble cutting oil will greatly increase blade life.

Figure 8-9   Power
hacksaw.

Because most power hacksaw vises are the swivel type, a periodic check for vise squareness is recommended (see Fig. 8-10). When cutting long lengths, an adjustable stock stand set at the same height as the saw will be needed to ensure a good square cut (see Fig. 8-11). After the workpiece is properly aligned and secured in the saw vise, start the saw and lower the blade slowly until the cutting starts. This will help prevent blade damage.

The band saw (Fig. 8-12) has the advantage of faster cutting speeds because of its continuous cutting action. No time is lost, as with the hacksaw, with a noncutting return stroke. Band saws, however, require a little more skill in blade setup and maintenance in order to function correctly.

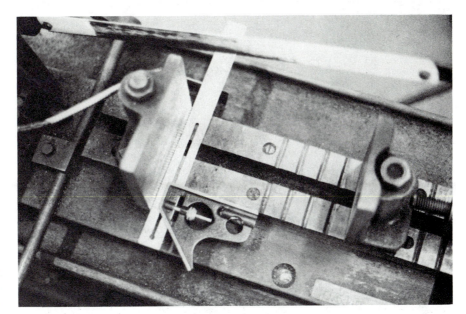

Figure 8-10 Squaring the power hacksaw vise.

Figure 8-11 Workpiece on an adjustable stock stand.

Figure 8-12 Band saw. (Courtesy of Emerson Electric Co., Special Products Div.)

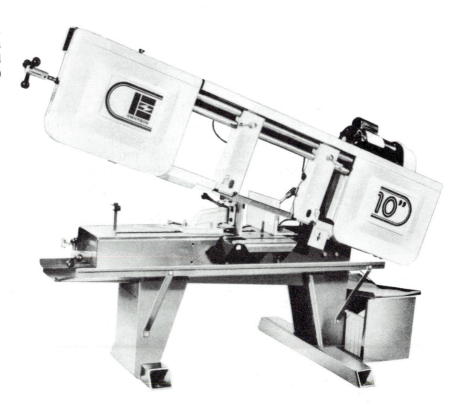

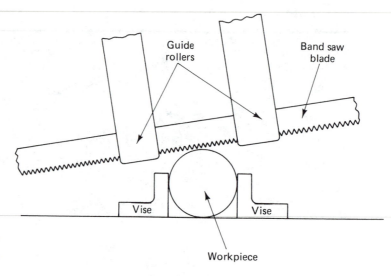

Figure 8-13 Band saw guide rollers.

Not only must the blade be kept taut, but the guide rollers must be kept in perfect working order to ensure a straight, accurate cut and prolonged blade life.

If the guide rollers are adjustable, they should be set as close to the work as possible (see Fig. 8-13). Blades having between 10 and 18 teeth per inch are recommended for cutting mild steel (see Chart 8·4).

CHART 8-4   Band Saw Blade Selection[a]

Teeth per inch	Material thickness (in.)
10	Over 1
14	¼ to ¾
18	⅛ to ¼
24	Less than ⅛

[a]Band saw blades less than 85 inches in length should be of a more ductile blade material to prevent frequent breakage.

Blade speed should be between 200 and 250 feet per minute. All hard-to-cut steels should be cut at the slower speed with a 24-teeth-per-inch blade. As with the hacksaw, use of a water-soluble cutting oil and blade coolant will greatly increase cutting efficiency and blade life.

Workpieces being cut in the band saw must be properly secured in the saw vise and long lengths must be supported by an adjustable stock stand. Proper cutting starts, particularly on thin cross sections, are essential with the band saw to prevent costly blade breakage.

Do not start the saw with the blade in contact with the workpiece. Start the saw in the raised position and lower it slowly onto the work.

Note: To realize the maximum efficiency of power saws, particularly on production runs, always stack or gang-cut material whenever possible. For example, if you have to cut a 20-foot length of 2-inch flat stock into 6-inch pieces, the first step should be to cut four 5-foot pieces and then gang all four together to make the 6-inch cuts (see Fig. 8-14).

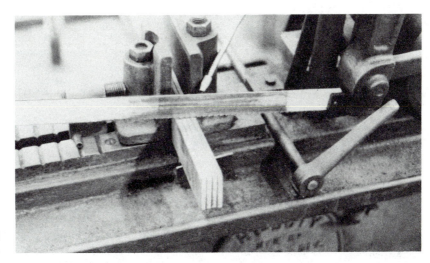

Figure 8-14 Gang cutting.

HYDRAULIC IRONWORKER The ironworker (see Fig. 8-15) is one of the most versatile tools in steel fabrication. It will perform a number of tasks, including plate and bar shearing, coping and mitering of structural shapes, punching, and bending operations. Machines of the type shown are capable of shearing mild-steel plate ¾ inch thick and 10 inches wide, 4-inch angle iron ⅜ inch thick, and punching holes 1¼ inches in diameter through ½-inch plate.

When using the shear blades it is absolutely essential that the workpiece be held securely under the hold-down bar (see Fig. 8-16). This will prevent the work from jumping up during the cutting operation and possibly causing damage to machine and shear blades. This is particularly important on flywheel-operated machines because of their rapid cutting action.

To ensure an accurate cut on flat stock, a soapstone guideline should be drawn along the full length of the cut. This will be needed to align the line of cut properly with the shear blades (see Fig. 8-17). When the cut is

Figure 8-15 Iron-worker.

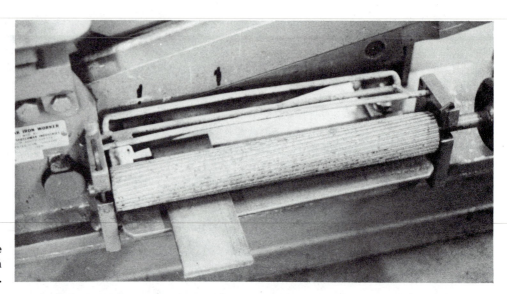

Figure 8-16 Workpiece
under a hold-down
bar.

Figure 8-17 Alignment
of ironworker shear
blades and the line
of cut.

properly aligned, lift up the back of the workpiece and hold it tightly against
the hold-down bar. This will prevent the workpiece from kicking out of
alignment during the shearing operation. (*Caution:* Keep hands and figures
clear of the hold-down bar and shear blades while the machine is in operation.) To increase cutting efficiency, cutting oil should be applied to the
blades after every 10 cuts.

The design of this machine may cause a rake change of the blades; therefore, different sections of the shear blades will yield different results. The
end of the blades closest to the pivot point (see Fig. 8-18) will apply the
maximum shear force, whereas the opposite end will cause the least amount
of distortion. When using the machine to its maximum capacity, always keep
this in mind.

The angle shear (see Fig. 8-19) is designed to make both square and
mitered cuts. Although most operate on the same principle as the bar and
flat stock cutter discussed previously, many of these shears are compound
cutters (the top blade comes down between two bottom blades). If this is
the case on the machine you are using, you must allow for the amount of
material lost. The angle shear shown in Figure 8-19 removes ⅜ inch of
material with each cut. When laying out your lines of cut, in these instances
it may be good practice to draw two sets of lines for each cut, with the dis-

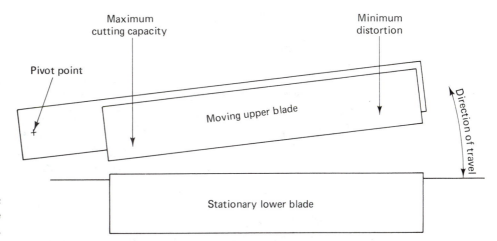

Figure 8-18   Hydraulic ironworker shear blade configuration.

Figure 8-19 Ironworker angle shear.

Figure 8-20   Layout lines for an angle-iron compound cutter.

tance between these two lines equal to the thickness of the upper shear blade (see Fig. 8-20). This will reduce the chance of a cutting error.

Most angle shears will also have guidelines on them for cutting 45-degree miters. Before cutting the actual production parts, make several practice cuts on scrap. Feed the scrap piece into the angle shear as shown in Figure 8-21 and carefully align it with the 45-degree guideline. Hold the piece securely during the cutting operation. With a little practice, fairly accurate miter cuts can be made easily and quickly.

The punching capabilities of the ironworker can be a tremendous work-

Figure 8-21   45° miter cutting.

and time-saver for the fabricator. Many of the punches and dies used are the flat-faced blanking type (no punch rake). The punch face has a center point (see Fig. 8-22) which is used for indexing or centering the punch accurately on the workpiece. Double-rake punches (see Fig. 8-23) are also widely used and have the advantage of requiring less punch tonnage because of the shearing action of the rakes.

To avoid tool damage, never punch a hole through material that is thicker than the punch diameter. For example, the smallest hole that should be punched through ½-inch plate is ½ inch. If smaller-diameter holes are required, they should be drilled.

Punch tonnage requirements are listed in Appendix 3. If a tonnage calculation must be made for a specific job, use the following formula:

$$F = \pi d T S$$

where F = required punch force
d = hole diameter
T = material thickness
S = material tensile strength

EXAMPLE: Find the tonnage required to punch a ½-inch-diameter hole through a piece of ½-inch stainless steel having a tensile strength of 90,000 psi.

Figure 8-22 Blank punch.

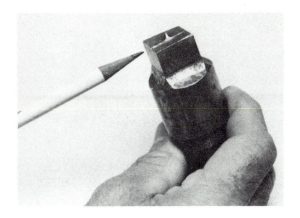

Figure 8-23 Double-rake punch.

$$F = \pi dTS$$
$$F = 3.14(0.5)(0.5)(90,000)$$
$$F = 70,650 \text{ pounds}$$
$$F = 35.3 \text{ tons}$$

Many tonnage charts are calculated using shear rather than tensile strength (shear strength is approximately 80% of tensile strength). A calculation of punch tonnage as a function of tensile strength will therefore be 20% higher than the minimum requirement. This increased margin will prevent machinery and tools from being pushed to the limit and possibly damaged. Installation and setup of punches and dies as well as punch and die clearance are discussed in Chapter 16.

Regardless of the type of punch being used, proper workpiece preparation and setup are essential for accuracy. Hole locations should be marked and center punched just as if they were being drilled. The stripper, which prevents the workpiece from being lifted up with the punch, must also be set. Clearance between the stripper bar and die table (see Fig. 8-24) should be slightly greater than the material being punched. Failure to use the stripper properly can cause workpiece and tool damage. Set the workpiece under the stripper bar, slowly lower the punch and align the punch center with the mark on the workpiece (see Fig. 8-25). When this is accomplished, punch the hole. This alignment procedure is quite easy with the hydraulic ironworker because of the ability to lower the punch slowly and stop it at any point on the cutting cycle simply by manipulating the lever pedal. As with any first operation, do a test punch on scrap.

Figure 8-24 Stripper bar clearance.

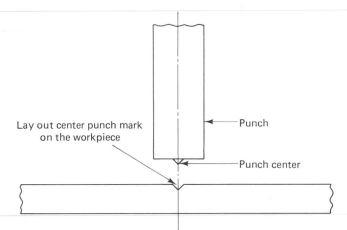

Lay out center punch mark on the workpiece

Punch

Punch center

Figure 8-25 Punch and workpiece alignment.

Figure 8-26 Setup guides for corner holes.

Figure 8-27 Setup guide for linear holes.

If a series of holes are to be punched as shown in Figure 8-26, setup guides can be clamped to the die table after the first hole is aligned and punched. This will allow you to punch all of the other, similarly placed holes without having to realign each one.

The use of a straightedge guide is imperative when punching a linear series of square holes, as shown in Figure 8-27. Not only must each be punched in the correct spot, but alignment of the sides of each hole must also be considered. If the spacing between all of the holes is the same, a simple indexer can also be employed. Punch the first two holes and leave the punch down in the second hole. Clamp or weld an indexing tab on the straightedge guide at the location of the edge of the first hole (see Fig. 8-28). Now, as each hole is punched, locating the next hole becomes a simple matter of moving the workpiece so that the previously punched hole lines up with the indexing tab. *Note:* Apply cutting oil to the punch and die before using and after every 10 holes punched.

Figure 8-28 Indexing tab.

MANUAL PUNCH Small, inexpensive hand-operated punches can be effectively used on thicknesses less than $\frac{3}{16}$ inch. If the machine being used is not rated for the material thickness of the workpiece, the punches can be raked to increase the capacity. To determine the maximum rake obtainable, lower the punch all the way down into the die and mark it flush with the die face (see Fig. 8-29). Remove the punch and grind a rake so that the trailing edge is $\frac{1}{16}$ inch below the marked line. This will give the maximum rake for that particular punch and die set. This method is recommended only for limited use, not high production runs. Apply a generous amount of cutting oil to the punch.

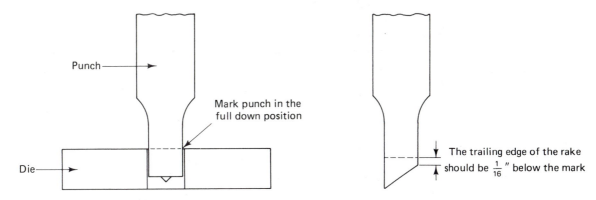

Punch

Mark punch in the full down position

Die

The trailing edge of the rake should be $\frac{1}{16}$ " below the mark

Figure 8-29 Maximum punch rake.

PLATE SHEARS   Power shears (see Fig. 8-30) are classified into two goups: hydraulic and mechanical. The mechanical flywheel type of shear has a faster cutting action, whereas the hydraulic is used for higher-capacity ratings. Fast cutting action may be desirable for production efficiency, but as the size of the workpiece increases, handling becomes more difficult and time consuming and the difference in cutting speeds between hydraulic and mechanical shears becomes insignificant.

Shear capacity is determined by the thickness of the mild steel the machine is designed to cut. For example, a ½-inch shear is rated to cut ½-inch-thick mild steel. If harder alloys such as stainless steel are to be cut, the rated capacity of the machine is reduced by as much as 50%.

Shears are available with capacities ranging from 16 gauge to 1½ inches and cutting blade lengths of 36 inches to 20 feet. Because of the high cost of these machines (a ¼-inch shear with an 8-foot cutting capacity can exceed $30,000), only larger companies will have shears with capacities greater than ⅜ inch.

Figure 8-30 Plate shear.

To ensure a clean and accurate cut, shear blades must be kept sharp and blade clearance properly adjusted. Most shear blades are reversible so that as one edge dulls, the blades can be removed and turned around. Blade sharpening must be done on a surface grinder equipped to handle such jobs. Refer to the operating manual for your particular machine for sharpening specifications. Blade clearance is an important adjustment because it affects cutting edge distortion. Depending on the manufacturer, ¼-inch-capacity shears will specify blade clearances of 0.007 to 0.012 inch. Again, consult the operating manual for machine specifications. Blade rake adjustment, not available on all machines, will also have an effect on cut distortion. If your machine has an adjustable rake and if the workpiece thickness is less than the rated capacity, the rake angle can be decreased to reduce plate distortion. The standard rake angle for shears of ¼ inch and less capacity is ¼ inch per foot of blade length.

Most shears provide two methods of measuring the material to be cut. The adjustable back gauge (see Fig. 8-31) indicates the distance from the cutting edge of the bottom blade to the back gauge bar. The front gauge (see Fig. 8-32), which consists of two measuring scales attached to the shear bed, is used for measuring distances from the bed to the lower-blade cutting

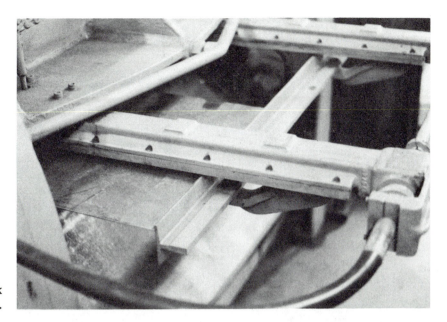

Figure 8-31 Back gauge.

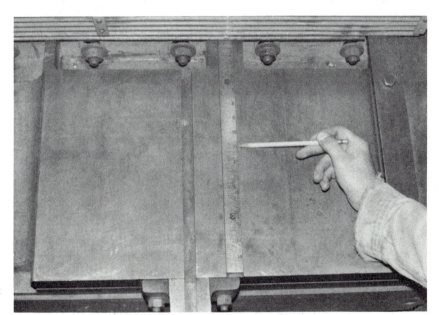

Figure 8-32 Front gauge.

edge. On each side of the bed are side gauge bars which are set at 90 degrees to the blades. All gauges should be checked for accuracy periodically.

The first step in making accurate cuts is squaring the workpiece. If you are going to use the back gauge for measuring the cuts, use method A. If using the front gauge or measuring from the front side of the shear, use method B.

METHOD A. Place the workpiece on the shear bed with one side squarely against the side gauge (see Fig. 8-33). Slide the workpiece under the hold-downs until the entire width of the edge to be cut extends at least ¼ inch beyond the lower blade. Shearing this edge will give a square starting point. Now, set the back gauge to the desired dimension, feed the workpiece into the shear until it comes in contact with the back gauge bar, and make the cut.

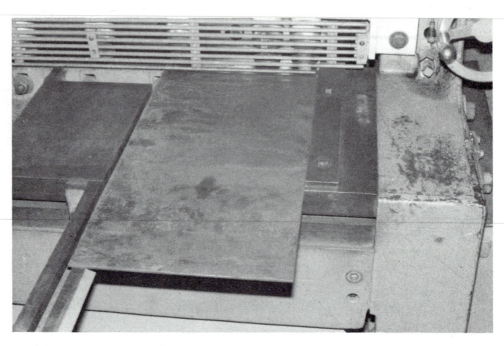

Figure 8-33 Squaring
cut.

METHOD B. Follow the steps outlined in method A for the initial squaring cut. After the cut is made, turn the plate upside down so that the same edge is still against the side gauge and the square cut edge is facing the front or bed side of the shear. Align the workpiece to the desired dimension on the front gauge scales. If several pieces have to be cut, clamp the front gauge bar onto the shear bed aligned with the desired setting on the gauge scales (see Fig. 8-34).

When working with pieces that extend beyond the shear bed, use a measuring tape to align the cut. Slide the end of the tape under the hold-downs until the end hook is fastened onto the lower blade cutting edge (see Fig. 8-35). When the workpiece is properly aligned, remember to remove the measuring tape before shearing.

An alternative method for setting up cuts is visual alignment. This is particularly useful when making angular cuts. The first step is to lay out the

Figure 8-34 Front
gauge bar.

Figure 8-35   Aligning a
cut with measuring tape.

entire line of cut with soapstone. Next, slide the plate under the hold-down
and visually line up the cut by looking down between the hold-down head
and the cross head. If the workpiece is narrow, make sure that it is positioned
under at least one of the hold-downs.

Although the newer plate shears have a cutting accuracy of 0.005 inch,
additional securing of the workpiece on older machines may be necessary
for close-tolerance cutting. Many times, particularly with mechanical shears,
the shearing operation will cause the workpiece to jump slightly out of alignment. This becomes a common problem when hold-downs are not properly
adjusted or the blades are dull. To prevent additional inaccuracy due to this
jumping, secure the workpiece to the shear bed with C clamps or clamping
dogs.

Note: Mechanical flywheel-type machines must be allowed to reach operating
speed before any cutting is attempted. Failure to do this may cause the shear
to jam halfway through the cutting operation. If this happens, shut off all
power to the machine and manually turn the flywheel in the reverse direction to raise the cross head. When this is accomplished, the workpiece can be
cleared.

Caution: Plate shears are very powerful machines which exert a tremendous
amount of force. Never place any part of the body under or between the
hold-downs or cross head. When performing any maintenance, always disconnect all electrical power and always block up the cross head when changing blades, particularly on hydraulic machines.

Chapter 9

BENDING and ROLLING

BENDING PLATE THICKNESSES   The bending of steel parts in a power press brake (see Fig. 9-1) can be done by either air or bottom bending. In the air bending process, the workpiece is formed to the desired angle between punch and die but is not bottomed against the die as in bottom bending. The advantage of air bending, particularly with plate thicknesses, is that it requires four to six times less tonnage than bottoming. For this reason most steel plate is formed by the air bending method. Bottoming is more widely used for sheet metal parts when very accurate bends are required and is discussed in detail in Chapter 15.

When forming 90-degree air bends on mild steel, the punch and die configuration will vary with plate thickness. As shown in Figure 9-2, the V-die opening should be at least eight times the material thickness (10 times the material thickness for steel over ½ inch) with a die angle of between 80 and 88 degrees. The punch should have an end radius equal to no less

Figure 9-1 Power press brake.

114

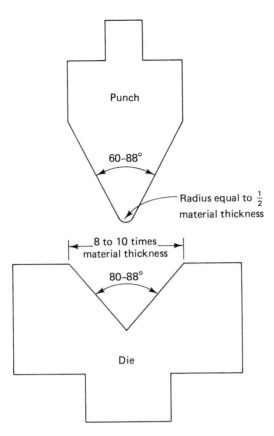

Figure 9-2 Punch and die configuration for 90° air bends.

[In figure: Punch / 60-88° / Radius equal to ½ material thickness / 8 to 10 times material thickness / 80-88° / Die]

than one-half the material thickness. This will produce the recommended inside bend radius equal to or slightly greater than the material thickness.

A bend allowance must be calculated into the workpiece layout to compensate for size expansion caused by material stretch during the bending operation. A bend allowance chart for bottom bending can be found in Chapter 17, but can be easily calculated for air bending by using the following formula:

$$\text{Bend allowance} = \frac{\pi}{2}\left(R + \frac{T}{3}\right)$$

where R is the inside bend radius and T is the material thickness.

EXAMPLE: Make a 90-degree air bend on a piece of ¼-inch plate as shown in Figure 9-3.

$$\text{Bend allowance} = \frac{3.1416}{2}\left(0.250 + \frac{0.250}{3}\right)$$
$$= 1.57(0.250 + 0.083)$$
$$= 1.57(0.333)$$
$$= 0.520$$

This calculation shows that the material will stretch approximately 0.520 inch. When cutting the workpiece to size, 0.520 inch must be subtracted. Instead of cutting the plate 14 by 18 inches, it would have to be cut 13.480 by 18 inches. The layout for the bend line would therefore be 6 inches minus one-half the bend allowance (6 − 0.260) or 5.740 (see Fig. 9-4). The workpiece can then be set into the press brake, aligned so that the bend line is centered under the punch (see Fig. 9-5), and bent to a 90-degree angle.

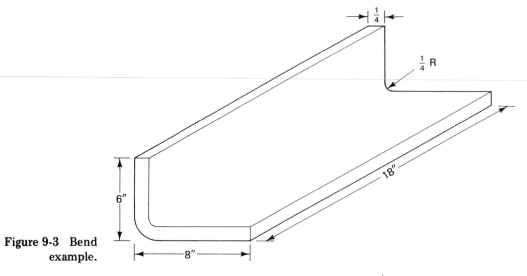

Figure 9-3 Bend
example.

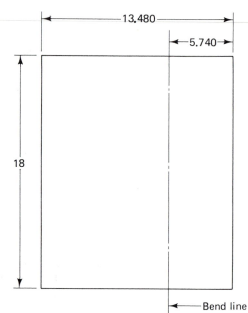

Figure 9-4 Bend line
layout.

Figure 9-5 Center-
ing the bend line
under the punch.

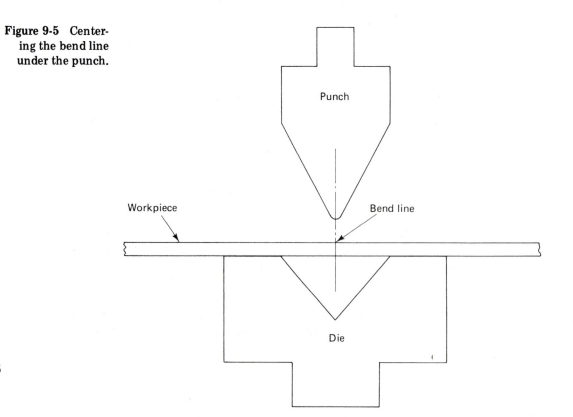

As mentioned previously, air bending is not the most accurate of forming operations. If the finished part must be an exact size, cut the material oversized and trim to the finished dimensions after bending.

Tonnage requirements for air bending mild-steel plate are given in Appendix 3. Power press brake setup is extensively discussed in Chapter 15.

ROLLING PLATE THICKNESSES

Power plate bending rolls (see Fig. 9-6) can be classified, according to roll configuration, into three basic groups: initial pinch, pyramid, and four-roll (see Fig. 9-7). Among the newer machines, the initial pinch type is the most common because of the ability to prebend workpiece ends to eliminate flat spots at the beginning and end of the rolled piece. The pyramid type of roll is the oldest design and gives the highest roll capacity for its size. The disadvantages of the pyramid roll are the flat spots left on the ends and the difficulty encountered in rolling small diameters. The four-roll type of machine offers the most versatility because of the ability to prebend on both sides of the drive rolls. Four-roll machines have the high work capacity of the pyramid roll and are excellent in forming conical shapes. This type of roll is also the most expensive to purchase. Layout procedures will be the same regardless of machine type.

As with bending, rolling a cylinder will cause the workpiece to stretch and this stretching must be considered in the layout. For example, the layout procedure for a cylinder with a 12-inch outside diameter, 48 inches long,

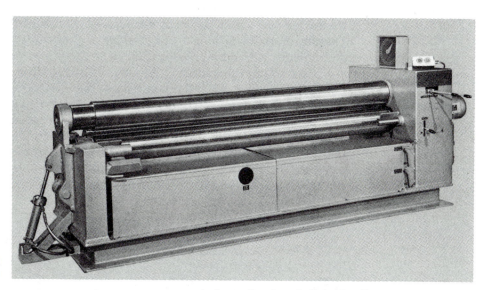

Figure 9-6 Plate roll. (Courtesy of Comeq Inc., Baltimore, Md.)

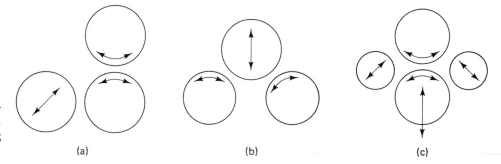

←→ Indicates direction of adjustable roll

Indicates drive roll

Figure 9-7 Roll configuration: (a) initial pinch; (b) pyramid; (c) four roll.

(a)   (b)   (c)

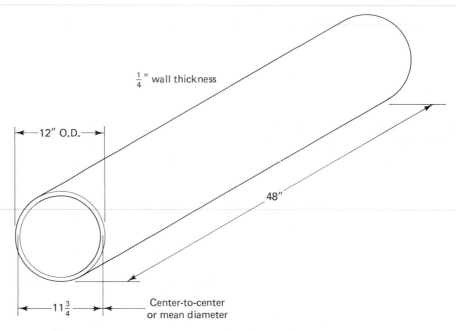

Figure 9-8 Center-to-center diameter.

$\frac{1}{4}$ " wall thickness

12" O.D.

48"

11$\frac{3}{4}$

Center-to-center
or mean diameter

and a ¼-inch wall thickness will be analyzed. If we use the 12-inch outside diameter to determine cylinder circumference, after rolling we would wind up with an overlap of approximately ¾ inch or an outside diameter slightly more than ¼ inch oversized. To compensate for material stretch, calculate circumference using the center-to-center or mean diameter (see Fig. 9-8). Therefore, the workpiece cut size prior to rolling would be ¼ inch by 36.9 inch by 48 inches.

The rolling procedure will vary with the different machine types (see Fig. 9-9). If a pyramid roll is being used, feed the workpiece into the machine as shown in Figure 9-10, and lower the top roll until the desired radius is formed (see Fig. 9-11). Keep in mind that the workpiece must be fed squarely into the roll and rolls must be perfectly parallel to prevent "spiraling." When the top roll is in position, run the machine in reverse and back the workpiece out. This will reduce the size of the end flat spot (an alternative method of eliminating flat spots is to prebend the workpiece ends in a press brake).

Figure 9-9 Rolling operation.

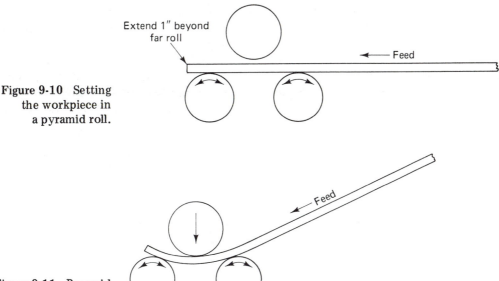

Figure 9-10 Setting the workpiece in a pyramid roll.

Figure 9-11 Pyramid roll-forming radius.

Refeed the workpiece squarely into the machine and complete the roll. Be conservative with your roll adjustments. It is safer to make several passes through the machine than to try to roll the cylinder in one shot and overroll it. Correcting an overroll, particularly on heavier plate, will often require many hours of extra work.

The setup for an initial pinch machine is slightly different. Feed the workpiece squarely into the machine and raise the lower roll until the material is clamped securely between the upper and lower rolls (see Fig. 9-12). Now raise the pinch roll to prebend the workpiece (see Fig. 9-13) and run it through the roll. Remember to be conservative with your adjustments. Before refeeding the workpiece, turn it around and feed the trailing end first. Completing this roll will remove most of the original leading-edge flat spot created by the initial set.

After a cylinder is formed, run it through the machine several more times to improve its uniformity. This can be done even after welding as long as the welds have been ground flush to the plate surface.

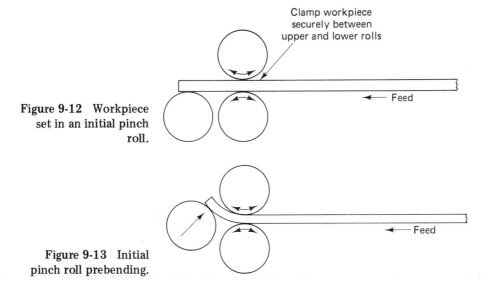

Figure 9-12 Workpiece set in an initial pinch roll.

Figure 9-13 Initial pinch roll prebending.

Some of the older machines do not have drop ends which allow for easy removal of the completed cylinder. Rolls of this type must be partially disassembled for cylinder removal, which can be a time-consuming operation. If this situation exists, you might consider rolling the cylinder in two halves.

Because of the wide variety of machine manufacturers and types being used in industry today, we suggest consulting the operator's manual for your specific machine for recommended adjustments and operating procedures.

Chapter 10

DRILLING and THREAD CUTTING

DRILLING Although many drilling techniques and drill-bit configurations are available in industry, this section deals primarily with methods most often used in structural steel fabrication.

The twist drill (Fig. 10-1) is the most common drilling tool. The drill body has two flutes which form a spiral. The lip or cutting edge of the drill does the actual cutting, but the flutes carry the chips out of the hole and away from the work and allows cutting oil to reach the lips keeping the drill cool. The margin of the drill provides clearance for the drill body. This reduces friction and excessive heat, which would cause the drill to bind in the hole.

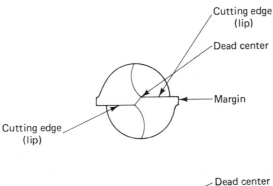

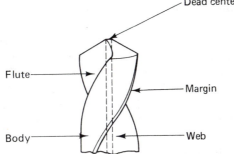

Figure 10-1 Twist drill.

Twist drills are available in three size classifications: fraction, letter, and number. Fraction-size drills are available from $\frac{1}{16}$ to $\frac{1}{2}$ inch in $\frac{1}{64}$-inch increments and from $\frac{1}{2}$ to $1\frac{1}{2}$ inches in $\frac{1}{32}$-inch increments. Larger and more intermediate-size drills are available but usually only by special order. Number drills range in size from number 1 (0.228) to number 80 (0.014) in diameter. Letter drills range from A to Z. An A-size drill is 0.234 inch in diameter and the Z size is 0.413 inch in diameter. See Charts 10-1 and 10-2 for a complete listing.

CHART 10-1 Decimal Equivalents of Number Size Drills

No.	Size of drill (in.)	No.	Size of drill (in.)	No.	Size of drill (in.)	No.	Size of drill (in.)
1	0.2280	21	0.1590	41	0.0960	61	0.0390
2	0.2210	22	0.1570	42	0.0935	62	0.0380
3	0.2130	23	0.1540	43	0.0890	63	0.0370
4	0.2090	24	0.1520	44	0.0860	64	0.0360
5	0.2055	25	0.1495	45	0.0820	65	0.0350
6	0.2040	26	0.1470	46	0.0810	66	0.0330
7	0.2010	27	0.1440	47	0.0785	67	0.0320
8	0.1990	28	0.1405	48	0.0760	68	0.0310
9	0.1960	29	0.1360	49	0.0730	69	0.0292
10	0.1935	30	0.1285	50	0.0700	70	0.0280
11	0.1910	31	0.1200	51	0.0670	71	0.0260
12	0.1890	32	0.1160	52	0.0635	72	0.0250
13	0.1850	33	0.1130	53	0.0595	73	0.0240
14	0.1820	34	0.1110	54	0.0550	74	0.0225
15	0.1800	35	0.1100	55	0.0520	75	0.0210
16	0.1770	36	0.1065	56	0.0465	76	0.0200
17	0.1730	37	0.1040	57	0.0430	77	0.0180
18	0.1695	38	0.1015	58	0.0420	78	0.0160
19	0.1660	39	0.0995	59	0.0410	79	0.0145
20	0.1610	40	0.0980	60	0.0400	80	0.0135

Courtesy of L. S. Starrett Company.

Whether the holes are drilled with a hand-held $\frac{1}{4}$-inch drill motor or large drill press, certain steps must be taken if a high-quality job is to be expected. Hole locations should always be center punched (Fig. 10-2). This will ensure an accurate drill start. Attempting to start drilling without a center punch, particularly with hand-held motors, will usually result in the drill wandering and the hole being made in the wrong spot.

If a large-diameter hole is being drilled (over $\frac{1}{2}$ inch in diameter), a technique known as pilot drilling should be employed. An initial pilot hole is made with a smaller drill. The pilot hole should be slightly larger in diameter than the dead center of the finish drill (see Fig. 10-3).

Caution must be taken not to make the pilot hole too large, as this will cause the finish drill to chatter and cut an out-of-round hole. The drill press

CHART 10-2   Decimal Equivalents of Letter Size Drills

Letter	Size of drill (in.)	Letter	Size of drill (in.)
A	0.234	N	0.302
B	0.238	O	0.316
C	0.242	P	0.323
D	0.246	Q	0.332
E	0.250	R	0.339
F	0.257	S	0.348
G	0.261	T	0.358
H	0.266	U	0.368
I	0.272	V	0.377
J	0.277	W	0.386
K	0.281	X	0.397
L	0.290	Y	0.404
M	0.295	Z	0.413

Courtesy of L.S. Starrett Company.

Figure 10-2 Hole location being center punched.

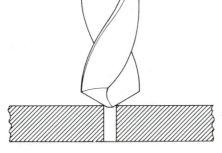

Figure 10-3 Pilot hole slightly larger than dead center of the finish drill.

provides the easiest and most accurate method of hole drilling and all fabricated parts of suitable size should be drilled this way. It also provides greater mechanical advantage, making the drilling of the largest hole quite effortless. The table and vise allow for accurate and secure clamping of the workpiece and a perfect 90-degree drill-to-work surface relationship. The most unique feature, not available on most portable drilling equipment, is a wide range of spindle speeds, which will greatly increase the efficiency of the drills. Smaller-diameter drills should be used at a much higher speed than the larger sizes (see Chart 10-3 for recommended drill speeds for various diameters).

CHART 10-3   Drill Speeds for Cast Iron and Steel[a]

Drill-bit diameter (in.)	Cast iron and low-carbon steel	Medium-carbon steel	High-carbon and alloy steels
$\frac{1}{8}$	2600	2200	1600
$\frac{1}{4}$	1300	1100	800
$\frac{3}{8}$	900	750	550
$\frac{1}{2}$	700	575	425
$\frac{5}{8}$	550	450	325
$\frac{3}{4}$	450	375	275
$\frac{7}{8}$	400	325	240
1	350	275	200

[a]For high-speed drills; approximate revolutions per minute.

Pieces which are small enough to be clamped in the drill press vise should be set up on parallel bars (see Fig. 10-4) to avoid damage to the vise or drill. The vise can be held by hand when drilling holes under $\frac{3}{8}$ inch. For drilling larger holes, clamp the vise securely to the table. Pieces too large for the vise can be clamped directly to the table (see Fig. 10-5).

A center drill or stub center can be used to align the center punch mark (see Fig. 10-6) properly. Set the spindle speed for the drill being used and check to make sure that the drill is properly secured in the chuck. If the

Figure 10-4 Workpiece clamped in a vise.

Figure 10-5 Workpiece clamped to a table.

Figure 10-6 Aligning the center-punch mark with a center drill.

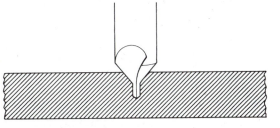

Figure 10-7 Starting a hole with a center drill.

finished hole diameter is greater than that of the center drill, the center drill can be used to start the hole. Drill until half of the tapered section is in the work (see Fig. 10-7).

As you are drilling the hole, keep in mind that you should lift out the drill periodically to clear chips and apply cutting fluid.* (*Caution:* Do not attempt to remove chips by hand. As the drill approaches the bottom of the work and is about to break through, reduce the pressure being applied. This will prevent the drill from being rapidly drawn through the work which may cause it to bind and break.)

*Use cutting oil for steel, and kerosene for aluminum and copper alloys.

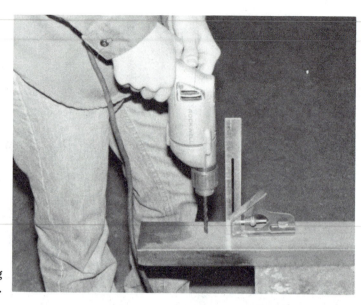

Figure 10-8 Aligning
the drill with a square.

Remove all burrs from the completed holes with a counter sink or deburring tool. Deburring can also be accomplished by cutting the ridge with a larger-size drill or by hand filing.

Often in structural fabrication, the work is too large for a drill press, or holes must be made in other than the flat position. In these instances portable hand drills or magnetic-base drills must be used. Small-diameter holes can be made easily with a ¼- or ⅜-inch drill motor. (Drill motor size is determined by its chuck capacity. A ¼-inch drill motor has a chuck that will accept drill shanks up to ¼ inch.) Two problems are usually incurred when using this type of drill. Excessive drill pressure, causing a deflection and breakage of smaller bits, and keeping a perpendicular alignment are probably the most critical aspects of accurate drilling. If you find difficulty in judging whether or not the drill is perpendicular to the work, use a small combination square for a line of reference (see Fig. 10-8).

Drilling large-diameter holes by hand can be physically difficult. Large drills require much more pressure to cut efficiently. Two things can help when using a ½- or ¾-inch drill motor: pilot drilling and the use of a "dead man." The dead man (see Fig. 10-9) is a simple gadget to make and will

Figure 10-9 Drilling
with the aid of a
dead man.

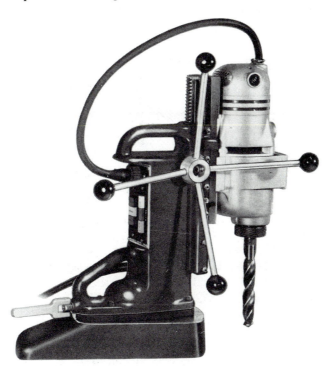

Figure 10-10 Magnetic base drill. (Courtesy of Black and Decker.)

greatly increase your mechanical advantage. One word of caution: when using a dead man, the drill motor must be steadied with one hand and the pressure applied with the other. Before breaking through the bottom of the hole, hold the drill motor firmly with both hands. An easy method of telling when the drill is about to break through is to listen for a change in the sound of the drill motor. The pitch will become deeper.

A tool that can be used to great advantage on flat steel surfaces is the magnetic base drill stand (see Fig. 10-10). When the drill is properly positioned, the electromagnet in its base holds it firmly in position, creating a portable drill press. When these machines are used at heights or in the vertical and overhead positions, they must be safety chained to the work. This is an extremely important safety precaution. The weight of this tool can be as much as 80 pounds and inadvertently unplugging it will disengage the magnetic base.

THREAD CUTTING   American standard threads are dimensioned and classified by a designation which specifies major thread diameter, number of threads per inch, and thread type.

EXAMPLE:

$$\frac{3}{8}'' - 16 \text{ NC}$$

thread type

threads per inch

major thread diameter (see Fig. 10-11)

Thread type will be one of the following:

NF, National Fine—also referred to as SAE (Society of Automotive Engineers)

NC, National Coarse—also referred to as USS (United States Standard)

NPT, National Pipe Taper

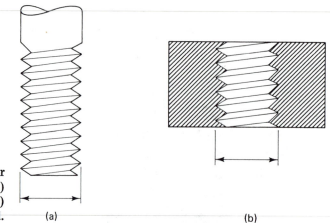

Figure 10-11 Major thread diameter: (a) external thread; (b) internal thread.

(a)   (b)

Metric thread designations are always prefaced by the letter M followed by the major thread diameter and thread pitch (distance from thread to thread; see Fig. 10-12).

EXAMPLE:

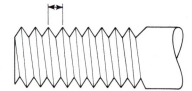

M 12 − 1.50
pitch (mm)
thread diameter (mm)
metric

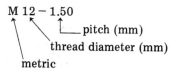

Figure 10-12 Thread pitch.

For left-hand threads the letters LH will follow the designation.

The difference between coarse and fine threads is the thread depth and number of threads per inch. As seen in Figure 10-13, both bolts are ⅜ inch in diameter. The bolt on the left has a fine thread that is shallow in cut but more numerous per inch. The coarse thread on the right has a much deeper cut but fewer threads per inch.

A coarse thread is most often used in steel fabrication because of its ability to withstand high-torque tightening. However, if resistance to vibration is the primary design consideration, the fine thread would be the better choice. A fine thread should also be used on thin cross sections to allow for a greater number of threads in contact. For example, Figure 10-14 shows a thin section with both coarse and fine threads. Under stress, the fine thread will prove to be the strongest because more threads are in contact between bolt and threaded cross section.

Figure 10-13 Coarse and fine thread comparison.

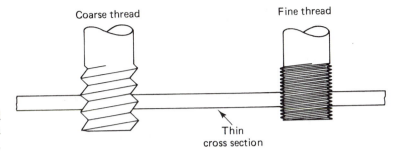

Figure 10-14 Thread selection for thin cross sections.

Coarse thread

Fine thread

Thin cross section

INTERNAL THREADS

Internal threads, when made by hand, are cut with taps which are made in sets of three styles: taper, plug, and bottoming (see Fig. 10-15). Because of its configuration, the taper tap is the easiest to start and is most often used on through holes. When a blind or dead end hole has to be threaded all the way to the bottom, the plug and bottoming taps are used to finish threads not fully cut by the taper tap.

Successful internal thread cutting begins with the selection of the proper tap drill size. A 75% thread cut is ideal; 100% thread cuts increase the strength of the thread by only 5%, but require three times the force to cut. This greatly increases the chance of breaking the tap and damaging the workpiece. Chart 10-4 lists the proper drill sizes for the most common Ameri-

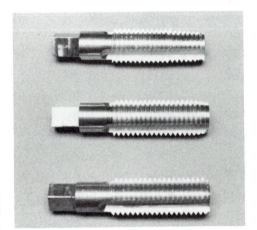

Figure 10-15 Taps. *(from top to bottom)* Taper, plug, and bottom tap.

CHART 10-4 Tap Drill Sizes

Size	Threads per inch NC UNC	NF UNF	Outside diameter (in.)	Pitch diameter (in.)	Root diameter (in.)	Tap drill approx. 75% full thread	Decimal equiv. of tap drill
0		80	0.0600	0.0519	0.0438	3/64	0.0469
1	64		0.0730	0.0629	0.0527	53	0.0595
1		72	0.0730	0.0640	0.0550	53	0.0595
2	56		0.0860	0.0744	0.0628	50	0.0700
2		64	0.0860	0.0759	0.0657	50	0.0700
3	48		0.0990	0.0855	0.0719	47	0.0785
3		56	0.0990	0.0874	0.0758	46	0.0810
4	40		0.1120	0.0958	0.0795	43	0.0890
4		48	0.1120	0.0985	0.0849	42	0.0935

CHART 10-4 Tap Drill Sizes (continued)

Size	Threads per inch NC UNC	Threads per inch NF UNF	Outside diameter (in.)	Pitch diameter (in.)	Root diameter (in.)	Tap drill approx. 75% full thread	Decimal equiv. of tap drill
5	40		0.1250	0.1088	0.0925	38	0.1015
5		44	0.1250	0.1102	0.0955	37	0.1040
6	32		0.1380	0.1177	0.0974	36	0.1065
6		40	0.1380	0.1218	0.1055	33	0.1130
8	32		0.1640	0.1437	0.1234	29	0.1360
8		36	0.1640	0.1460	0.1279	29	0.1360
10	24		0.1900	0.1629	0.1359	26	0.1470
10		32	0.1900	0.1697	0.1494	21	0.1590
12	24		0.2160	0.1889	0.1619	16	0.1770
12		28	0.2160	0.1928	0.1696	15	0.1800
1/4	20		0.2500	0.2175	0.1850	7	0.2010
1/4		28	0.2500	0.2268	0.2036	3	0.2130
5/16	18		0.3125	0.2764	0.2403	F	0.2570
5/16		24	0.3125	0.2854	0.2584	I	0.2720
3/8	16		0.3750	0.3344	0.2938	5/16	0.3125
3/8		24	0.3750	0.3479	0.3209	Q	0.3320
7/16	14		0.4375	0.3911	0.3447	U	0.3680
7/16		20	0.4375	0.4050	0.3726	25/64	0.3906
1/2	13		0.5000	0.4500	0.4001	27/64	0.4219
1/2		20	0.5000	0.4675	0.4351	29/64	0.4531
9/16	12		0.5625	0.5084	0.4542	31/64	0.4844
9/16		18	0.5625	0.5264	0.4903	33/64	0.5156
5/8	11		0.6250	0.5660	0.5069	17/32	0.5312
5/8		18	0.6250	0.5889	0.5528	37/64	0.5781
3/4	10		0.7500	0.6850	0.6201	21/32	0.6562
3/4		16	0.7500	0.7094	0.6688	11/16	0.6875
7/8	9		0.8750	0.8028	0.7307	49/64	0.7656
7/8		14	0.8750	0.8286	0.7822	13/16	0.8125
1	8		1.0000	0.9188	0.8376	7/8	0.8750
1		12	1.0000	0.9459	0.8917	59/64	0.9219
1 1/8	7		1.1250	1.0322	0.9394	63/64	0.9844
1 1/8		12	1.1250	1.0709	1.0168	1 3/64	1.0469
1 1/4	7		1.2500	1.1572	1.0644	1 7/64	1.1094
1 1/4		12	1.2500	1.1959	1.1418	1 11/64	1.1719
1 3/8	6		1.3750	1.2667	1.1585	1 7/32	1.2187
1 3/8		12	1.3750	1.3209	1.2668	1 19/64	1.2969
1 1/2	6		1.5000	1.3917	1.2835	1 11/32	1.3437
1 1/2		12	1.5000	1.4459	1.3918	1 27/64	1.4219
1 3/4	5		1.7500	1.6201	1.4902	1 9/16	1.5625

Courtesy of L.S. Starrett Company.

Figure 10-16 Aligning a tap with snub center.

can standard threads. Always deburr both ends of the drilled hole with a countersink prior to tapping.

Holes drilled on a drill press can also be tapped in the same operation. After the tap drill hole has been made, remove the drill from the chuck and install a snub center. Secure the tap in the tap handle and place it in position on the hole. Lower the drill press chuck so that the snub center fits into the centering hole on the top end of the tap (see Fig. 10-16). This will hold the tap in perfect aligment as the threads are being cut. Apply cutting oil liberally to the tap. Failure to do this can result in damage to the tap and workpiece. Turn the tap handle while applying light pressure with the down feed handle. Reverse the tap after each quarter revolution to break the chips. Continue this procedure until the thread is completed.

When tapping a thread without the aid of a centering device, care must be taken to ensure the correct 90-degree tap-to-work surface relationship. Position the tap on the hole and visually check for proper alignment. Apply pressure while turning the tap handle. Check a second time for alignment. Once the tap is started, reverse it slightly after each quarter revolution to break the chips. Remember to apply a liberal amount of cutting oil. Care must be taken with small-diameter taps not to use excessive force, as they will break quite easily.

EXTERNAL THREADS The tool used to hand cut an external thread is a die and they are available in two styles: solid hex and round adjustable (see Fig. 10-17). Adjustable dies are designed to allow for a slight oversize or undersize thread cut. Like taps, dies are tapered on one end to facilitate easy starting.

The die is mounted in a die stock (handle) which has an adjustable guide to aide in thread alignment (see Fig. 10-18). Prior to cutting the threads, the end of the work should be chamfered (see Fig. 10-19). If an adjustable die is used, tighten the setscrew on the die stock to open the die so that approximately 40% is initially cut. This initial cut will prevent the die from cocking as it bites into the material. The setscrew can then be

Figure 10-17 Hexagon and round dies.

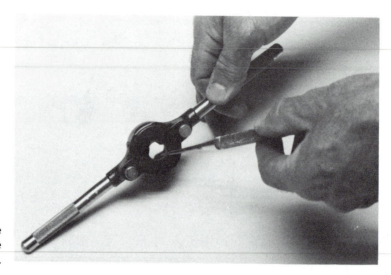

Figure 10-18 Die stock with adjustable guide.

Chamfered edge

Figure 10-19 Preparation of the workpiece for external thread cutting.

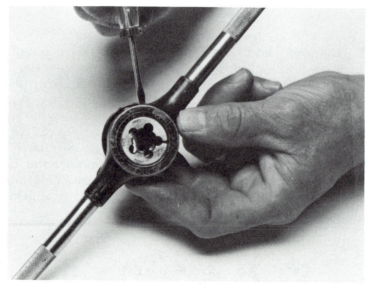

Figure 10-20 Die stock with die.

132

backed off and the final cut made. Secure the work firmly. Fasten the die in the die stock with the tapered end toward the adjustable guide (see Fig. 10-20). The tapered side of the die will also have "start from this side" stamped on it. Place the die stock and die on the workpiece and adjust the guide to the size of the work. Turn the die stock clockwise while applying a slight amount of pressure. Apply plenty of cutting oil and reverse direction

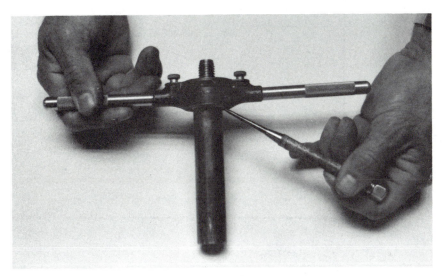

Figure 10-21 Reversing the die stock to complete the thread.

slightly after each quarter-turn to break the chips. If the thread has to be cut to a shoulder, thread as close to the shoulder as you can get. Then back off the die and turn it over so that the finished side is toward the work and complete the thread (see Fig. 10-21). Dies can also be used to restore damaged threads, but care must be taken to start the die on the original thread.

THREAD GAUGES Thread gauges are used to determine the number of threads per inch (thread pitch for metric sizes) of a nut or bolt. When the proper-size gauge is held against the thread, all of the teeth on the gauge will align perfectly with the

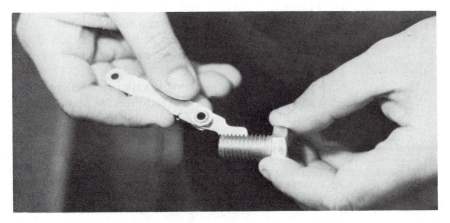

Figure 10-22 Thread gauge.

threads (see Fig. 10-22). Each set of teeth on the gauge has its corresponding number of threads per inch stamped on it. Metric gauges have the thread pitch stamped on them.

Chapter 11

JOINING OPERATIONS

The final step in many metal fabrication jobs will involve some type of welding or bolting operation. The choice of joining method will depend on one or more of the following factors: (1) job specifications, (2) equipment availability, (3) production efficiency, (4) strength requirements, (5) welding compatibility of joining surfaces, and (6) whether or not the members being joined are to be permanently connected or removable.

WELDING A knowledge of the various types of welding processes will prove to be extremely helpful in determining which process will give the best results (see the readings in Appendix 2). The key to production efficiency is proper weld-joint preparation and the ability to determine the optimum weld size. Overwelding will only waste time and material.

Most welds made on structural steel and heavy plate can be classified as groove or fillet welds. Groove welds are used when the surfaces being joined are on the same plane (see Fig. 11-1). Fillet welds are employed when the edges being welded are perpendicular to each other.

If maximum strength is required for plate or structural shapes connected by groove welds, the joint must be prepared so that 100% weld penetration can be obtained. This is accomplished by forming a bevel on one or both of the joining surfaces (see Fig. 11-2). The suggested angle for these bevels is between 30 and 37½ degrees. This will produce an included angle of 60 to 75 degrees on V-groove joints. If the exact bevel angle is not specified, it will be left to the welder's preference. The bevels can be made by grinding, flame cutting, or beveling machine.

If the weld can be done on both sides, use the sequence in Figure 11-3. This will reduce the chance of severe weld distortion. If all of the welding must be done from one side, secure the parts with clamps or strong backs to reduce distortion due to weld shrinkage (see Fig. 11-4). Weld the strong back on one side only so that they can be easily removed after the welding operation.

134

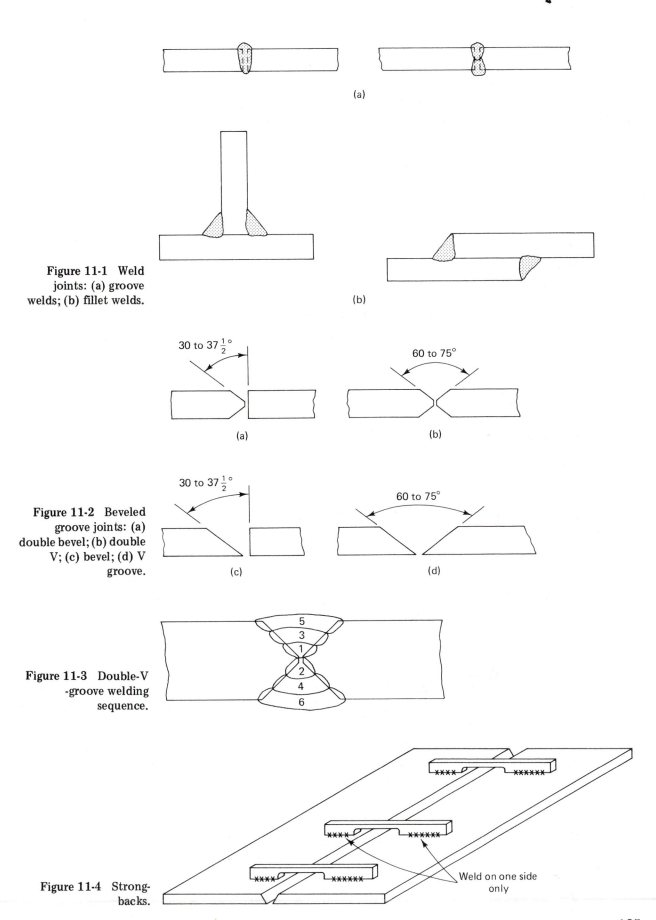

Figure 11-1 Weld joints: (a) groove welds; (b) fillet welds.

(a)

(b)

30 to $37\frac{1}{2}°$

60 to 75°

(a)

(b)

30 to $37\frac{1}{2}°$

60 to 75°

Figure 11-2 Beveled groove joints: (a) double bevel; (b) double V; (c) bevel; (d) V groove.

(c)

(d)

Figure 11-3 Double-V -groove welding sequence.

Figure 11-4 Strong-backs.

Weld on one side only

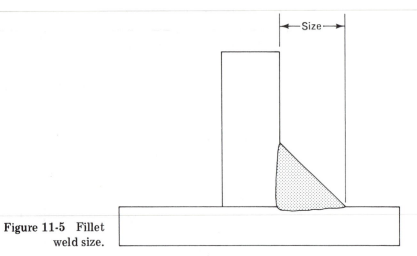

Figure 11-5 Fillet weld size.

Fillet weld size is measured from root to toe (see Fig. 11-5). To achieve maximum strength from a fillet weld, the joint must be welded on both sides and the size of the weld equal to three-fourths of the material thickness. Use Chart 11-1 as a guide.

CHART 11-1   Filler Weld Size-to-Strength Relationship

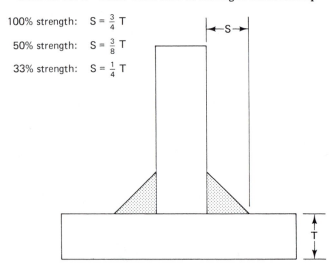

100% strength: $S = \frac{3}{4} T$

50% strength: $S = \frac{3}{8} T$

33% strength: $S = \frac{1}{4} T$

If the weld cannot be made on both sides and maximum strength is required, the upright member of the joints in Figure 11-6 can be beveled. Care must be taken to clamp this type of joint securely because of the increased problem of weld distortion.

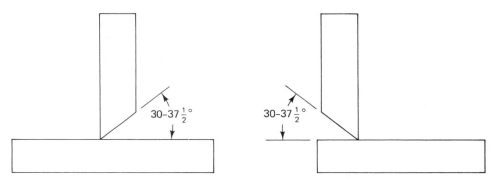

Figure 11-6 Beveled fillet welds.

SPLICING Occasionally, structural shapes, particularly beams, will have to be spliced together to form extra-long lengths. The method of splicing is crucial if these members are to be load bearing and not directly supported under the splice. A method that works quite well is a modified version of square joints (see Fig. 11-7). Bevel all mating edges to allow for maximum weld penetration. For additional strength, fishplates should be welded to the web or flange

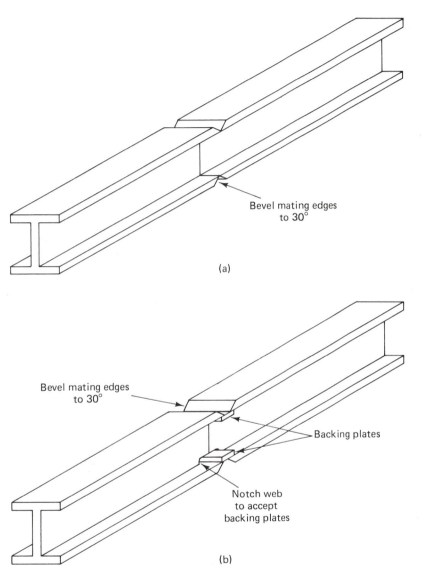

Figure 11-7 Beam splice joints.

(see Fig. 11-8). The weld directly under the fishplates must be ground flush to permit solid contact between fishplate and structural member.

The joining of two or more large pieces of plate to form a thicker section calls for the use of plug or slot welds to prevent buckling between the plate surfaces. For example, two ⅜ inch by 48-inch by 96-inch plates are spliced together to form a plate ¾ inch thick. If the plates were simply welded together around the perimeter, the weld would not be adequate enough to prevent surface buckling. As an alternative, take one of the plates and cut a series of holes approximately 1 to 1½ inches in diameter through it (see Fig. 11-9). The plates can then be clamped together and the holes filled with weld. These plug welds will maintain intimate contact between plate surfaces and eliminate the problem of buckling.

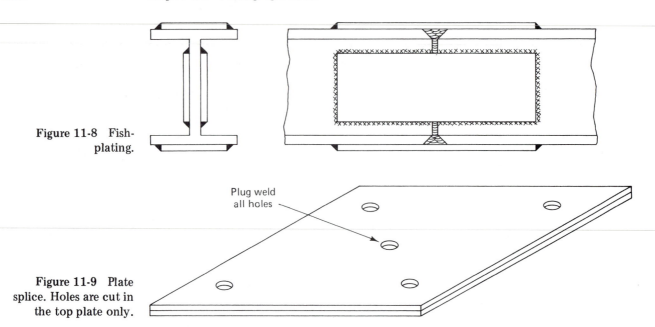

Figure 11-8   Fish-plating.

Figure 11-9   Plate splice. Holes are cut in the top plate only.

Plug weld all holes

When laying out a lap joint (one member overlapping the other) as in Figure 11-10, the overlap should be five times the thickness of the thinnest member being joined. Since these members are joined with fillet welds, refer back to the paragraph on fillet weld size to determine the appropriate weld size.

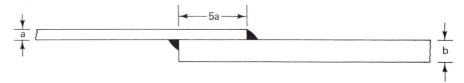

Figure 11-10   Lap joint.

BOLTING   Making a bolted connection is more expensive and time consuming than a welded one because of the many steps required. Pieces must be clamped together, hole patterns marked, holes drilled and deburred, and nuts and bolts set in place. However, a joint or connection often cannot be welded. In many field assembly operations or on connections that must be able to be taken apart, welding would be impractical.

BOLTS AND MACHINE SCREWS   Bolts and machine screws are identified by head shape, thread diameter and type, length, and grade. Figure 11-11 shows the head configurations for the most commonly used threaded fasteners. The choice of bolt or machine screw type used will be determined by the amount of load that the connection is subjected to, if the connection is to be a tight, snug fit or highly torqued, frequency of disassembly, and whether or not the heads must be flush with the finished surface.

Most standard assembly fastenings are made with hexagon-head bolts when large diameters, speed of assembly, or high-torque tightening is required. Square-head bolts are generally used in the construction field. The various slotted-head bolts are used when high-torque tightening is not required. In the case of the flat, oval, or fillister heads, the finished connection has a smooth surface (see Fig. 11-12). Joint designs of this type should be considered when appearance is a primary consideration or for applications

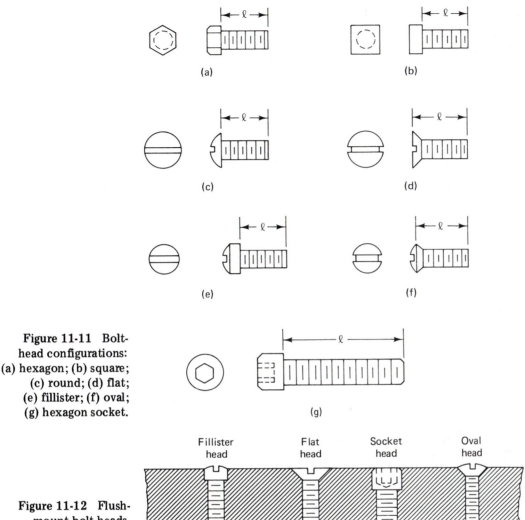

Figure 11-11 Bolt-head configurations: (a) hexagon; (b) square; (c) round; (d) flat; (e) fillister; (f) oval; (g) hexagon socket.

Figure 11-12 Flush-mount bolt heads.

such as catwalks and stair treads, where bolt-head protrusion would create a safety hazard.

Socket-head cap screws (Allen screws) give the combined advantage of a concealed head and high-torque capabilities. Cap screws are widely used in machine fabrication.

Thread size and type are discussed in Chapter 10. The length of bolts and machine screws is determined by the measurement (l) as shown in Figure 11-11.

Bolts are available in various lengths, with thread sizes from ¼ to 3 inches. Available thread diameters for socket-head cap screws range in sizes up to 1½ inches and machines screws to ⅜ inch in diameter. Machine screws are manufactured in diameters up to ¾ inch, but these are specialty items and not readily available.

BOLT GRADING The Society of Automotive Engineers (SAE) and the American Society for Testing and Materials (ASTM) have established a bolt grading system which groups bolts by the material they are made from, minimum tensile strength, and proof load (see Chart 11-2). Proof load is the amount of tensile force a bolt can withstand without being permanently stretched.

CHART 11-2 Bolt Grading System

Head markings	SAE grade	ASTM grade	Material	Nominal bolt diameter (in.)	Minimum tensile strength (psi)	Proof strength (psi)
No marks	1	A 307	Low-carbon steel	¼ to 1½	55,000	33,000
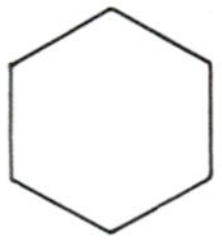	2		Low-carbon steel	¼ to ¾ Over ¾	64,000 55,000	52,000 28,000
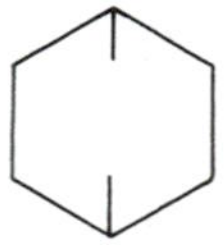	3		Medium-carbon steel	¼ to ½ Over ½	110,000 100,000	85,000 80,000
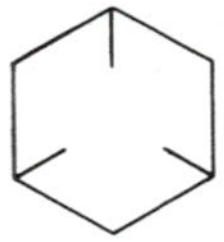	5	A 440	Medium-carbon steel, heat treated	¼ to ¾ ¾ to 1 1 to 1½	120,000 115,000 105,000	85,000 78,000 74,000
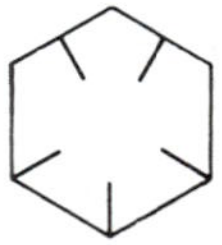	7		Medium-carbon low-alloy steel, heat treated	¼ to 1½	133,000	105,000
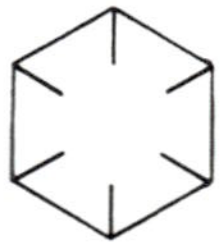	8	A 354	Medium-carbon alloy steel, heat treated	¼ to 1½	150,000	120,000

Notice when looking at the chart that the tensile strength rating of a bolt will often vary with its diameter.

Low-carbon steel bolts (SAE grades 1 and 2) are the least expensive to purchase and the most widely used for general fabrication. The higher-strength bolts, however, should always be used for all critical high-strength connections. Building and bridge construction are covered by specific code guidelines (see the readings in Appendix 2).

NUTS Nuts are usually made from very ductile steel. This ductility allows the nut to yield while being tightened, enabling the internal thread to distribute the tensile load evenly. The stripping strength of steel nuts is approximately 90,000 psi.

Nuts commonly used in industry can be classified into five groups: hex, square, slotted, castellated, and jam (see Fig. 11-13). Hex and square nuts are also available in heavier grade. These nuts are larger in size across the flats and are used for heavy work loads, where increased surface contact is required.

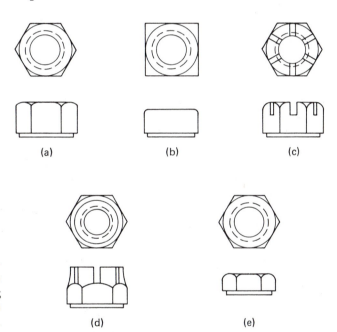

Figure 11-13 Commonly used nuts: (a) hexagon; (b) square; (c) slotted hex; (d) castellated; (e) jam.

Slotted nuts are used on fast-moving rotating assemblies such as shaft connections or aircraft parts. They have the advantage of being cotter-pinned or safety-wired through the bolt to prevent loosening.

Castellated nuts have a slotted crown top which has a tendency to tighten itself against the bolt and act as a self-locking device. Nuts of this type are widely used in the automotive industry.

Jam nuts have a very thin profile and are used for jamming or locking the primary nut in place. The primary nut must first be tightened to the desired torque. The jam nut is then spun down against it, and while the primary nut is held with one wrench, the jam nut is tightened against it with another.

WASHERS Although many different types of washers are commercially available, the three types most commonly used in steel fabrication are flat, lock, and beam washers (see Fig. 11-14). The primary function of the flat washer is to dis-

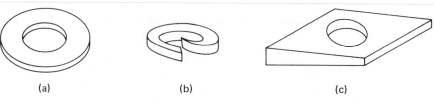

Figure 11-14 Washers:
(a) flat; (b) lock; (c)
tapered beam.

(a)   (b)   (c)

tribute the compressive force of the nut and bolt over a larger area, thereby
producing a more rigid joint. Flat washers are also used when bolting an
oversized or slotted hole, particularly if the hole is the same or larger than
the bolt head. Use only hardened washers under both nuts and bolt heads on
high-strength connections.

The split-spring lock washer is made of heat-treated alloy steel and designed to exert force between the nut and the workpiece. The use of this
type of washer is extremely important on assemblies subjected to rotary
movement or vibration.

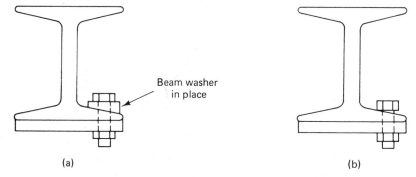

Figure 11-15 Tapered
flange bolt joint: (a)
correct; (b) wrong.

(a)   (b)

Beam washers are wedge-shaped (see Fig. 11-15) and designed to
compensate for the tapered flanges on structural shapes such as I beams and
channels. These washers should always be used when bolting through tapered
flanges. If not, the bolt head or nut will not have a square surface to seat on
and tightening will cause the bolt to bend and possibly fail.

DRILLING   The key to a high-quality bolted connection is the drilling of proper-sized
BOLT HOLES   holes. The holes must be slightly larger in diameter than the bolts being used
but not so large as to cause excessive play. If holes are too sloppy, movement

CHART 11-3   Bolt Clearance Holes

Bolt diameter (in.)	Clearance hole diameter (in.)
$\frac{1}{4}$	$\frac{17}{64}$
$\frac{5}{16}$	$\frac{21}{64}$
$\frac{3}{8}$	$\frac{25}{64}$
$\frac{7}{16}$	$\frac{29}{64}$
$\frac{1}{2}$	$\frac{17}{32}$
$\frac{5}{8}$	$\frac{21}{32}$
$\frac{3}{4}$	$\frac{25}{32}$
$\frac{7}{8}$	$\frac{29}{32}$
1	$1\frac{1}{16}$
$1\frac{1}{4}$	$1\frac{5}{16}$
$1\frac{1}{2}$	$1\frac{9}{16}$

can occur in the connection and cause an additional shearing force on the bolts. If holes are drilled with exactly the same diameter as the bolts, alignment of parts and insertion of bolts will be extremely difficult. Use the information given in Chart 11-3 as a guide for clearance hole diameters. *Important*: Always deburr all drilled or punched holes to ensure complete contact between mating surfaces.

BOLT PATTERNS   If bolt-hole patterns are not specified, the following examples can be used as a guide.

Single bolt connections of the type used for cross bracing or pivoting joints not only place stress on the bolt, but will also have the tendancy to elongate the hole. To help compensate for this, an additional plate can be welded at the location of the hole to increase the cross section (see Fig. 11-16).

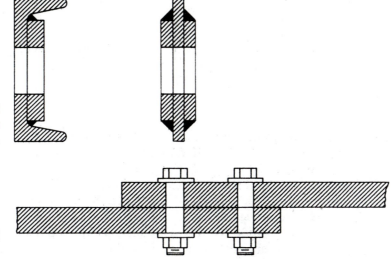

Figure 11-16 Increased cross section for a single-bolt pivot joint.

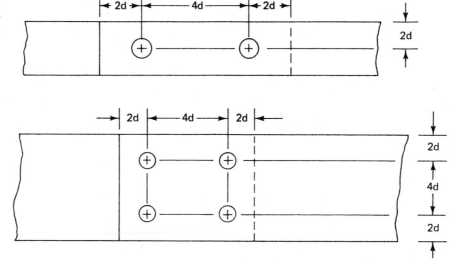

Figure 11-17 Bolted lap joint.

Lap joints (see Fig. 11-17) have a tendency to bend under heavy loads due to the eccentricity of the joint. The overlap should be sufficient enough to allow at least two bolts in each row. The holes should be set in at a distance equal to twice the bolt diameter and each row separated by approximately four times the bolt diameter (see Fig. 11-18).

Figure 11-18 Lap joint bolt patterns. d, bolt diameter.

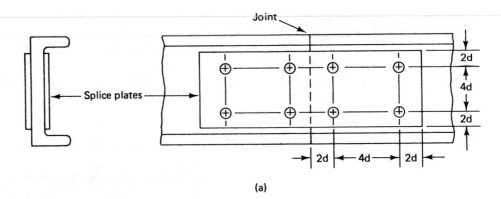

(a)

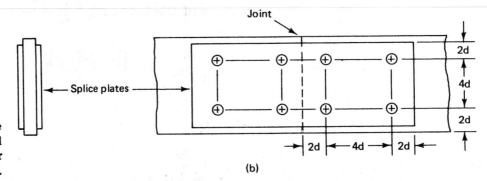

Figure 11-19   Splice joints: (a) structural shape splice; (b) flat bar splice. d, bolt diameter.

(b)

Splice joints should be made with a splice plate on both sides of the joint (see Fig. 11-19). If not otherwise specified, the splice plates should never be less than half of the thickness of the member being spliced. Use the bolt pattern in Figure 11-19 as a guide. In all nut-and-bolt assemblies, at least two full bolt threads should protrude beyond the nut after tightening.

If torque tightening is not specified, the following rule of thumb can be used as a guide for heavy structural bolts: Snug up the bolted assembly (if lock washers are being used, make sure they are fully compressed) and tighten the nut an additional half-turn. *Note*: Use at least a grade 3 bolt for all high-strength connections.

Chapter 12

HEATING and FLAME-CUTTING OPERATIONS

Before discussing these basic thermal operations which are often required in metal work, the safe use and proper setup of oxygen and acetylene equipment must be understood. If basic skill development is needed in this area, see the readings in Appendix 2.

The use of heating and cutting torches will become increasingly important as material thickness and need for portable cutting increases. The torch can be used not only for cutting or applying heat for forming but also for straightening, curving, and shrinking. The oxyacetylene process is the most common and efficient because the combination of oxygen and acetylene produces a flame with the highest heat output, approximately 6300°F. Alternate fuel gases, such as MAPP and propane, can also be successfully used. The major consideration for the use of the alternate gases is usually economic. In certain areas the use of MAPP gas or propane can result in considerable cost savings. Your local welding gas distributor would be the best source for information on availability, cost, and recommendations. Special cutting nozzles must be used for alternate fuel gases.

OXYACETYLENE EQUIPMENT USE   The following checklist can be used as a guide for safe oxyacetylene equipment use.

SETUP

1. Be sure that the regulator thumbscrews indicate that the regulator is closed, turned out counterclockwise, and loose.
2. Crack open acetylene valve on the torch.
3. Standing to one side, open the acetylene cylinder valve ½ turn. Leave the cylinder wrench in place.
4. Adjust the regulator to the desired working pressure by turning the thumbscrew clockwise. Never adjust higher than 15 pounds.
5. Close the acetylene valve on the torch.

6. Open the oxygen valve on the torch.
7. Standing to one side, open the oxygen cylinder valve all the way until seated in the fully open position.
8. Adjust the regulator to the desired working pressure.
9. Close the oxygen valve on the torch.

LIGHTING THE TORCH

1. Unwind the hose to get a reasonably safe distance away from the cylinders.
2. With safety glasses and/or welding goggles in place, open the acetylene valve on the torch and light with a spark lighter only. Quickly add some oxygen to the flame now by opening the oxygen valve.
3. Open the acetylene valve still further until full flow is feeding the flame. Add more oxygen until the desired flame type is obtained.
4. Turn off the torch by turning off the acetylene first. This will safely extinguish the flame at the tip. Then turn off the oxygen valve.

BLEEDING DOWN (NEVER STORE OR TRANSPORT WITHOUT SHUTTING DOWN OR BLEEDING CYLINDERS)

1. Close both cylinder valves tightly.
2. Open the acetylene torch valve and let the gauge readings fall to zero. Close the torch valve and do the same with the oxygen line. Do not bleed both lines at the same time.
3. Close the regulators by turning the thumbscrews counterclockwise.
4. Wind up the torch hoses on the cart handle and lay the torch in the tray.
5. Make sure that the hot tip is away from the hoses and cylinders.

ADDITIONAL SAFETY POINTS

1. When hooking up a new cylinder, always crack the valve open slightly to blow out any dirt that may have collected in it.
2. Be sure that the regulator is closed when turning on a fresh cylinder, and open the valve slowly.
3. Never oil the regulators and keep the hoses free of grease.
4. Periodically check the system for leaks.

FLAME CUTTING STRUCTURAL SHAPES The key to accurate flame cutting is accurate layout. This is particularly important with structural shapes because several surfaces must be marked and cut to produce one uniform edge. Lay out all cutting lines with soapstone. Use the following procedures as a guide for the various structural shapes commonly worked with. Remember that the torch must always be held perpendicular to the surface being cut (see Fig. 12-1).

ANGLE IRON. Mark both legs of the angle with soapstone and a combination square. Make the cut using the sequence shown in Figure 12-2.

CHANNEL. Again, using the combination square and soapstone, mark both flanges and the web of the channel. Cut the flanges first, from the bottom up, and then the web (see Fig. 12-3).

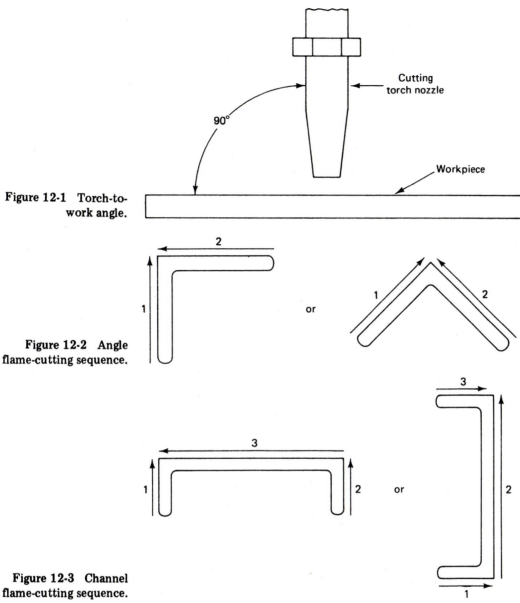

Figure 12-1 Torch-to-work angle.

Figure 12-2 Angle flame-cutting sequence.

Figure 12-3 Channel flame-cutting sequence.

I BEAMS.   Lay out I beams using the following sequence (see Fig. 12-4).

1. Strike a mark across the top flange.
2. Use the combination square to transfer this line to the bottom flanges.
3. Strike a line on the bottom flanges.
4. Transfer this line, using tri-square or triangle, onto the web.

Make the cut using the sequence in Figure 12-5. Cutting I beams from the bottom up will prevent flying sparks and molten metal from burning off layout lines.

PIPE AND MECHANICAL TUBING.   The easiest way to lay out a line of cut on pipe or tubing involves the use of a wraparound marking guide (see Fig. 12-6). These marking guides can easily be made from a piece of sheet metal or flexible plastic approximately 2 inches wide and slightly longer than the circumference of the piece being marked.

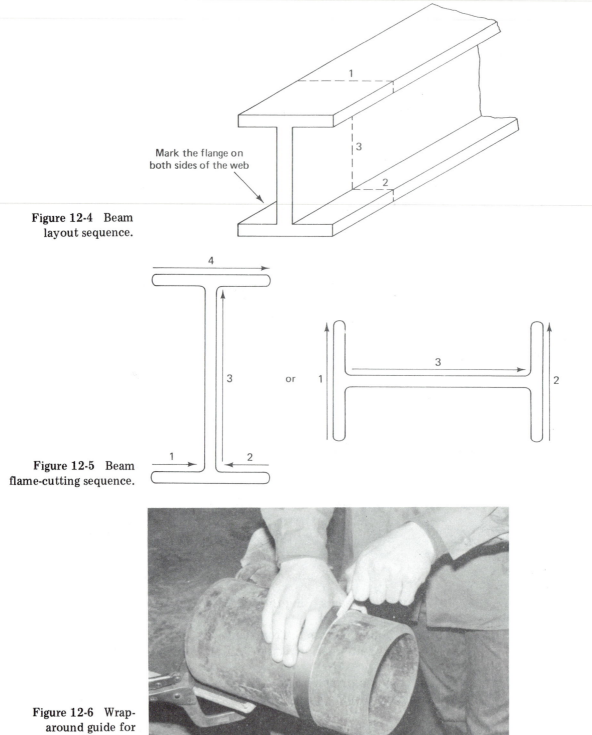

Figure 12-4 Beam layout sequence.

Mark the flange on both sides of the web

Figure 12-5 Beam flame-cutting sequence.

or

Figure 12-6 Wrap-around guide for marking pipe.

If the workpiece has to be cut lengthwise, a piece of angle iron held securely against the pipe wall (see Fig. 12-7) will produce a very accurate longitudinal guideline. If the workpiece can be rotated during the cutting operation, make the cuts across the top section and keep rotating it until the cut is complete (see Fig. 12-8). If the workpiece cannot be rotated, start the cut on the bottom and progress up each side (see Fig. 12-9).

If large-diameter pipe has to be accurately flame cut in any quantity, a hand-operated or power pipe cutting machine (see Fig. 12-10) should be

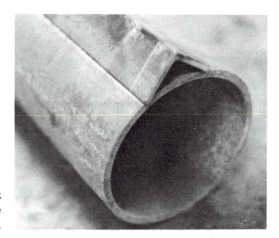

Figure 12-7 Layout of a line along the pipe wall.

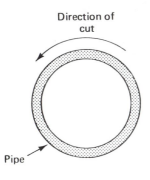

Direction of cut

Figure 12-8 Cutting sequence for rotating pipe.

Pipe

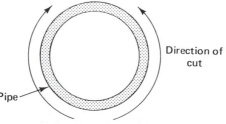

Direction of cut

Figure 12-9 Cutting sequence for fixed pipe.

Pipe

Figure 12-10 Pipe beveling machine.

used. Machines of this type are designed to cut pipe from 1½ to 60 inches in diameter and are particularly efficient for cutting good-quality beveled edges.

FLAME CUTTING PLATE AND FLAT STOCK

When cutting plate or flat stock always lay out lines, as previously discussed, with a combination square or straightedge. Simple cutting guides should also be employed.

In Figure 12-11, a piece of angle iron is clamped to the workpiece during the cutting operation. Keep in mind that the guides must be set back one half the diameter of the cutting nozzle (see Fig. 12-12). This same angle-iron guide can also be set corner up and used for making 45-degree bevel cuts (see Fig. 12-13). Cutting speeds must be reduced for bevel cuts.

When laying out straight-line patterns on plate, it is always a good idea to center punch each corner. This will give you a permanent reference for aligning cutting guides in the event that the layout lines are accidentally burned or rubbed off. When hand cutting irregular curve patterns, make a center-punch mark approximately every ½ inch along the entire layout (see

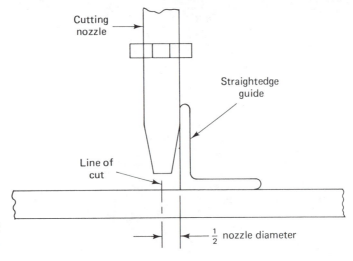

Figure 12-11 Angle-iron cutting guide.

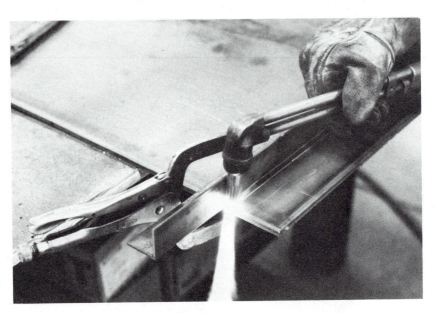

Figure 12-12 Cutting guide setback.

Figure 12-13 Angle-iron guide for a bevel cut.

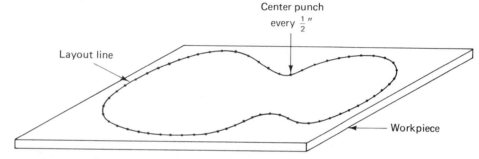

Figure 12-14 Layout for irregular shapes.

Figure 12-15 Circle-cutting attachment.

Fig. 12-14). Many times during cutting operations, particularly on patterns, the fabricator will inadvertently rub off layout lines with the gloved hand used to steady the torch. The center-punch marks eliminate this problem.

Circles and radii can be accurately cut with the use of a circle cutting attachment (see Fig. 12-15). These attachments can be purchased commercially or easily made. The first step in making this type of cut is to center punch the center of the radius or circle. Next, mount the attachment onto

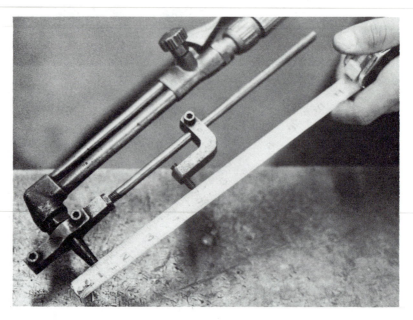

Figure 12-16 Setting the radius of cut.

the cutting torch and set the desired radius (see Fig. 12-16). Measure the radius between the adjustable center point on the circle-cutting attachment and the center of the cutting nozzle.

MACHINE CUTTING

Flame-cutting machinery is available in a wide variety of sizes, ranging from the compact track-mounted units up to the very sophisticated fully automatic shape-cutting machines (see Fig. 12-17). In this unit we limit our discussion to the most affordable and widely used smaller track-mounted portables (see Fig. 12-18).

Portable cutting machines are fairly easy to use and will cut steel up to 4 inches thick. Most have only two adjustments for travel speed and direction and a clutch to activate the drive motor. The key to an accurate setup is positioning the track so that it is perfectly parallel with the line of cut. It should be set back between 6 and 12 inches from the cut (see Fig. 12-19) and dimensions checked on each end of the track to ensure that it is parallel.

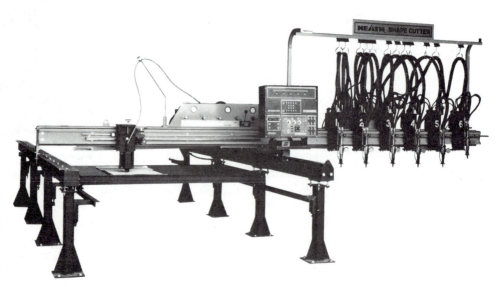

Figure 12-17 Automatic shape cutter. (Courtesy of ESAB North America, Incorporated, Heath Gas Cutting Division.)

Figure 12-18 Portable flame-cutting machine.

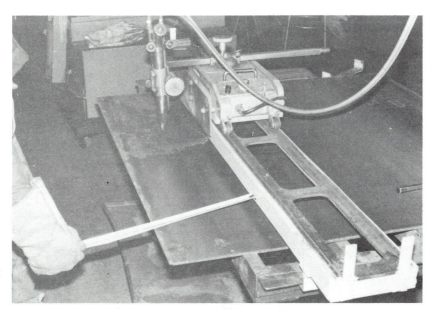

Figure 12-19 Cutting machine parallel with the line of cut.

Machine travel speed is measured in inches per minute. Consult Chart 12-1 for recommended cutting speeds. The torch assembly can also be easily rotated for bevel cutting (see Fig. 12-20). Before the cut is started, make sure that the track is securely in position and that the cutting machine carriage is properly seated on the track. Finally, check for correct nozzle-to-work distance (see Fig. 12-21).

Another optional accessory available for machines of this type is a circle-cutting attachment. The typical attachment can be adjusted to cut circles ranging from 4 to 48 inches. Before attempting to cut a circle, the swivel casters on the machine carriage must be unlocked.

Other important considerations in all flame-cutting operations are kerf (material lost in the cut) and gas consumption. Production flame cutting, particularly on heavy plate may require a gas cylinder manifold system to

CHART 12-1 Cutting Nozzle and Gas Pressure Selection

Metal thickness (in.)	Nozzle size		Acetylene (psi)	Oxygen (psi)	Cutting speed (in./min)	Kerf width (in.)	Acetylene consumption (CFH)	Oxygen consumption (CFH)
	Preheat Orifice Drill Size	Cutting Orifice Drill Size						
$\frac{1}{4}$	71	64	5	30	20	0.075	9	50
$\frac{3}{8}$	69	57	5	35	19	0.095	12	75
$\frac{1}{2}$	69	57	5	40	17	0.100	13	90
$\frac{3}{4}$	68	55	5	45	15	0.110	14	120
1	68	55	5	50	14	0.115	15	140
2	66	53	5	55	10	0.130	17	200
4	63	47	5	60	7	0.170	22	380

Source: R. H. Carr and R. L. O'Con, Welding Practices and Procedures. Englewood Cliffs, N.J.: Prentice-Hall, 1983.

Figure 12-20 Cutting machine set for bevel cuts.

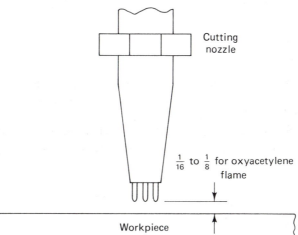

Cutting nozzle

$\frac{1}{16}$ to $\frac{1}{8}$ for oxyacetylene flame

Workpiece

Figure 12-21 Nozzle-to-work distance.

avoid frequent, time-consuming cylinder changes. Refer to Chart 12-1 for kerf and gas consumption information.

FLAME STRAIGHTENING AND BENDING Being able to use the torch as a tool to bend or straighten structural shapes will allow you to form curves without the need for expensive and specialized rolling equipment or transform bent structurals into usable straight lengths. Straightening long lengths of beams is quite common. Structural shapes will often bend under their own weight if not properly lifted or stored. There are no cut-and-dried formulas for flame straightening and bending; most of it is done by trial and error. The principle of the operation is heating a section of the structural member cherry red and rapidly quenching it with a strong, steady stream of water. A garden hose or water-charged fire extinguisher works best. The rapid quenching causes the metal in the heated area to contract or shrink and pull the member in that direction.

Most often the bending in a structural shape occurs laterally across the narrowest cross section (see Fig. 12-22). As in the example shown in Figure 12-22, both members have to be pulled to the right in order to be straightened. Support the pieces to be straightened along the entire length on wood chocks spaced approximately 5 feet apart (see Fig. 12-23). At this time you

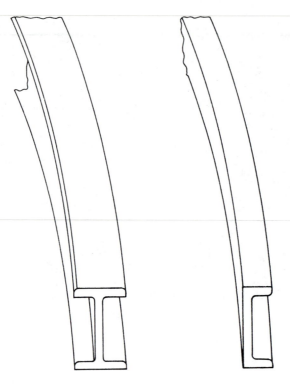

Figure 12.22 Bent structural shapes.

must visually determine the best points to do the straightening. Do not try to make the entire correction in one spot. Select several evenly spaced locations along the bend.

Mark a wedge-shaped area with soapstone on both upper and lower flanges 1 to 2 inches wide at each location (see Fig. 12-23). Heat the upper

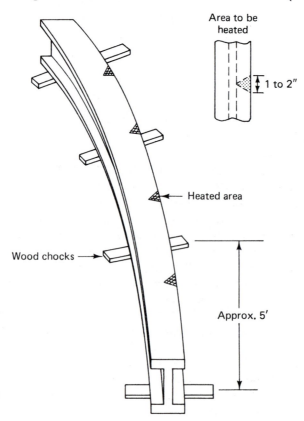

Figure 12-23 Layout for flame straightening.

and lower flange in the marked area until both are cherry red and quench rapidly. Before moving to the next location, check the amount of movement in the member. Remember that this is a trial-and-error method and adjustments in the number of heating locations or their size might have to be made. The same method is used for curving structurals. If radical curves have to be made, the member should be supported only on the ends so that its weight will work in your favor (see Fig. 12-24). This is particularly important if the member has to be curved along the widest cross section. The area heated for this type of curve is much larger (see Fig. 12-25).

In any curving operation a template should be made and used to check the progress of the bend. The flame-shrinking operation can also be used to correct a bow or oil-can bend in plate (see Fig. 12-26). Attempting to re-

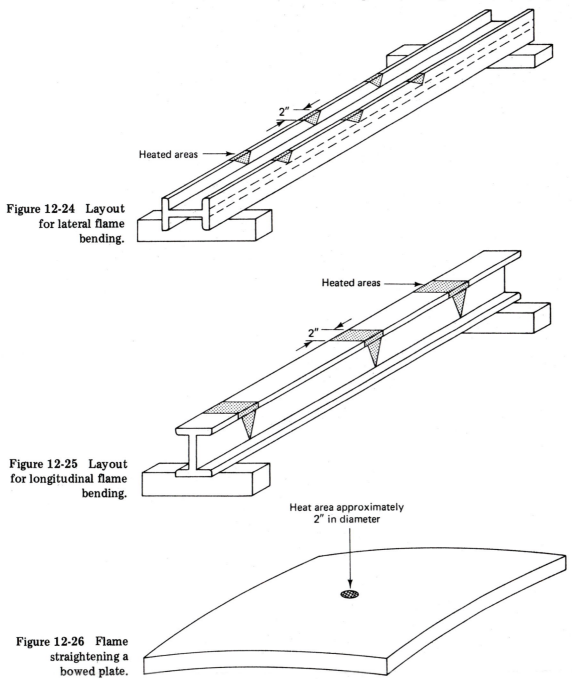

Figure 12-24 Layout for lateral flame bending.

Figure 12-25 Layout for longitudinal flame bending.

Figure 12-26 Flame straightening a bowed plate.

move a bow of this type on a press, particularly if the plate is part of a welded assembly, will usually result in the plate bowing in the opposite direction, thus producing the "oil canning" effect.

Mark an area about 2 inches in diameter in the center of the bend, heat it to a cherry red, and rapidly quench. Check the amount of correction. Do not reheat the same spot if additional correction is required. Select another spot on the bowed surface. Repeat this procedure until the bow is removed.

Chapter 13

GRINDING and FINISHING

The grinding and finishing operations discussed in this chapter are those most commonly used in structural and steel plate fabrication shops primarily for the removal of burrs, rust and scale, and "smooth to the touch" sanding.

SIDE WHEEL GRINDERS　The majority of this work is done with side wheel (angle) grinders (see Fig. 13-1). Machines of this type will turn at approximately 6000 rpm and produce a steady stream of sparks, particularly when using hard-grinding disks. For this reason the tool should be handled carefully and always used with its wheel guard in place. The operator must always be aware of the potential hazard not only to himself or herself but to those in the immediate area. Full face protection in the form of a safety face shield should always be worn. Also keep in mind that when you are holding the grinder, the wheel

Figure 13-1　Side wheel grinder. (Courtesy of United Abrasives Inc.)

Figure 13-2 Grinding disks. (Courtesy of United Abrasives Inc.)

will turn in a clockwise direction and throw sparks and metal particles to your right. Position yourself so that these particles will not hit other workers in the area.

The 7- and 9-inch aluminum oxide grinding disks (see Fig. 13-2) are generally used in all rough grinding and deburring operations. The disks are classified in two groups: fast cutting or long life. If grinding speed is the primary consideration, the fast-cutting disk would be the best choice; however, they wear down quite fast and require frequent changing. The long-life disks grind at a slower rate but last much longer.

The first step taken prior to changing a disk is unplugging the grinder. Next, set the machine upside down on a table with the handle against your left leg. With gloves on hands, press the spindle lock button (turn the disk slowly until it engages) and turn the disk counterclockwise (see Fig. 13-3). If the disk cannot be loosened, a disk spanner wrench will have to be used. Install the replacement disk, place the grinder handle against your right leg, press and engage the spindle lock, and tighten the disk securely by hand (see Fig. 13-4). The rotation of the grinder during normal operation has a tightening effect on the disk.

Hard-grinding disks work most efficiently when grinding on or near the outer edge. For this reason, the grinder should be held at an angle as shown in Figure 13-5. Always start the machine before bringing the disk in contact with the work. The disks are fairly durable but will crack and break if slammed violently onto the workpiece. Bring the disk in contact with the

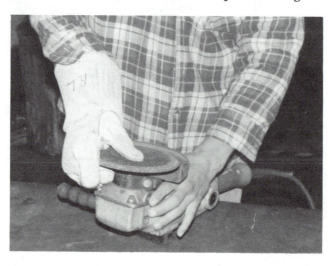

Figure 13-3 Loosening a grinding disk.

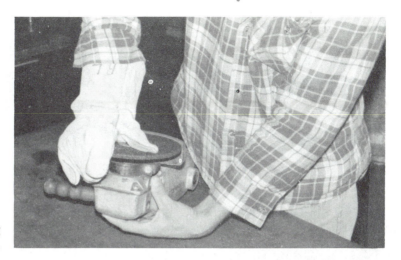

Figure 13-4 Tightening
a grinding disk.

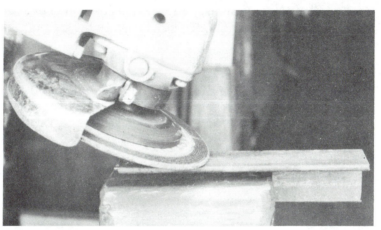

Figure 13-5 Grinding
with the edge of
the grinding disk.

workpiece slowly and apply only a slight amount of pressure. Let the machine
do the work. Keep the grinder moving with a back-and-forth motion to prevent surface gouges.

A wire cup brush can be mounted on the grinder (see Fig. 13-6) for
rapid removal of paint, rust, and scale. A word of caution. This is usually a
very dirty, dusty operation and should be done only in well-ventilated areas
or while wearing respirators.

Figure 13-6 Wire cup
brushes. (Courtesy of
United Abrasives Inc.)

Figure 13-7 Four-inch angle grinder. (Courtesy of Black and Decker.)

When grinding small surfaces or tight spaces, a smaller 4-inch side wheel grinder can be used (see Fig. 13-7). These machines are small and lightweight and excellent for out-of-position work where portability is the primary concern.

Because grinding disks are designed for rapid rough grinding, surface scratches will always be quite evident. If a smoother finish is required, an aluminum oxide sanding disk will have to be used. Sanding disks are thin and flexible and must be used with a backing disk (see Fig. 13-8). Because of its thin cross section, the disks can be very easily broken and care must be taken when in use. Unlike the grinding disk, the sanding disk is designed to flex and operate most efficiently on a wider outer area (see Fig. 13-9). The best method of engaging sanding disks with the workpiece is by backing it on.

Figure 13-8 Backing disk.

Figure 13-9 Using the outer surface of the sanding disk.

Engaging the disk in a forward direction will increase the chance of snagging the edge and breaking the disk. The medium grits of 60 and 80 are most commonly used.

DIE GRINDERS Heavy-duty die grinders (see Fig. 13-10) are frequently used to remove material or smooth areas with irregular curves or inside walls of pipe or mechanical tubing. The machine can be adapted with a variety of stones, small-diameter (2½-inch maximum) grinding wheels and cutting disks (see Fig. 13-11). Die grinders operate at high speed (14,500 rpm) and must be handled carefully. Wrenches supplied with the machine should always be used to securely fasten the grinding stones and disks. When using the machine, particularly in tight areas, it should be held firmly with light pressure applied to the work. Avoid making violent contact with the workpiece, as this can cause the grinding wheel to shatter. Die grinders equipped with thin cutting disks are excellent for notching and breaking weld beads without damaging the metal surfaces.

If fine sanding or smoothing of curved surfaces is required, a flap wheel (see Fig. 13-12) can be installed. Grits of 60 to 80 will produce excellent results.

Figure 13-10 Die grinder. (Courtesy of Black and Decker.)

Figure 13-11 Die grinder with assorted attachments.

Figure 13-12 Flap wheels. (Courtesy of United Abrasives Inc.)

FILING   The last step in finishing operations usually will involve some form of hand filing. Although files are made with four distinctive tooth patterns, we will limit our discussion to the single- and double-cut variety (Fig. 13-13). Curved tooth and rasp files are primarily used for rough cutting on the softer non-ferrous metals such as aluminum and lead and are impractical for use on cast iron or steel.

A single- or double-cut file can be further categorized by its coarseness. The file cuts most applicable for steel are the bastard, second cut, and smooth (see Fig. 13-14). Each of these file cuts is available in a variety of shapes and lengths, with the longer lengths of 10 to 16 inches being the most applicable in steel fabrication. The shape of the file selected would naturally be determined by the shape or contour of the surface being worked.

Figure 13-13 File tooth patterns. (*From left to right*) Single cut, double cut, and curved tooth.

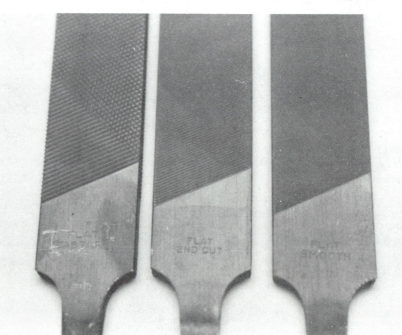

Figure 13-14   (*From left to right*) Bastard, second cut, and smooth files.

Selection of the most efficient file cut is determined by (1) the amount of material to be removed, (2) material hardness, and (3) the desired finish. Bastard files will remove material at the fastest rate on low-carbon steel; however, on the harder medium-carbon and alloy steel, second cut files will cut faster. If a smooth, scratch-free finish is desired, the final touches are done with a smooth or dead smooth cut.

When filing the edge of a plate or structural shape, always work lengthwise (see Fig. 13-15). Working crosswise is very inefficient and frequently results in the surface being cupped or scalloped.

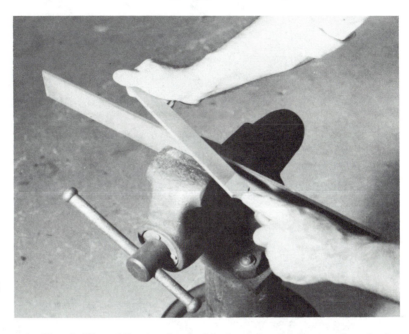

Figure 13-15 Filing lengthwise along the workpiece.

Hand files, like hacksaw blades, should be used only in one direction. Apply pressure on the forward stroke (see Fig. 13-16) and raise the file off the work surface on the return (see Fig. 13-17). Keeping pressure on the file during the return stroke will cause a premature wearing and dulling of the file teeth. The only exception to this recommendation is draw filing. Draw filing (see Fig. 13-18) is a technique in which the file is drawn back and forth across the work surface. Moderate pressure is applied in both directions. The

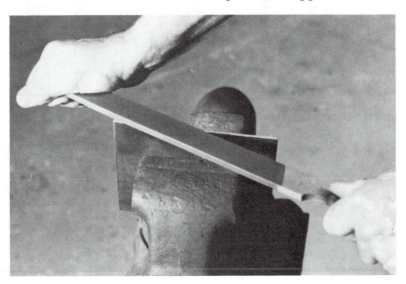

Figure 13-16 Forward stroke.

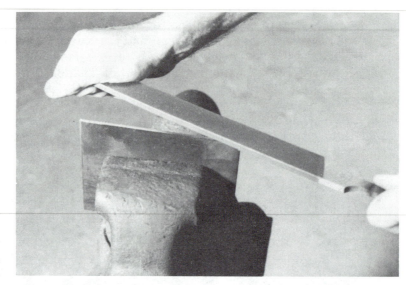

Figure 13-17 Return stroke.

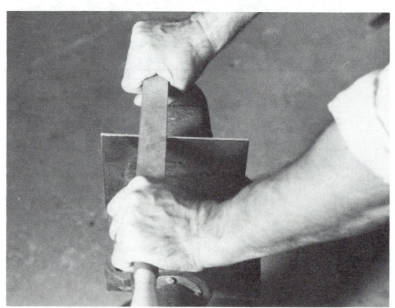

Figure 13-18 Draw filing.

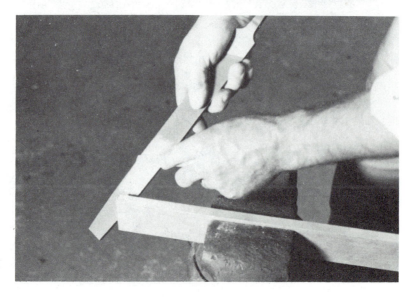

Figure 13-19 Cleaning the file with a file card.

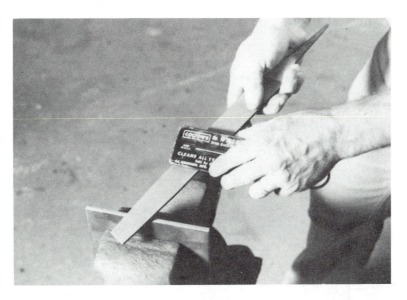

Figure 13-20 File rubbed with soapstone.

lateral file movement will not damage the teeth. This method of filing is excellent for producing a true flat and very smooth surface. Care must be taken to hold the file perfectly flat. Any rocking motion will cause the surface to be curved.

Files should be cleaned frequently with a file card (see Fig. 13-19) or a wire brush and, in the interest of safety and personal comfort, always be used with handles installed.

If you are working with a soft material and file clogging becomes a problem, rub the file down with soapstone (see Fig. 13-20). This will tend to give it a self-cleaning action.

Chapter 14

INTRODUCTION and STOCK SIZES

The word "precision" as used in fabrication terms means working to very close tolerances. In precision sheet metal, as used in the aerospace and electronic industries, working to tolerances of 0.010 to 0.015 of an inch are common. Occasionally, the fabricator may have work as close as 0.005 of an inch (five thousandths).

It would naturally follow then that the tools and machinery used would be in themselves "precision." The definition of precision used in conjunction with tools and machines that are or can be used on all kinds of work, both precision and nonprecision, must then be expanded to include "not being worn." Take, for instance, a shearing operation. In multiple shearing for parts that must be manufactured to within a final 10- or 15-thousandth tolerance (Fig. 14-1), each sheared piece should be within at least 0.005 of

Figure 14-1 Multiple shearing operation requiring close-tolerance accuracy.

the required flat pattern development size. Most power shears have a movable back gauge that is mechanically cranked out for any given dimension from the cutting blades. To accomplish this movement requires an arrangement of worm and bevel gears plus a chain drive sprocket assembly.

Proper procedure requires that the mechanic crank past the required dimension and then move the back gauge back in toward the shear blades, stopping at the actual required dimension. This method takes up the normal backlash between the parts of the gear train so that the back gauge is mechanically locked in position. A shear in good condition can now cut any number of pieces to identical dimension without significant variation. However, if through use or just plain abuse, the gear train is so worn and sloppy that the back gauge cannot be mechanically locked in position and bounces in and out as the shear cycles, the cut pieces will vary in size according to the movement of the back gauge. It will then be impossible to use the shear for close-tolerance accuracy.

So it must be with the other equipment in the precision sheet metal shop. In addition, the sheet metal mechanic must bring to the job a certain degree of sensitivity and fastidiousness. The first-class mechanic is somewhat of a perfectionist and just a little fussy about the condition of personal tools and the accuracy of the setups that have been made.

SHEET METAL DIMENSIONS Thicknesses of less than ⅛ inch are generally defined as being "sheet metal." When purchasing either hot- or cold-rolled steel sheets, a gauge thickness is specified. These thicknesses are close to, but not exactly an even fractional dimension. Thus 11 gauge, which is nominally thought of as ⅛-inch material, is, according to the U.S. (revised) standard gauge chart (see Chart 14-1)

CHART 14-1 Standard Gauge Decimals

Gauge and equivalent in decimals of an inch.
For accuracy always specify by decimal.

Ga. No.	Brass Brown & Sharp	Steel Sheets Mfrs. Std.*	Strip & Tubing Birmingham or Stubs	Steel Wire Steel Wire Ga.†	Steel Wire Music Wire
6-0's	.5800			.4615	.004
5-0's	.5165	. . . .	.500	.4305	.005
4-0's	.4600	. . . .	.454	.3938	.006
3-0's	.4096	. . . .	.425	.3625	.007
2-0's	.3648		.380	.3310	.008
0	.3249	. . . .	.340	.3065	.009
1	.2893	. . . .	.300	.2830	.010
2	.2576	. . . .	.284	.2625	.011
3	.2294	.2391	.259	.2437	.012
4	.2043	.2242	.238	.2253	.013
5	.1819	.2092	.220	.2070	.014
6	.1620	.1943	.203	.1920	.016
7	.1443	.1793	.180	.1770	.018
8	.1285	.1644	.165	.1620	.020
9	.1144	.1495	.148	.1483	.022
10	.1019	.1345	.134	.1350	.024
11	.0907	.1196	.120	.1205	.026
12	.0808	.1046	.109	.1055	.029
13	.0720	.0897	.095	.0915	.031
14	.0641	.0747	.083	.0800	.033
15	.0571	.0673	.072	.0720	.035
16	.0508	.0598	.065	.0625	.037
17	.0453	.0538	.058	.0540	.039
18	.0403	.0478	.049	.0475	.041

CHART 14-1   Standard Gauge Decimals (continued)

Gauge and equivalent in decimals of an inch.
For accuracy always specify by decimal.

19	.0359	.0418	.042	.0410	.043
20	.0320	.0359	.035	.0348	.045
21	.0285	.0329	.032	.0317	.047
22	.0253	.0299	.028	.0286	.049
23	.0226	.0269	.025	.0258	.051
24	.0201	.0239	.022	.0230	.055
25	.0179	.0209	.020	.0204	.059
26	.0159	.0179	.018	.0181	.063
27	.0142	.0164	.016	.0173	.067
28	.0126	.0149	.014	.0162	.071
29	.0113	.0135	.013	.0150	.075
30	.0100	.0120	.012	.0140	.080
31	.0089	.0105	.010	.0132	.085
32	.0080	.0097	.009	.0128	.090
33	.0071	.0090	.008	.0118	.095
34	.0063	.0082	.007	.0104	.100
35	.0056	.0075	.005	.0095	.106
36	.0050	.0067	.004	.0090	.112
37	.0045	.0064	...	.0085	.118
38	.0040	.0060		.0080	.124

*Replaces U.S. Standard (Revised) Gauge.
†Replaces Washburn and Moen Gauge.
Source: Joseph T. Ryerson and Son, Inc.

actually 0.006 less than ⅛ inch or 0.119. Similarly, a thickness of 16 gauge is not nominally ¹⁄₁₆ inch but actually 0.059 according to the same standard.

When purchasing aluminum sheet, both decimal sizes and fractions are specified. Thicknesses such as 0.040, 0.050, 0.070, and 0.080 are available in addition to the common ¹⁄₁₆, ³⁄₃₂, and so on, fractional sizes. Other alloy types generally fall into this category.

Standard sheet sizes are 48 inches wide by 120 inches long. Aluminum sheet is often 144 inches long, while cold-rolled steel and alloy sheet is commonly supplied in 36-inch widths by 96 inches long. In planning a sheet metal job it must be remembered that although a catalog or data book may list a wide variety of stock sizes as being available, your local distributor may actually stock only a portion of sizes that are listed. Ordering special sizes, though listed as stock sizes in a manufacturer's catalog, may prove to be prohibitively expensive.

Chapter 15

SHEARING and BENDING

POWER SHEARS   For fast, precision cutting of sheet stock, a power squaring shear is needed (see Fig. 15-1). The shear should be equipped with an adjustable back gauge which will provide an accurately sheared drop-off piece. The back gauge setting is accomplished in one of two ways. As shown in Figure 15-2, a front-reading vernier gauge is mounted on the operator side of the shear. This device allows an infinite adjustment, in thousandths of an inch, up to 24.000.

Figure 15-1   Typical power squaring shear for up to 10-gauge material.

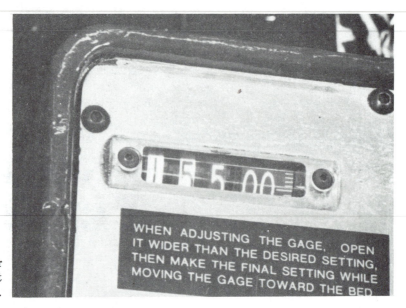

Figure 15-2 Vernier
back gauge readout at
the front of the shear.

An alternative arrangement is shown in Figure 15-3. Moving to the back of
the shear, the operator cranks the back gauge to position in increments of
0.007 inch by means of a spring-loaded pin which locks into an adjusting
ring. Each full revolution of the crank moves the back gauge ¼ inch. Also,
⅛-inch, ¹⁄₁₆-inch, ¹⁄₃₂-inch, and ¹⁄₆₄-inch graduations are marked with detents
for each. The final detent falls between the ¹⁄₆₄ or 0.015 position, allowing a
setting as fine as 0.0075. Although not quite as accurate as the vernier gauge,
it is fine enough for most precision shearing. The power shear is also equipped
for "front gauging." This means that accurate dimensional shearing can be
accomplished in front of the shearing blades and the drop-off piece falls
behind the machine. There is a metal scale installed in the bed of the shear.
This scale is set so that the graduations visible represent actual dimensions
from the cutting blades. This arrangement can be extended well beyond the

Figure 15-3 Mechan-
ism for setting dimen-
sions of backqauge
at the rear of
the shear.

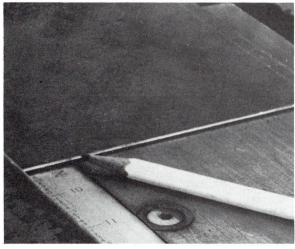

Figure 15-4 "Front gauging" with the setup dimension being (a) read and (b) set in front of the blades.

front of the shear so that with the use of appropriate "stops," large dimensions can be accurately cut (see Fig. 15-4).

FOOT-OPERATED SHEARS
Foot-operated shears of the type shown in Figure 15-5 can be used for precise shearing even though they are not designed specifically for such use. To make precision cuts, the pieces must be "front gauged." Assume, for example, that the desired dimension of the first cut is 10 inches, 430 thousandths (10.430). First, a rough cut of approximately 11 full inches must be made. The basic back gauge device that comes with this type of shear can be used for this initial cut. This cut is needed to prevent the weight of a large drop-off section from dragging the needed piece under the hold-down fingers and away from the dimensioned stop. Next, as illustrated in Figure 15-6, a combination square with an 18-inch blade is used to set the stop bar across the

Figure 15-5 Foot-operated squaring shear by front gauging.

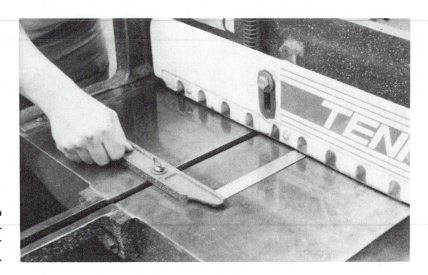

Figure 15-6 Setting up the final cutting dimension on a foot shear by front gauging.

bed of the shear. As 430 thousandths is just 0.007 shy of $\frac{7}{16}$ (0.437), the blade must be carefully set in the square frame. The dimension should be set on both the left and right ends of the bar to ensure an even cut along the width of the sheet. The precut sheet is now held firmly against the stop bar and trimmed to its final dimension.

USING THE POWER SHEAR For an illustration of proper shear use, assume that 15 pieces of sheet metal, 12.800 inches by 7.252 inches, are required. Using sheets 48 inches in width, the first logical dimension to cut is the wider one, 12.800. This will result in a smaller drop-off piece as waste when the other dimension is cut. Set the back gauge to 12.800 and cut three strips that width by 48 inches long. After verifying the setting and accuracy of the cut with a caliper, one end of the strip must now be squared. For this operation always use the left side of the machine. The shear blades are angled so that the stock is pushed against the squaring bar as it is cut (see Fig. 15-7). Trim approximately ¼ inch off the strip, which should now be checked for square as shown in Figure 15-8. The 7.252-inch dimension is now set with the back gauge. Each squared strip is now fed into the shear up to the back gauge and will yield six pieces with

Figure 15-7 Squarng the strip end before cutting the final dimension.

Figure 15-8 Checking the trimmed strip for squareness.

only about 4 inches left as a drop-off. The three extra pieces are used as set-up pieces in subsequent operations.

Proper Use and Safety

The shear must always be used within its rated capacity. The typical sheet metal power shear is usually made for up to 10-gauge mild steel. The foot-operated shear can be used on mild steel up to 20 gauge and 48 inches wide. Narrower pieces up to 16 gauge may also be cut with accuracy. Such shears will also cut aluminum up to 0.093 thick with good accuracy.

Keeping in mind that precision shearing means cutting to within 0.005 tolerance, the gapping or clearance between the knife blades is extremely important as well as the overall condition and sharpness. High-volume, precision sheet metal shops that shear a wide variety of material thicknesses will often have more than one shear, each gapped for a particular range of thicknesses. Improperly gapped or dull blades can cause the poorly sheared edges shown in Figure 15-9. When the gap is too narrow or close for the material thickness being sheared, excessive wear to both the blades and the whole machine will result. Always refer to the manufacturer's recommendations.

When feeding large sheets into the shear, care must be exercised in several ways. When handling the sheet, always wear gloves, as the flexing of a 10- or 12-foot sheet will almost always result in razor-like cuts to the hands and fingers. Two pairs of hands should grip the sheet as indicated in

Figure 15-9 Effect of the blade gap setting on the sheared edge: (a) excessive rake caused by blade deflection due to lack of gap clearance; (b) material rollover caused by excessive blade gap; (c) minimum edge rake—proper blade gap for material being sheared.

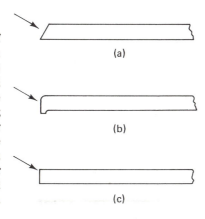

(a)

(b)

(c)

Figure 15-10 Safe
handling of sheet stock.

Figure 15-10. The material should be brought gently into contact with the
back gauge (see Fig. 15-11). Rather than ramming it squarely into the back
gauge and possibly knocking it out of adjustment, one corner is gently
brought into contact and then the other. This ensures that the sheet is
squarely under the blades.

Shears designed for sheet metal thicknesses are flywheel actuated. This
means that the energy to cycle the blades is generated by a rapidly spinning
flywheel. When either an electrical or mechanically operated clutch is en-
gaged, the ram moves down and shears the material. For this reason no

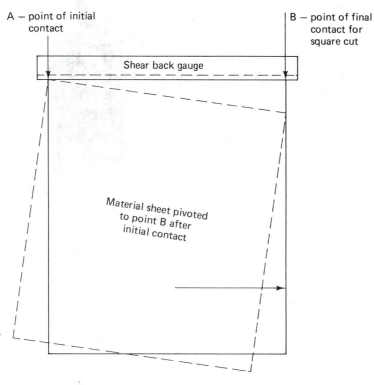

A — point of initial
    contact

B — point of final
    contact for
    square cut

Shear back gauge

Material sheet pivoted
to point B after
initial contact

Figure 15-11 Points of
contact for accurate
back gauge shearing.

attempt should be made to operate the machine until the flywheel is up to full speed. In fact, the material should not even be placed under the blades until after the machine is turned on and ready to use. If the clutch is in the tripped position, the blades will start to move as soon as the machine is turned on. With not enough flywheel speed, the machine will jam partway through the cut.

You should never attempt to shear double layers of material, and you should never try to cut a piece that is narrower than the material thickness. Both of these will cause springing and excessive wear on the blades. When cutting narrow dimensions, usually 1 inch or less from full 48-inch-wide sheets, the cut pieces will often twist and curl. They will then get stuck between the bed of the shear and the back gauge. If such narrow cuts are necessary, crank the back gauge back after the desired setting is made and the sheet is positioned. This will allow the drop-off to fall through while the hold-down fingers maintain the accuracy of the material position.

There is a guard in front of these hold-down pins to prevent injury by either the hold-downs or the moving blades. Although there might be production justifications for removing this guard, it is not at all advisable.

HAND-OPERATED BENDING BRAKES Like squaring shears, bending brakes are both powered and hand-operated. Although not considered a precision device, the hand or finger brake in Figure 15-12 can be made capable of very accurate bending operations.

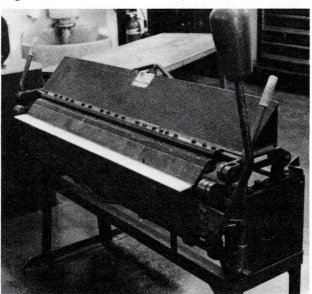

Figure 15-12 Sheet metal hand-operated finger brake.

There are three basic setup adjustments that are made on a hand brake. These adjustments are illustrated in Figure 15-13. In adjusting for the material thickness to be bent, the whole mounting frame that holds the individual dies or fingers is moved either in or out so that the dimension between the nose of the die and the bending leaf is that of the material thickness as shown. The next adjustment is that of material hold-down pressure. A turnbuckle arrangement (see Fig. 15-14) is located on both the left and right sides of the brake. When the locking lever is pulled toward the operator, the material is clamped between the die-holding frame and the bed of the brake. Proper adjustment allows the material to be held firmly under the dies while the bending leaf is operated. This adjustment must not be so tight as to mark or crease the material.

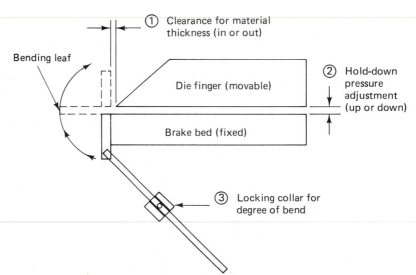

Figure 15-13 Three basic finger brake adjustments.

Figure 15-14 Turnbuckle adjustment for material hold-down pressure.

The third adjustment limits the travel of the bending leaf and thus determines the degree of bend. In typical use, a sliding lock is tightened at a point that allows the leaf to bend a flange of 90 degrees. This adjustment usually requires some trial and error.

USING THE HAND BRAKE

To bend a flange of a certain dimension, a bend line must be laid out on the flat stock. For a fairly accurate bend with a zero internal-bend radius (see Fig. 15-15), this line, for all practical purposes, can be considered the "inside" dimensional line of the flange. The stock is clamped in a position under the die as shown. Notice how a stop piece can be placed behind the dies. Clamped in the proper position on the bed of the brake, this stop will allow repetitive bends to be made without laying out each piece.

For more precise bending a slightly different approach is used. A zero internal radius is in reality a theoretical condition. However slight, some amount of radius is always present. The exact amount depends on the accuracy of the die, the bending leaf space adjustment, the condition of the die nose contour, and the degree to which the brake is used within its capacity. For precise hand brake bending and when the part requires specified internal

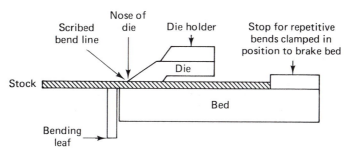

Figure 15-15 Setting up the finger brake for a zero-radius bend.

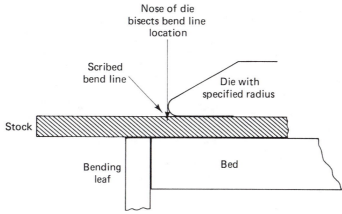

Figure 15-16 Setting up the finger brake for a dimensioned bend radius.

bend radius, the laid-out bend line must be considered the center of that bend radius. The more accurately a theoretical line drawn from the nose of the die bisects the scribed bend line, the more accurate the bent flange dimension will be (see Fig. 15-16).

Proper Use and Safety

The finger brake is limited in the thickness of the stock that can be accurately bent. Hand brakes which are used at or near the limits of their capacity will eventually spring out of shape, making accurate work very difficult. This results in the condition shown in Figure 15-17. Notice how the sharp or

Figure 15-17 Excessive radius develops at the center of the flange when the brake is used beyond capacity.

Figure 15-18 Limitation of a hand brake in forming a deep box.

minimum radius is maintained at the ends of the flange, while toward the middle a prominent radius has developed.

When bending a three- or four-sided box, the hand brake is limited in the depth of such a box. As shown in Figure 15-18, the previously bent flanges prevent the third flange from being bent to the full 90 degrees. The typical finger brake can bend a box to a maximum depth of 4½ inches.

The brake shown has an accurate bending capacity of up to 20-gauge mild steel, across its full width of 48 inches. The bending of narrower widths of thicker as well as softer materials such as aluminum are possible. Finger brakes that bend up to 12-gauge material are available.

Even though this machine is hand-powered, there are possibilities for injury to occur. Avoid having someone else operate the hold-down lever while you are lining up the stock under the dies. This will prevent accidental pinching of the fingers. Large sheets can be supported with a roller stand. When operating the bending leaf, be sure that it clears your body as you push the leaf handle away from you and the leaf comes up to bend the part (see Fig. 15-19).

The hand-operated finger brake is a necessary supplement to the power press brake. In multiple bending operations the finger brake can be used to

Figure 15-19 Make sure that your body is clear of the bending leaf as it rises to complete the bend.

complete or initiate a particular bend without forcing a change of setup or die arrangement in the press brake.

POWER PRESS BRAKE The press brake as pictured in Figure 15-20, uses a variety of V-type dies to perform very precise bending. The setup of the press brake is essentially mathematical, rather than by eye as with the finger brake. The bend line on the part is lined up between the center of the upper and lower V dies through a series of simple mathematical computations. The "stop" is often mechanized so that any setting can be made from the front of the brake, to within thousandths of an inch (see Fig. 15-21). However, in precision work, these settings or readouts should always be proven by making test bends on scrap.

Figure 15-20 Typical power press brake.

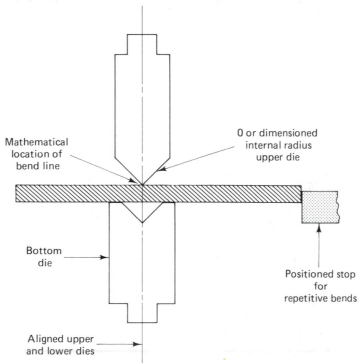

Figure 15-21 Location of the bend line with the use of press brake V dies.

Mathematical location of bend line

0 or dimensioned internal radius upper die

Bottom die

Positioned stop for repetitive bends

Aligned upper and lower dies

**AIR BENDING,
BOTTOMING,
AND FORMING**

These are terms used in press brake work. Air bending means simply that the material is not forced completely into the bottom die and there is some "air space" between the underside of the material and the bottom of the V die. As shown in Figure 15-22, the internal radius formed is usually close to the material thickness even with a zero radius on the upper die. Also, the degree of the bend is determined by how far the upper die pushes the material into the lower die. Air bending may be a desirable objective or an unavoidable result. Whereas even in sheet metal work, plate thickness of from ⅛ to ¼ inch may be encountered, air bending lessens the chance of plate fracture on these thicknesses and on thinner but harder alloys. However, because of the possi-

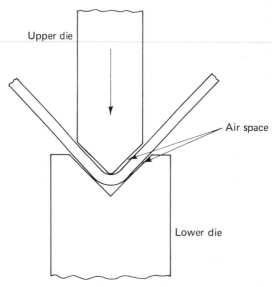

Figure 15-22 Air bending diagram.

ble variations in internal bend radii, precisely accurate bends become somewhat of a hit-or-miss affair. Air bending may also be the result of a combination of die sizes available and brake tonnage limitations. The narrower bottom die (see Fig. 15-23) requires more tonnage for the material to be pressed into it than the wider one. Even though it was not intended, air bending was unavoidable and the possible variations in radius and flange dimension may not meet the requirements of precision and repeatability. Appendix 3 contains a bending tonnage chart for making air bends on mild steel. Note the change in tonnage requirements with the change in bottom die width.

Figure 15-23 Wider bottom dies require less tonnage to achieve an equal degree of bend: (a) 1¼-inch bottom die—more tonnage required; (b) 2-inch bottom die—less tonnage required.

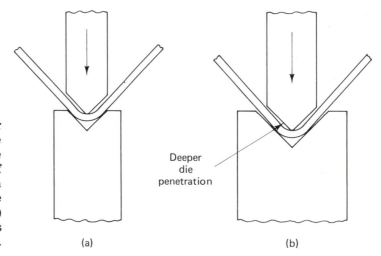

(a)   (b)

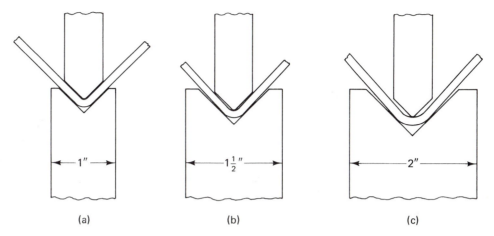

Figure 15-24 Example of a "bottoming" bend and how larger bottom dies can lead to an air bend situation: (a) "bottoming" with formed internal radius; (b) slight air bend; (c) more air bending due to excessive die clearance, unreliable internal radius dimension.

Bottoming means that the material is bent or more properly "formed" between the upper and lower dies, which close completely, with only the thickness of the material separating them (see Fig. 15-24). Notice how the internal-bend radius is now actually being determined by the radius on the upper die. Also in the figure, the selection of progressively larger bottom die sizes can be seen as leading to an "air bend" condition.

In precision sheet metal work "bottoming" is required for repeatable, precise bending; therefore, the selection of die types and sizes becomes most important.

DIE SELECTION Figure 12-25 shows some standard punch and die sets with the dimensions that form the basis for selection and setup. The upper dies, which are labeled "88 degrees," are typical of those used for bending plate thicknesses. The slight overbending is an advantage in bending plate and material which has a

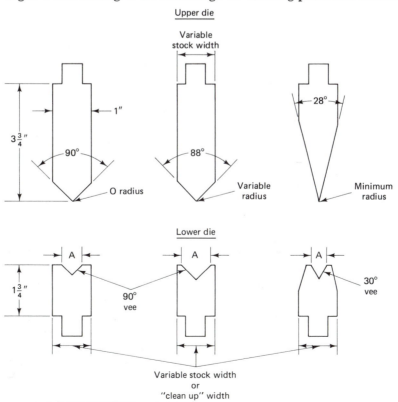

Figure 15-25 Some typical press brake die sets.

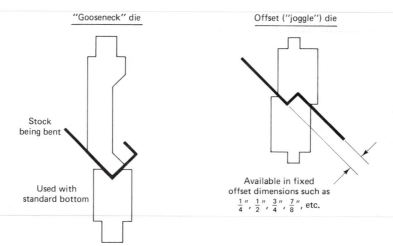

tendency to "spring back," such as with some grades of aluminum. Used with a standard 90-degree bottom die, the material will return to a perfect 90-degree angle as the upper die is raised. The application of still other die types is covered in Section II (Chaps. 6 through 13).

In specifying the size of the bottom dies, dimensions given refer to the measurement at the top of the V. In Figure 15-25, these dimensions are labeled A. The generally accepted rule for die width selection is that the die width (A) be at least eight times the thickness of the material being bent. Thus, when bending 16-gauge material, 0.060 is multiplied by 8, equaling 0.480. A ½-inch die width is then called for. Similarly, when bending ³⁄₁₆-inch material, multiply 0.187 by 8. A die opening of 1½ inches would be needed.

DIE CUTTING AND DIE MODIFICATION

When forming complicated sheet metal assemblies which require multiple bending sequences, it soon becomes apparent that no single set of dies will be able to complete the job. Some of the die types that have been shown might have found use in their existing shape and length, but more often it is necessary to alter them in some way (see Fig. 15-26).

The dies are supplied in a case-hardened condition. As shown in Figure 15-26, only the shaded area is hardened; the working surfaces remain smooth and polished, so as not to mar the material being bent. The remaining body of the die is fully machinable.

Die stock can also be purchased as fully hardened alloy material. These types are intended for high-tonnage, production bending and are considerably more expensive than the case-hardened variety. These dies are not meant to be altered in any way.

Die stock is purchased in random lengths of from 2 to 12 feet. Sooner or later, most shops will find it necessary to cut them into shorter lengths. This should not be done without careful consideration, as gathering up many small pieces to make one long bend is time consuming and makes alignment difficult when installing the pieces in the brake. Dies that have been cut should be squared and their mating edges marked to facilitate such piecing together. When considering the need to cut or otherwise alter a die, the mechanic must first decide on a bending sequence. Also to be considered is the width of each flange to be bent in that sequence. Such careful planning

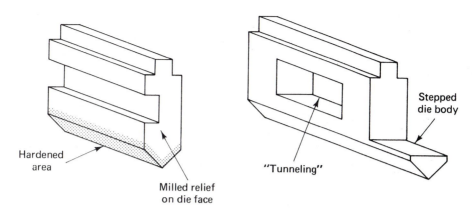

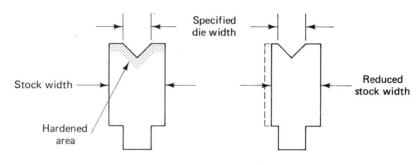

Figure 15-26 Altering standard dies to achieve particular results.

Bottom die "shaving"

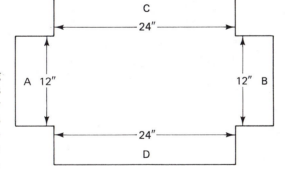

Figure 15-27 Bending the shorter flanges (A, B) first will allow the longer flanges (C, D) to be bent without shortening the upper die.

will not only avoid the need for extra die changes and setups, but may also indicate the possibility of completing the job with existing die lengths.

The flat pattern in Figure 15-27 can serve as an illustration. A die length of 2 feet is selected and the first two flanges to be bent are the narrow 12-inch ones. The remaining 24-inch flanges are bent last. If the wider flanges were bent first, the die would have to be cut to fit the remaining short flanges. Although this may appear to be very obvious in this simple illustration, more complex jobs will require a strategy similar to that used in a game of checkers, where the moves are planned several times ahead.

Similarly, the bottom dies may also require cutting to a specific length. The flat pattern in Figure 15-28 uses "reverse" flanges as an example. Here, flanges A, B, C or D must fit over the bottom die in order for the final bends to be made.

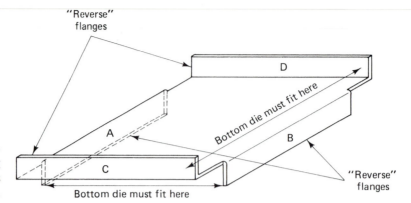

Figure 15-28 "Reverse" flange bending must take into account the bottom die width.

BENDING SEQUENCES   The sequencing of the bends, which bend is made first, second, and so on, presents other problems beyond merely one of die length. The mechanic must be careful to avoid getting "locked out." This means that the completing of one bend prevents a second bend from being completed or possibly even from being started. As shown in Figure 15-29, flanges 1, 2, 3, and 4 must be completed before flanges 5, 6, 7, and 8.

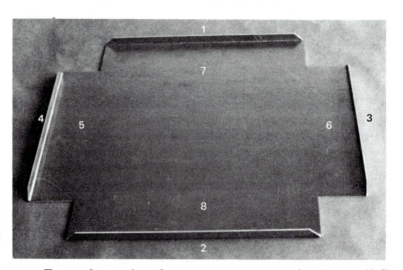

Figure 15-29 Proper sequencing of bends to avoid being "locked out."

Even when using the proper sequence, the "return" flange A may prevent the primary flange B from being completed to 90 degrees. The solution to this problem depends on the relative dimensions of each flange. As the width of flange A increases in relation to the width of flange B, altering or changing the upper die type (see Fig. 15-30) may allow the bending sequence to be completed.

Figure 15-30 Changing the upper die type or modifying the **upper** die can allow completion of the bending sequence.

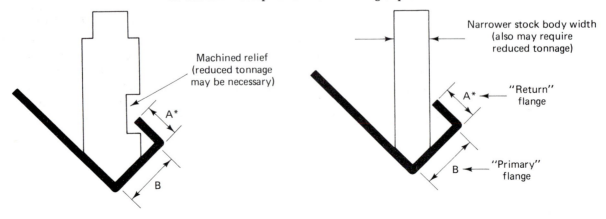

Figure 15-31 Completing a problem bend in the hand-brake.

Figure 15-31 shows still another alternative in the use of the finger brake previously described. But again the relative dimensions of the flanges as well as the capacity of the brake may require, in the final analysis, a complete redesign of the unit wherein the flange in question is fabricated as a separate part.

PRESS BRAKE LIMITATIONS   The press brake is limited in application due to several other parameters beyond bed width and tonnage. Figure 15-32 illustrates these variables which would influence the selection of any particular model.

The throat depth is not always a true restriction if the work can fit between the upright frames of the brake (see Fig. 15-33). The ram stroke travel and the ram adjustment travel on brakes typically used in sheet metal work range from 2 to 4 inches and 3 to 6 inches, respectively.

The die space or "shut height" is a most important consideration when selecting both standard and nonstandard die arrangements and when contemplating the limits in forming four-sided boxes. This dimension of shut height is defined as being the distance between the upper die holder and the bottom die bed with the ram at the bottom of its stroke and with the ram

A = Throat depth
B = Ram stroke travel
C = Bottom die bed height
D = Total die space or "shut height"

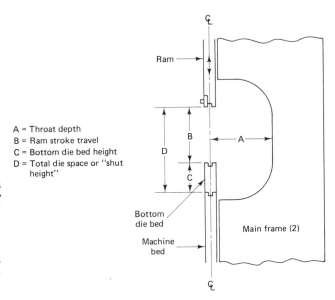

Figure 15-32 Various dimensional aspects of the typical press brake. A, throat depth; B, ram stroke travel; C, bottom die bed height; D, total die space or "shut height."

Figure 15-33 Bending
a wide flange that fits
between the upright
frames.

adjustment all the way up (see Fig. 15-34). Some brake models allow for the
removal of the bottom die bed (see Fig. 15-35). Thus the shut height can be
increased by 2, 4, or even 6 inches. Then with the use of the die extensions
shown, the depth of any four-sided box, which could be bent, is significantly
increased.

The careful mechanic will always make a complete search of the shop's
die rack before cutting or altering any die. Together with careful bending
sequence planning, the mechanic will ensure that the dies on hand will be
used efficiently and that any die modification will not be a duplication.

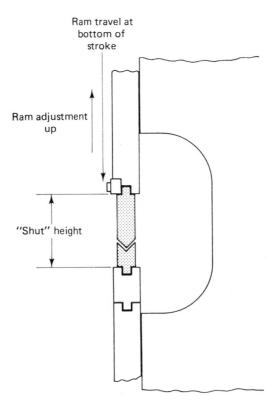

Figure 15-34 Press
brake "shut height."

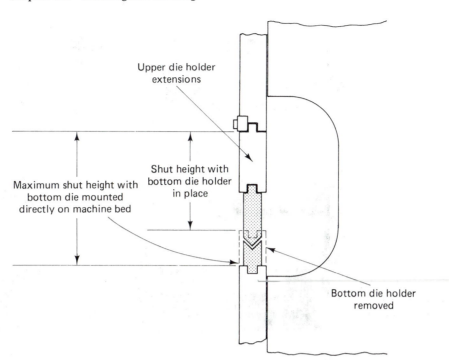

Upper die holder extensions

Shut height with bottom die holder in place

Maximum shut height with bottom die mounted directly on machine bed

Bottom die holder removed

Figure 15-35 Use of die extensions along with the removal of the bottom die bed.

PRESS BRAKE USE AND SAFETY

The procedures and recommendations that follow are to be considered as basic in the use of the typical press brake. The variation in equipment design and capacity as determined by different manufacturers and their various models within a product line may either make invalid portions of what is included in this section, or even impose still other considerations not mentioned. As with any type of machinery, the user must be familiar with the particular characteristics of the individual machine as outlined in the operator's manual supplied with the equipment.

The first step is the selection and installation of the dies. It is critically important before any die installation is attempted that the ram be set at the bottom of its stroke and the power be turned off. The ram adjustment, which is independent of the stroke, can now be used to facilitate insertion of the dies. The reason for this procedure is that if the brake is accidentally cycled while changing or setting up dies, the ram, which is at the bottom of its stroke, can only go up, not down to crush the hands and fingers, which are supporting the dies (see Fig. 15-36).

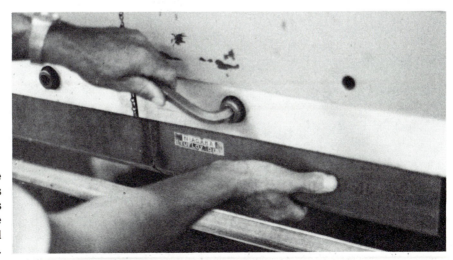

Figure 15-36 Make sure that the ram is at the bottom of its stroke before attempting to install dies.

An extra note of caution: If the brake is a hydraulic model, the ram will not go either up or down with the power off. However, a flywheel type of brake is a different affair. The ram, at the top of its stroke, is held in position by a mechanical clutch. Even with the power off, accidentally releasing the clutch will allow the ram to cycle down.

Figure 15-37 illustrates the method of lining up the upper and lower dies. While the upper die holder merely clamps the die in position, the lower bed setscrews are used for positioning the lower die and locking it in place. The most precise method is to use two pieces of stock, of the same thickness as the material to be bent, as shims. Either adjust the ram down or the bed (on some press brakes) up until the shims are gripped equally on both sides of the V. Once the bottom die is locked in position, readjust, if necessary, the ram distance between the upper and lower dies to reflect the material thickness.

At this point it is best to check if the stroke travel will give the required degree of bend. This should be done with a piece of scrap of the same width as the flange to be bent. If the material being bent is one of the strain-hardenable aluminum alloys, pay particular attention to the grain direction. Pieces bent with the grain at right angles to the die will require a deeper stroke than if the grain direction is parallel to the die (see Fig. 15-38).

Whether or not the brake will bend the flange to the required angle in one stroke depends on several factors. Among these are flange width, material type, die condition, overall brake condition, and most significantly, how much of the brake capacity is being used to make the bend. As flange width increases across the dies, there will be a tendency for the ram and the bed to sag in the middle. Imperceptible as this "give" might be, it may be enough to affect the degree of bend, especially toward the center of the flange. Increas-

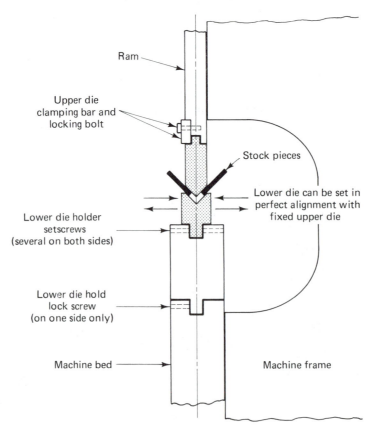

Figure 15-37 Upper and lower die alignment.

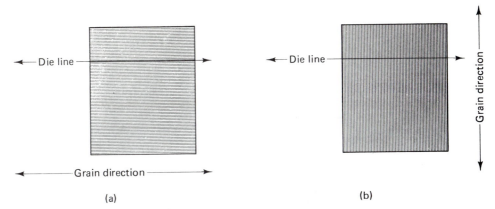

Figure 15-38 Bending
(a) "with" and (b)
"against" the grain.

(a)   (b)

Figure 15-39 Making
the second "hit" at a
more rigid section of
the die bed: (a) first
"hit"; (b) second "hit."

ing the depth of the stroke is not always the right approach. This might cause
excessive strain on both the die and the brake itself as well as actually crushing the material. Figure 15-39 demonstrates a method of "multiple hits" to
overcome the problem. Notice how the center of the flange, which does not
bend completely, is moved to the more rigid point on the bottom die bed.
Another way to increase the depth of the stroke temporarily is to use a

Figure 15-40 Using a paper shim to increase the press stroke temporarily.

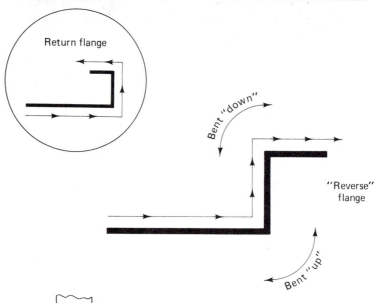

Figure 15-41 "Reverse" flange.

Return flange

Bent "down"

"Reverse" flange

Bent "up"

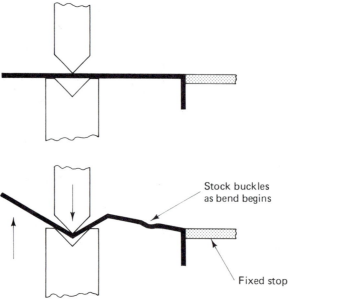

Figure 15-42 Interference with a back gauge stop.

Stock buckles as bend begins

Fixed stop

shim at the point where the flange is not being bent to 90 degrees. A piece of heavy paper or manila envelope is ideal for this purpose (see Fig. 15-40).

So far, setups for both straight flange bends as well as return flange bends have been discussed. Figure 15-41 illustrates the reverse flange bend, which imposes still other setup requirements.

The movement upward of flange B will cause the previously bent flange A to strike the setup stop bar (see Fig. 15-42). To overcome this, a hinged stop bar can be used. Another method would be to employ a spacer which would be free to just flip out of the way as the reverse flange moves in the direction shown (see Fig. 15-43). Still another approach would be to turn the part around and hang the reverse flange A over the front of the bottom die. As shown in Figure 15-44, this may not prove feasible if the balance of the part does not easily fit behind the dies and between the upright frames. This method, which is similar to the "front gauge" use of the shear, will require some deviation from the setup methods that follow.

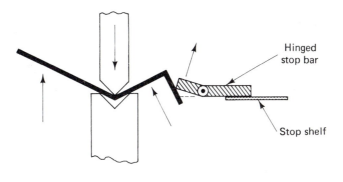

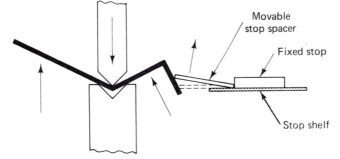

Figure 15-43 Allowing for movement of the reverse flange during bending.

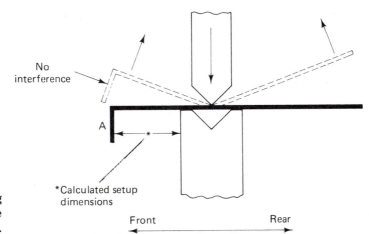

Figure 15-44 Bending with the reverse flange in front of the die.

PRESS BRAKE SETUP   The procedures to be described are basic to press brake operation. There are several setup systems and devices available which can eliminate one or more steps and reduce the need for certain repetitive calculations. The function of those devices is based on what will be detailed here which is intended primarily for the precision job shop mechanic who typically produces short-run production and prototype work.

Press brake setup is predicated on the placement of a "bend line location" directly over the center of the bottom vee die and under the center line of the upper die (refer to Fig. 15-21).

To determine the dimension of a bend line from any given edge or zero location, the following procedure is used. Assume that the dimension of the flange to be bent is 1½ inches, better expressed as 1.500 thousandths. From that figure, deduct one-half of the bend deduction number used in the flat pattern development of the part.* If that bend deduction number is, for example, 0.110 thousandths, the new number is 1.500 minus 0.055 or 1.445. This dimension is not marked on the part. Recall that the setting up of the press brake is mathematical rather than setting up to a scribed line as on the hand brake. To this dimension (1.445) is added one-half the full width of the bottom die used—not the vee width, but the full stock width of the whole die. Note that in Figure 15-25, this width is labeled "cleanup." This means that although the nominal stock width may be 1 inch, it will have been reduced by a final grinding and finishing of the die stock during manufacture. Thus any particular run of die stock may have had anywhere from 30 to 50 thousandths ground off and unless there has been additional reworking of the die, it can be assumed that it has been ground equally on both sides.

To continue the example, say that the bottom die is 0.960 thousandths when measured with a vernier caliper. One-half of that, or 0.480 thousandths, is added to the bend line dimension of 1.445. This gives a *bend line setup dimension* of 1.925.

Rule: *To calculate the bend line setup dimension for the press brake, determine the flange dimension, subtract one-half of the bend deduction figure, and to this add one-half of the full body width of the bottom die.*

This final dimension is used to locate a stop bar so that when the material is placed between the dies, the original bend line location (1.445) is directly centered over the V (see Fig. 15-45).

Figure 15-46 shows how this setup is actually done. Using the depth extension rod of the caliper, set the blade of a combination square to the required dimension (1.925). This could also be accomplished by a direct reading of the square blade graduations to the nearest 64th. By laying the square as shown against the front face of the die, a stop bar can be accurately clamped in position. The setting should be checked on both left and right extremes of the flange width (see Fig. 15-47).

With careful setup and accurate die alignment, the first test bend should be within 10-thousandths or even 5-thousandths tolerance. It would not be uncommon to see parts with several bends that must be within 10- or 15-thousandths overall tolerance. As illustrated in Figure 15-48, each of the four bends would actually have to be within 3 thousandths. In light of this, the mechanic should proceed to make whatever fine adjustments are needed to bend as close to nominal as possible.

*The use of bend deduction and bend allowance is described in Chapter 17.

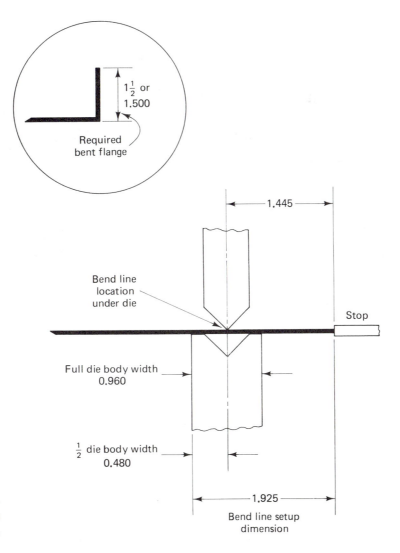

1½ or
1.500

Required
bent flange

1.445

Bend line
location
under die

Stop

Full die body width
0.960

½ die body width
0.480

1.925

Bend line setup
dimension

Figure 15-45 Mathematics of the press brake setup.

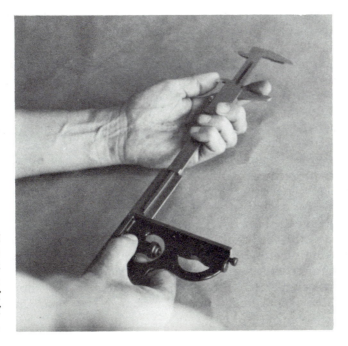

Figure 15-46 Setting the bend line setup dimension, 1.925, first on the caliper, then on the square, by means of the extension rod of the caliper.

Figure 15-47 Setting up the bend line setup dimension stop.

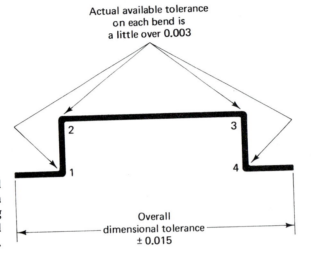

Actual available tolerance
on each bend is
a little over 0.003

Figure 15-48 Actual tolerance allowed on a four-bend part having a 0.015-inch overall tolerance.

Overall
dimensional tolerance
± 0.015

One well-proven method of making such fine adjustments, not only in bending brake operations, but in all precision setup work, is the use of feeler gauges. Figure 15-49 shows the type with individual blades graduated in 1-thousandth increments. Disassembled, each blade is used as a precision shim. If the flange dimension is 0.005 of an inch short, clamp the test piece to the shelf against the stop. Unclamp the stop, place the shim as shown, and reclamp the stop bar in the new position. Removing the shim will allow the part to move that much farther in under the dies. If the flange dimension is 0.005 of an inch too long, the 0.005 shims can be left propped against the square-edged stop bar or be used to permanently reposition the stop bar that much farther in toward the dies.

The remaining setup operation pertains to obtaining the proper degree of bend. This is normally accomplished during the initial setup stage for the flange dimension. Obviously, a close tolerance dimension check cannot be made for a right-angle bend unless the bend is indeed 90 degrees or whatever angle is called for.

Once the stroke distance has been adjusted, the practical aspect of making repetitive bends both with and across the material grain will require careful attention on the part of the mechanic. This is particularly so in using flywheel-operated press brakes. On this type, "slipping" of the clutch by treadle bar manipulation will influence how hard the material will be "hit" by the ram.

Figure 15-49 Positioning of the feeler gauge shim to make precise bending adjustments.

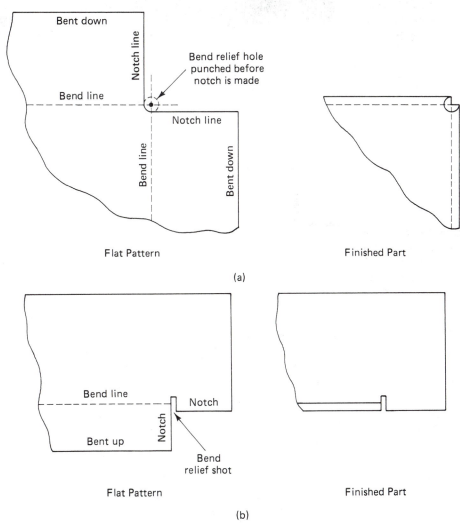

Figure 15-50 Bend relief holes and slots.

The accurate and repetitive bending of flanges may require the use of bend relief holes or slots, especially if the material is crack sensitive and exhibits a springiness that requires a slight overbending to achieve a 90-degree angle.

Figure 15-50a shows the typical use of a bend relief hole in the notched corners of a flat layout. These holes should be at least twice the material thickness. If the bend radius is larger than the material thickness, the holes may have to be even larger. Figure 15-50b illustrates the use of a slotted relief to prevent tearing of the stock in situations where the flange dimension must be equal to an adjacent edge.

It is in these areas of precision fabrication that both experience and touch become so important. The mechanic who has the responsibility to make setups for less experienced help must endeavor to make the operation as foolproof as possible. The dies must be carefully aligned and secured tightly. The bend line stops must be proven accurate and also made tight and in all ways immobile. The ram stroke must give the proper angle bend without crushing the material. In this respect the die selected must be correct for the job.

Chapter 16

PUNCHING, NOTCHING, and DRILLING

PUNCHING MACHINES Shown in Figure 16-1 are a variety of machines designed for the sole purpose of punching a hole. It is not the purpose here to describe in any intimate detail their operation, as that is more properly the role of the operator's manual supplied with any particular model and type.

What is to be taught in this section is both the mechanics of hole punching and the principles of accurate setup methods. This will be done within the context of precision sheet metal work. To demonstrate many of these principles and methods, a basic hand-operated punch, typical of the kind used in a short-run prototype shop, will be used. Thus it will soon become apparent that the theory behind these same methods are used in any number of sophisticated, automatic, and high-speed production punching machines.

A hole whose diameter exceeds the material thickness should never be drilled if its location, diameter, and concentricity are typical of what is required in close-tolerance precision work. The difficulty lies in the fact that before the body of the drill can effect a proper hole, the point is already through the material and no longer guiding the rest of the drill (see Fig. 16-2a). Figure 16-2b shows the correct method.

The preceding paragraph all but eliminates drilling as a viable sheet metal operation. On many blueprints, draftspersons always seem to specify the work "drill." A common notation is "drill 25/64 (0.390)-diameter hole." Such instruction should not be taken literally. A hole should never be drilled if it can be punched. Punching is faster, produces a clean hole, and most important, is more accurate in location. Of course, any number of situations can arise that could require drilling, but careful planning and operation sequencing should be carried out in advance so as to minimize such situations. On the other hand, the punching of holes where the diameter is less than one-half of the material thickness is not always recommended in sheet metal work. There are problems in both stripping the punch-out of the material and in small-diameter punch breakage. In these cases drilling may be the only method left. Drilling operations will be covered later.

Figure 16-1 Punching machines.

Figure 16-1 Punching machines (continued).

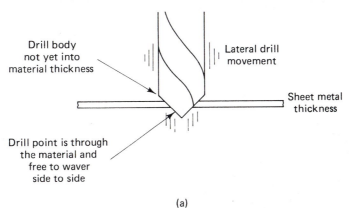

Drill body not yet into material thickness

Lateral drill movement

Sheet metal thickness

Drill point is through the material and free to waver side to side

(a)

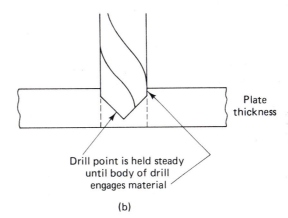

Plate thickness

Drill point is held steady until body of drill engages material

(b)

Figure 16-2 (a) A drill point clears the material thickness too soon; (b) the correct method.

PUNCH AND DIE TYPES   As in drills, round punches are available in fractional, number, and letter sizes. Additionally, punch and die sets come in an infinite variety of sizes and shapes. The more common ones can be purchased as stock items (see Fig. 16-3a). The dimensions indicated, length (L), width (W), radius (R), and Diameter (D), are typical of those punches which would be called "standards" in that they coincide with various types of industrial hardware to be discussed later.

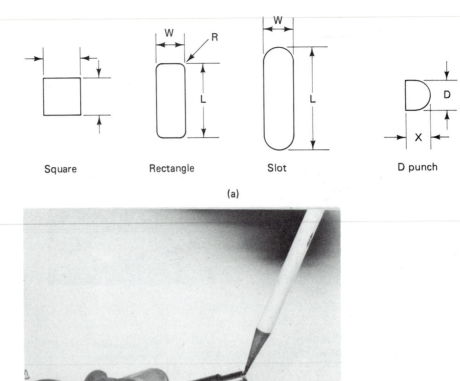

Square   Rectangle   Slot   D punch

(a)

(b)

Figure 16-3 (a) Some standard shape punches with typical dimensions; (b) round punch with a center point.

The precision sheet metal shop soon accumulates a large inventory of punches and dies and it becomes imperative that provision be made to catalog and store them for quick locating and to keep them in good condition. Included in this inventory would also be those called "specials" in that they were made by the in-house toolroom for any special application or tooling requirements.

Another aspect of type is the punch face condition. Elsewhere in this text the use of "rake" is discussed. Rake is the angling of the face of the punch in order to reduce the tonnage required to pierce the material. Generally in sheet metal work, this is not required. Most often the holes are "blanked." This means that tonnage alone pushed the flat face of the die through the work. Blanking is desirable not only because of greater setup accuracy, but there is less tendency for the work to distort as it is punched.

Most round punches have a center point on the face. This point is used in conjunction with a center punch mark on the work, as shown in Figure 16-3b. This makes possible very accurate hole locations. Most shaped punches, squares, ovals, and so on, will present only the flat face to the work. Setup is then accomplished by lining up the punch to scribed lines on the work.

DIE CLEARANCE AND TONNAGE REQUIREMENTS

The hand-operated punching machines used in a precision sheet metal shop are capable of generating anywhere from 3 to 5 tons of pressure. Power punches of up to 30-ton capacity are also employed. Their basic value is in their increased tonnage capacity and speed.

In aircraft and electronic short-run production, which is often considered the standard work load in the typical job shop or the in-house prototype shop, tonnage considerations are reduced to academics, especially as the work is often on soft aluminums and light-gauge mild steels and hole sizes are mostly under a ½-inch diameter. Holes requiring higher tonnages are punched on machines such as the multi-station Rotex-type punch or a power punch press.

However, a useful formula for calculating tonnage requirements is as follows: $C \times T \times S$, with C being the circumference or periphery dimension of the hole, T the thickness of the material, and S the tensile strength of the alloy. To find the tonnage required for any hole, simply multiply the three factors. For example, to find the tonnage required to punch a 1-inch round hole in 16-gauge mild steel: C (1 inch $\times$ 3.141) $\times$ T (0.059) $\times$ S (50,000) equals 9265 pounds or approximately 5 tons. Similarly, to punch a 1½-inch square hole in 20-gauge stainless steel, multiply (1½ inch $\times$ 4) $\times$ 0.035 $\times$ 90,000 which equals 18,900 pounds of just over 9 tons.

Although discussions of die clearance are related to tonnage needed, our concern in precision sheet metal is primarily one of hole quality. It must be remembered that the many holes one sees in an electrical chassis or panel are receptacles for a variety of closely dimensioned rivets, locking devices, and other assorted hardware, the proper installation of which is dependent on an accurately sized hole.

The maximum accepted punch-to-die clearance when piercing ⅛-inch-thick material or less is 10%. As shown in Figure 16-4, this means for example, that the die diameter must be, 204 thousandths (No. 6 die) for a 3/16 (0.187)-diameter punch.

Figure 16-5 shows the mechanics of hole punching and illustrates the importance of proper die clearance. As the die clearance dimension increases, so does the area labeled "shear zone." The illustration also details a punched hole. The objective in precision punching is to get the maximum straight-side wall dimension. Both "rollover" and "break-out" dimensions will increase with increases in punch and die clearance. In sheet metal punching where

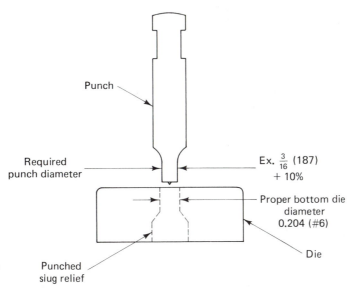

Figure 16-4 Punch and die clearance factors.

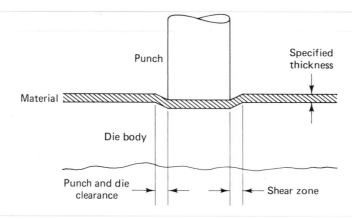

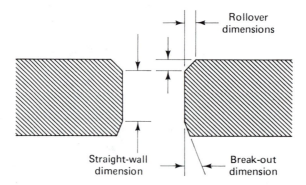

Figure 16-5 Punched-hole characteristics.

both location and hole quality are of equal importance, die clearances may often be held to an absolute minimum (below 10%) and consistent only with proper punch operation and without undue wear and tear on the punching machine.

PUNCH AND DIE INSTALLATION

Figure 16-6 shows a typically installed punch and die setup. The adapters are required to accommodate a variety of punch shank and bottom die diameters.

If installation is on a power-operated punch, be sure that the power is off. The mechanic should always avoid the temptation to make die changes or even minor setup changes with the machine running as unexpected cycling could prove disastrous both to the tooling and to the hands and fingers.

To begin, install the punch in the punch adapter, making sure that the setscrew is engaging the flat relief on the punch shank. This keeps the punch from slipping out of the adapter even if the setscrew is jarred loose, which it often is. The assembled adapter and punch is then attached to the ram, usually with a yoke device. The two nuts on the yoke should be tightened both evenly and securely.

The bottom die is now inserted in its adapter and once again the locking setscrew should be engaging the flat relief on the die body. The assembled adapter and die are now installed into the die holder. Notice in Figure 16-7 how the setup table is attached to the die holder containing the die and die adapter, which should each be tightly held in place by their respective setscrews.

The setup table can now be used to move the die and adapter assembly into place under the punch.

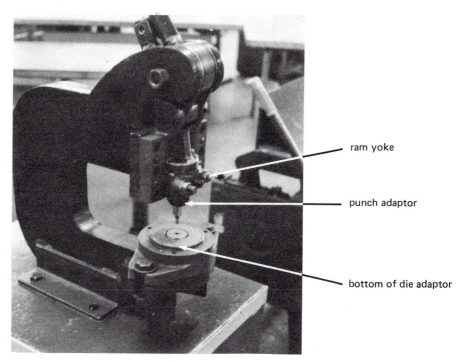

ram yoke

punch adaptor

bottom of die adaptor

Figure 16-6 Sheet metal hand punch showing both punch and die in their respective adapters.

Figure 16-7 Setup table being attached to the die holder assembly.

The next operation is to "home" the punch. This is done to seat the punch and punch adapter in the ram, for no matter how tightly the setscrews and locknuts are, there will always be some movement the first time that pressure is brought to bear on the assembly. To do this, place an extra-heavy piece of stock in position as if it were to be punched. Stroke the machine manually several times. The thick material, rather than being pierced through, will force the punch to seat in its holders. Now the die can be aligned to the punch. Stroke the machine so that the punch just enters the die and see that the punch is centered in the die opening. Now the locknuts, which hold the die holder to the machine bed, can be securely tightened. A good punching setup will use hardened bolts and setscrews, so the mechanic must not hesitate to apply some muscle when tightening them.

The depth of the punch stroke should now be checked. The method of

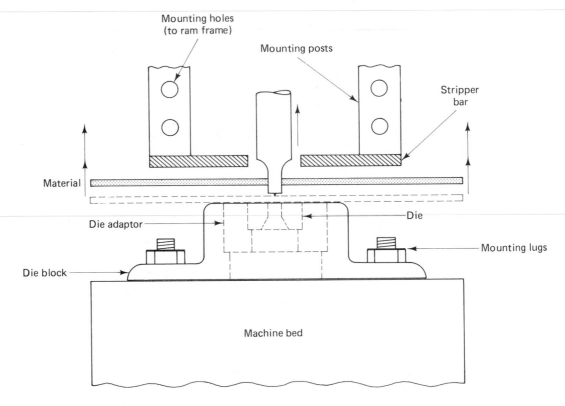

Figure 16-8 Punch stripping diagram.

doing this will vary with machine type, but adjust so that just enough stroke is achieved to punch the hole. Excessive punch penetration may enlarge or distort the hole in soft materials.

Practically all punching operations will require some way of keeping the material down while the punch cycles upward. This is referred to as "stripping" (see Fig. 16-8). There are any number of ways that such stripping bars can be installed and just as many configurations in relation to punch size and type and hole locations. Figure 16-9 illustrates some of these variations. Part (b) shows a hard-rubber bushing which compresses during the punch stroke. As the punch rises, it then expands, pushing the work off the punch body. Basic considerations for stripping include the following:

1. The stripping bar should be thicker than the material to be stripped.
2. The stripping bar should be high enough to allow adequate stock movement but not so high as to interfere with the punch stroke.

Figure 16-9 Punch stripping devices mounted in place.

3. The stripping bar should engage enough of the material surrounding the hole so that the punch can be withdrawn evenly.
4. The stripping bar should be parallel to the work so that there is no cocking of the stock as the punch is pulled out. Such uneven movement can distort the hole or even break the punch.
5. Apply some lubrication to the punch body to aid the stripping operation.

To complete the installation, with the power on, cycle the punch to ensure proper operation and punch several holes in some appropriate scrap. Now turn off the power and manually cycle the punch, checking to see if proper punch and die alignment is being maintained.

The difference between an "operator" and a "mechanic" will now become apparent, as the mechanic will check to see if the punched hole is within the size specifications on the print and will also, periodically during the run, check the punch and die alignment and tightness of all the locknuts.

PUNCHING SETUPS As will be described in Chapter 17, a hole location is a coordinate which can be labeled X and Y. The dimensions originate from similarly designated X and Y bank edges (see Fig. 16-10). In order to punch the hole in the required location, the coordinate must be placed directly under the punch center.

In hand-operated punching of one- or two-piece jobs, this is simply accomplished by center punching the laid-out coordinates and engaging them to the center point on the punch face. More often with either the hand punch or especially with the power punching of many holes, stop bars must be clamped to the setup table, which will facilitate such repetitive positioning. Figure 16-11 shows a typical setup. Note that the stop labeled Y only touches one spot on edge Y. To engage the whole edge, as does the X stop, would require undue reliance on stock squareness, which will not have the strict tolerance requirement the hole location carries.

The setup is made to a center-punched template or first piece. Using just enough pressure for the template to be held in place by the punch, the mechanic then clamps the X and Y stops in position on the setup table

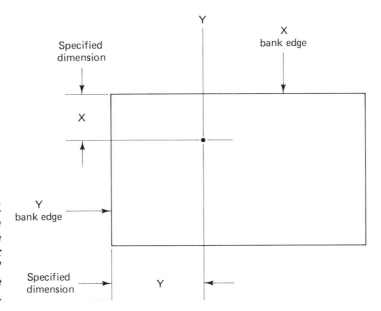

Figure 16-10 The X and Y coordinate dimensions from the layout are the basis for determining "bank" edge locations on the punch setup table.

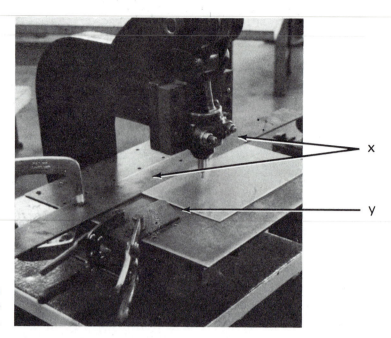

Figure 16-11 Setup stops mounted on the punch table.

against those edges designated on the original layout as "bank." This last point is very important, for if in subsequent punching of any number of pieces, the blanks get rotated or flipped over, the hole pattern as laid out on the template will be changed. Figure 16-12 shows a punching operation with the parts being stacked in such a way as to prevent their being misoriented.

As for stock material to be used as stops, most any piece of random material can be used for this purpose as long as the edges are square and smooth and it is at least as thick as the material being punched.

The first piece punched should now be dimensionally checked against the blueprint locations. The hole could be checked to the template, but going back to the blueprint and recalculating the flat pattern dimension is the proper way. The hallmark of a good mechanic is that he or she will

Figure 16-12 Careful orientation of parts being punched. Note alignment of previously punched holes.

always devise a different way of checking the same dimension. If the hole is not close enough to the nominal dimension, feeler gauge shims can be used as described in Chapter 15 to make minor adjustments.

SETUP VARIATIONS　　There are any number of hole pattern configurations that would make it practical to attempt to punch two or more holes with a single setup. This can be accomplished as long as the "bank" does not change. In other words, if the layout dimensions come from any given edge, the setup on the punch must come from the same edge. Figure 16-13 shows the affects of "flipping" the bank edge. Notice how bank edge Y has been reversed in part (b). If the overall dimension of the flat piece is 5 inches and has a tolerance of 0.015 and the piece was 0.010 over size or 5.010, it will be impossible to punch the holes to within the 0.005 tolerance allowed. By flipping the oversize but still acceptable piece, the tolerance between the holes is already used up. In another case, let's assume that there is a pattern of holes to be punched, as shown in Figure 16-14.

　　The phrase "tolerances nonaccumulative" on the print dictates that although there might be 15 thousandths tolerance between holes, that tolerance cannot actually be used because the 8-inch dimension must also be within the 15 thousandths specified. Thus the actual allowed error between holes is just over 3 thousandths.

　　Let us also assume that this job is a 500-piece run. This means that

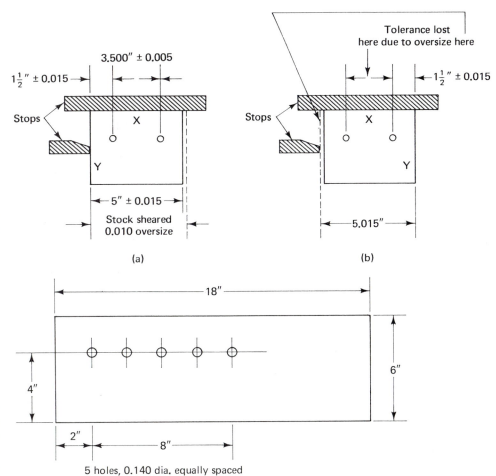

Figure 16-13　Dimensional error as a result of "flipping" the bank edge.

Figure 16-14　Punching a line of holes with accuracy required not only between holes but in the overall pattern dimension. Tolerances ±0.015.

Figure 16-15 High-
capacity and high-speed
punching machine.

2500 holes will have to be punched and because of the close tolerance required, each of the 500 blanks will have to be handled five times. Thus each
hole will require a separate setup as the line of holes progresses along the
8-inch dimension.

It is this recurring hole-punching situation that has given rise to the
popularity of high-speed Strippit-type machines (see Fig. 16-15). Both as
manual or numerically controlled units, these machines are fast and extremely
accurate. The blanks are gripped by their bank edges and mechanically
moved along the X and Y coordinates to the proper position under the
punch.

Lacking such machines, multiple punching setups can be made with the
use of either step or pin gauges. A step gauge is merely made up of several
strips of metal (steel) which are spot-welded in position to each other, as
shown in Figure 16-16. The illustration also shows how the step gauge is
used on the setup table. Notice how the die may have to be elevated above
its adapter in order to keep the work level under the punch. This can be
accomplished with spacer washers shop-made for that purpose.

The pin gauge (see Fig. 16-17) has the advantage of being more
permanent and can be made more accurately, especially for a longer line of
holes. As shown in the illustration, hardened drill bushings and dowel pins

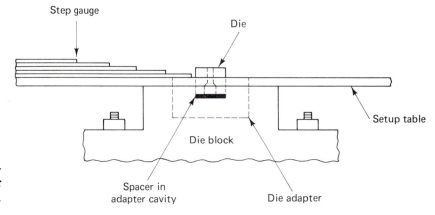

Figure 16-16 Shop-
made step gauge for
punching a line of holes.

Figure 16-17 Pin gauge setup. Note the predrilled hole pattern which receives the pin stop.

are used. Properly used, they can make repetitive hole patterns with remarkable accuracy.

Another method of reproducing hole patterns is known as transfer punching. This method can be very accurate on short runs if properly executed. The transfer template, usually of sheet steel, is ⅛ inch thick. On it, the layout is made with all the holes punched ⅛ inch in diameter. An accurately made transfer punch is made and used as shown in Figure 16-18. Note how the stops for the bank edges duplicate what would otherwise be the setup on the punch table. All of the hole locations are now center punched and one of the blanks is marked or coded as a master to indicate which center-punched location gets what diameter hole. The blanks are then carefully stacked and oriented as to bank edges and sequentially punched using only the center punch mark and an appropriate stripper bar.

In the making of such reproducing templates and gauges, it must be remembered that they must be made to tolerances only half that allowed on the finished part. Such close work usually requires a mechanic competent in close-tolerance layout techniques. These techniques are discussed in the section describing layout methods.

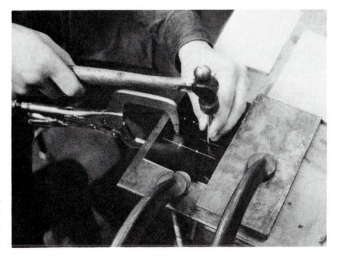

Figure 16-18 Using a transfer punch to punch mark a hole pattern.

Figure 16-19 Setting up the punch body to irregular hole pattern layout lines.

When setting up oval, square, rectangular, and other flat-faced punches, a square must be used. At least one of the straight sides of such odd-shaped holes and cutouts must be parallel or square to a bank edge. The hole outline must be laid out on the piece; then as shown in Figure 16-19, the punch is located on the laid-out lines. To ensure absolute squareness to the edge, a square is used with the blade placed flat against the punch body.

NOTCHING AND NIBBLING

Sheet metal operations require the making of large cutouts of often intricate shapes. This also includes the removal of relatively large amounts of material in the making of corner reliefs to facilitate the bending of flanges. Figure 16-20 shows examples of each of the operations to be discussed here.

Notching is accomplished with the hand-operated machine as shown in Figure 16-21. There are power-operated versions, but a "hand notcher" is more commonly seen in the precision sheet metal shop. The unit shown will handle up to 16-gauge mild steel and up to ⅛-inch thickness of the softer

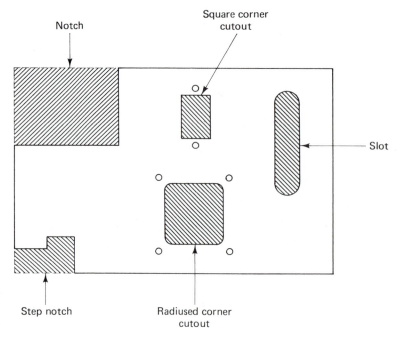

Figure 16-20 Examples of notching and nibbling operations.

Figure 16-21 Hand notching machine.

aluminums. Large notches should be done in stages (nibbled) both for accuracy and to prevent undue wear and tear on the machine (see Fig. 16-22).

The notching is done according to scribed lines on the work or if identical, multiple notches are to be made, setups are made according to scribed lines on a template or first piece.

Figure 16-23 shows the positioning of stop bars on the setup table of the notcher. If tolerances and the function of the notch allows, two or four identical notches can now be made by merely flipping and rotating the blank piece. As notches are most often used for bending reliefs and as such are welded closed, the tolerances are not as strict as if they were dimensioned on the print. If the dimensions of the notch are indeed called out on the print, the mechanic is obliged to maintain the "bank edge orientation" to ensure the required accuracy.

Figure 16-22 Method of nibbling a large notch rather than forcing the machine to cut in one stroke.

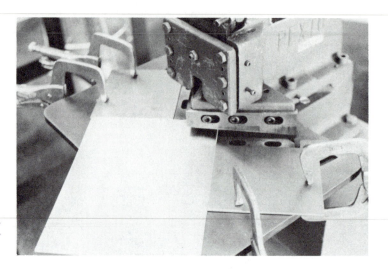

Figure 16-23 Stops clamped to the notcher table.

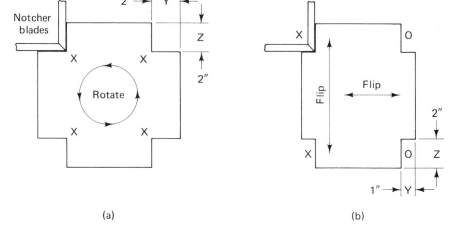

Figure 16-24 Notching symmetrical and asymmetrical cut outs: (a) dimensions Y and Z are equal; (b) dimensions Y and Z are unequal.

Figure 16-24 illustrates some aspects of multiple notching to a setup. The notched part in Figure 16-24a has four identical and symmetrical notches A single setup will allow the making of all four corners labeled X by simply flipping and rotating the part. The part in Figure 16-24b has four identically dimensioned notches, but they are not symmetrical. Thus only the corners labeled X must be flipped in the direction shown. The corners labeled 0 will require another flip to place them in the X position.

The notcher is also used to make the cutout required for flange mitering. Figure 16-25 shows the finished part and the required flat pattern with the notch being formed by the 90-degree nose of the notching machine. Figure 16-26 illustrates how, with repositioned notcher blades, the

Figure 16-25 (a) Notching required for a mitered flange; (b) typical machine set-up for a miter notch.

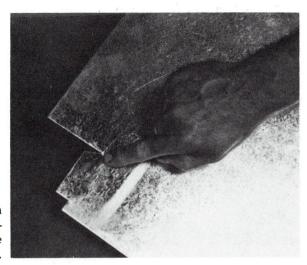

Figure 16-26 Notch made possible by repositioning the notching blades.

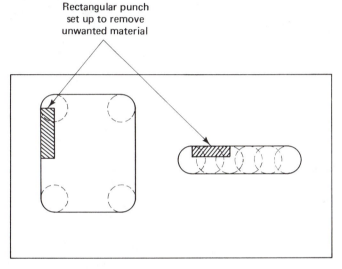

Figure 16-27 Method of nibbling a radiused square cut out and a large slot.

tab which is bent inside the flanges for either spot welding or brazing is notched. The notcher is also useful in certain cutoff and back shearing operations that are too small to be done on the power shear.

Large notches that cannot be done in the notching machine, or repetitive notching that requires power application, can be accomplished in the punch press with dies of the appropriate size and shape.

Typical punch-nibbling operations are shown in Figure 16-27. The radiused corners are punched holes. The setup is then made so that the perimeter of the cutout is made by sliding the work along under the punch, making slightly overlapping hits. The large slot is made by punching a hole at both ends and nibbling out in between.

USING THE DRILL PRESS IN SHEET METAL OPERATIONS

As discussed, the drilling of material thinner in dimension than the intended diameter of the hole produces holes that are out of round and of inaccurate dimension and location. The hole, rather than being bored by the drill body, is torn by the drill point. Yet the drill press is a valuable piece of shop equipment in precision sheet metal work if it is used properly and with the proper tooling.

Safety in using the drill press, besides the use of eye protection, consists mainly of preventing the work from spinning with the drill or cutter as it

Figure 16-28 Safety stop clamped to the drill press table to prevent spinning.

breaks through the back side of the material. While clamping the work to the table is a basic procedure, it is not often practical in precision work, nor needed in every instance. Figure 16-28 shows the position of a stop bar clamped to the back edge of the table. If the work does grab the cutter, the stop bar prevents its full rotation.

Drilling Holes

If a hole has to be drilled that is significantly larger in diameter than the thickness of the material, there are several approaches that can be taken. First would be the use of a twist drill specially ground for sheet metal applications. As shown in Figure 16-29, the drill on the right has been altered so that the outer cutting lips begin to cut into the stock just after the point takes hold in the center point location. This is similar to the auger bit used in drilling wood.

The use of a counter bore is illustrated in Figure 16-30. A smaller pilot hole is drilled (or punched) before the larger hole is bored through the stock. To prevent the creation of a large burr on the back side of the work, the first side is bored only halfway through the work; then the part is flipped over and the bore completed.

Still larger-diameter holes can be made with a flycutter. Figure 16-31 illustrates the making of a relatively large hole. Note the use of clamps to hold the stock steady. If the stock is very thin and cutting from both sides to eliminate the breakout burr is impractical, use a piece of plywood under the work. This will protect the tool's cutter and the drill press table. This operation requires extra slow spindle speeds, steady pressure, and lubrication of the cut. Kerosene and mixtures of kerosene and light motor oil make excel-

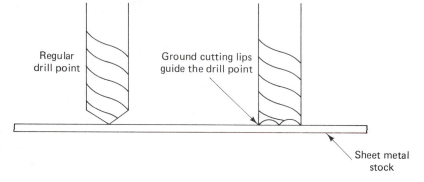

Regular drill point

Ground cutting lips guide the drill point

Sheet metal stock

Figure 16-29 Regular drill and reground drill for sheet metal drilling.

Figure **16-30** Using a counter bore.

Figure **16-31** Using a flycutter.

lent lubricants, especially on aluminum. Lubricants should always be used, mainly to prevent loading up of the cutting edges of any tool used in precision work. Such loading will cause an inaccurate hole to be made.

COUNTERSINKING The need for countersinking is shown in Figure 16-32. The dimensional tolerance for the countersunk hole is usually quite strict. Besides the obvious need for providing a flush surface as with rivets and screws, other hardware and terminals require critical dimensional accuracy for proper installation. Countersinks, which are not properly made, will affect the installation and performance of the hardware they are to receive and can cause problems during painting and other finishing operations. Figure 16-33 illustrates the use of a simple device to ensure accurately sized countersinks. The smaller surface area of the block overcomes any bow or twist in the whole piece,

Figure **16-32** Examples of hardware that required countersunk holes.

Common flat-head screw	Allen-head screw	Rivet	Electrical standoff	Pressed locknut
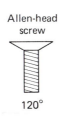	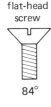			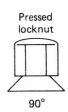
84°	120°	100°	60°	90°

Figure 16-33   Using a bushing as a standoff to overcome workpiece distortion. A typical countersink is in the chunk.

Figure 16-34   Automatic stop-countersking tool.

Figure 16-35   Automatic tapping head.

Figure 16-36 Hardened drill bushing in a fixture allows accurate drilling of smaller-diameter holes.

which would become apparent if the entire piece was laid on the drill press table.

The use of the stop-countersink (see Fig. 16-34) eliminates the need to rely on the totally inadequate depth-setting devices built onto the typical drill press. Countersinking, like flycutting, is always done with spindle speeds slower than those used in drilling.

TAPPING The drill press shown in Figure 16-35 is equipped with an automatic tapping head. This clutch-activated device will turn clockwise, cutting the thread when downward pressure is exerted, and reverse itself, removing the tap as the drill press spindle is raised.

Coupled with the use of drill bushings (see Fig. 16-36), the drill press can still be used to drill holes accurately placed, but of limited diameter.

Chapter 17

PRECISION LAYOUT

What follows here is a sequential narrative for making a precision layout for either a first piece or a template. These basic procedures are applied to all kinds of sheet metal problems regardless of complexity. However, as this type of construction is used primarily in aircraft and electronic fabrication, many of the more familiar sheet metal shapes are not referred to. Those typical heating and air-handling sheet metal shapes are the subject of texts dealing exclusively with that trade.

While "sheet metal" is still "sheet metal," the point of departure between the two forms is the accuracy of the dimensioned part. Whereas the application of machinery in such precision work has been described, so too must the methods of layout and template making.

The electronic chassis shown in Figure 17-1 will be used as an in-

Figure 17-1 Typical electronic chassis to be made in one piece.

structional vehicle. To this, the basic rules for layout will be highlighted so that they can be applied to any typical fabrication assignment.

Also, to illustrate the principles explained, some very simple and basic layouts will be shown. *It is strongly recommended that the reader follow along, performing along with the text, the actual computations and sketching.*

FLAT PATTERN DEVELOPMENT

Figure 17-2 is a facsimile of the actual blueprint for the part shown in Figure 17-1. From this and only this, the mechanic must envision the appearance of the flat pattern outline. The object on the blueprint must be mentally unfolded and a sketch made of the pattern.

Figure 17-3 illustrates a paper representation of the mental unfolding of the part. Actually, what is done in the making of the sketch is the separate drawing of each of the views on the print. But unlike the print, the separate views are connected to each other along the appropriate mating edges. This is done with dashed rather than solid lines. The dashed line on the flat pattern is used only to denote the location of a bend. As this is a flat layout, it cannot represent any hidden surface as it normally does on a blueprint. To complete the layout, any view not included on the blueprint must also be made part of the flat pattern.

Figure 17-4 is the complete flat pattern sketch of the part to be made. This initial "one-piece format" will immediately present several important questions to the mechanic.

1. Can the part actually be made in one piece?
2. A bending brake of what size and capacity is required?
3. Where are the bends located, and where are the seams or mating edges located?
4. What joining methods will be required?
5. What subsequent special tooling will be needed as the job progresses?
6. Does it (the layout) contradict or confirm the original time and material estimate?

The completed sketch should include all the details shown on the print. A "detail" can be a hole, a notch or cutout, a countersink, and whatever else the print shows and dimensions. It is a philosophical and practical matter of fact that if the part cannot be drawn by the mechanic, it cannot be built by the mechanic, at least not in the form in which it was originally drawn on the blueprint.

In reviewing Chapter 4, one must remember that the essence of blueprint reading is in the basic premise that the print is drawn as to its function: what does the part do? where does it fit? what must be mounted on it? and so on. What is actually required in blueprint reading, beyond the obvious reading of the words and symbols and computing dimensions, is in reinterpreting the print as to "how" the part is to be built.

The making of the flat pattern sketch shown, and in its subsequent dimensioning, will soon indicate if the part can be made in the shop with the equipment at hand. For instance, if an electronic chassis is 6 inches deep and the print shows that the flanges are to be formed by bending, it becomes readily apparent that a one-piece layout may not be possible. The typical finger brake has a depth capacity of just over 4 inches, and without sufficient tonnage and the correct die tooling, even a press brake could not do the job. The result is that now the one-piece layout sketch is useless. But as the

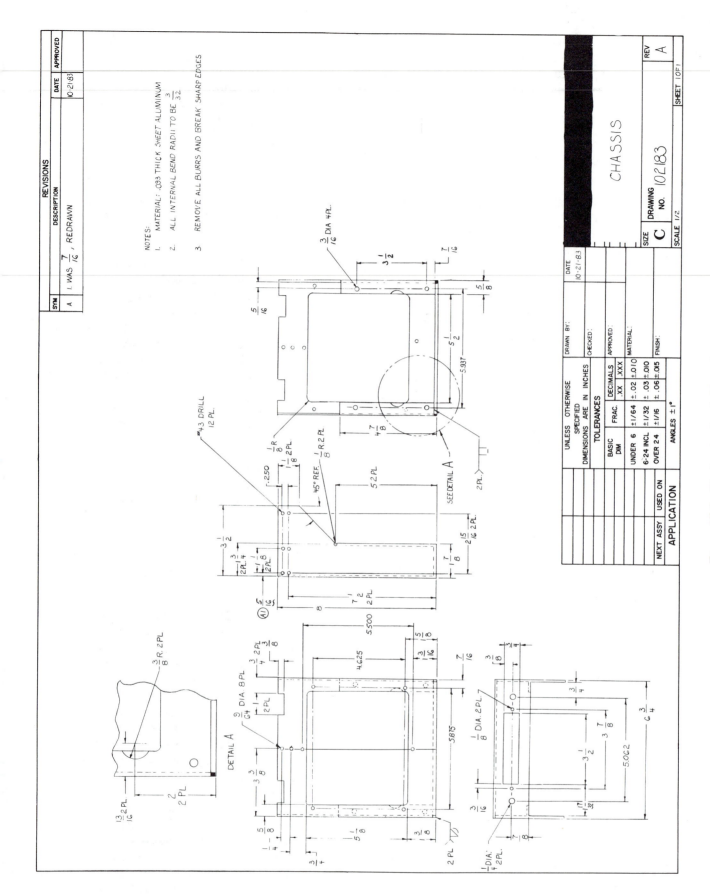

Figure 17-2 Electronic chassis blueprint.

222

Figure 17-3 Envisioning the flat pattern of the part.

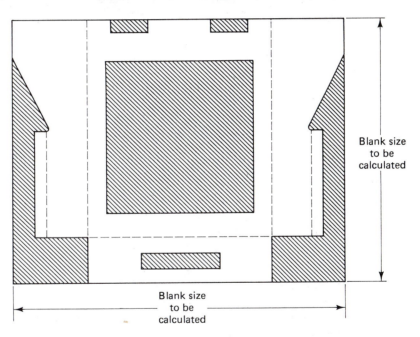

Figure 17-4 Flat pattern blank of the part showing major cutouts and notches. Shaded area, areas to be notched or nibbled away, *after* other holes and details are completed.

Blank size to be calculated

Blank size to be calculated

cheapest materials in the shop are still pencils and paper, there is no real loss of time or materials. If a design change is necessary, there may be a host of possible manufacturing implications. Such changes will often require some sort of approval or an engineering change order on the blueprint. In this respect there is a clear advantage in having both design and drafting personnel familiar with the shop facility and its operations so that work orders can be intelligently assigned.

The flat sketch need not be dimensionally accurate as long as it is in some proportion to the dimensions given. This means that if the pattern forms a rectangular shape, it should not be drawn as a square. Or if one flange is 6 inches and an adjacent flange is 5 inches, that relationship should be apparent in the sketch. The sketch should also be large enough for clear and complete detailing and dimensioning.

DETERMINING THE DEVELOPED SIZE

If it proves feasible to make the part in one piece, the next step is to calculate the length and width of the sheared blank. This is known as the developed size or in many shops, simply the shear size.

If one were to tear out this page and bend it into the U shape shown in Figure 17-5, it is obvious that the outer surface of the paper is being stretched. Similarly, any piece of metal being so bent will stretch along its "outside" dimension. Figure 17-6 illustrates the dimensional considerations involved in determining the shear size.

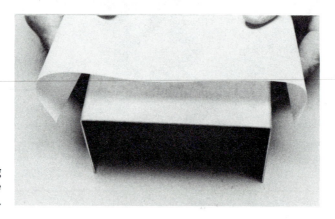

Figure 17-5 Bending causes the outer surface to stretch.

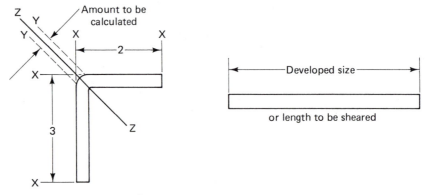

Figure 17-6 How the developed or "shear size" is derived.

The extension lines labeled X are the actual dimensions of the finished part and are often referred to as the "outside mold lines." At the point of tangency where the mold line separates from the actual part, two dashed lines labeled Y are drawn. These are drawn parallel to an imaginary line Z which bisects the internal angle over which the part is bent. What is to be calculated is the amount the material will stretch, as indicated by the distance between the lines labeled Y. That dimension or amount of metal must be deducted from the flat length of the material. In layout work that dimension is known as the "bend deduction figure."

The three constants required to determine the bend deduction figure are the material thickness, the internal bend radius, and the degree to which the part is bent. Chart 17-1, the bend deduction chart, is one that the authors have used for many years. The reader may be familiar with charts that give different deductions. The conflicting figures do not indicate that any chart is wrong, but rather that they have been derived from different bases.

Bend deduction charts are in circulation that are based on either the J chart system, the neutral line computation, or the empirical bend formula. The chart used here is based on the latter, which may be expressed as the equation $0.0714R + 0.0078T = 1$ degree of bend allowance. In the equation, R represents the internal radius and T represents the material thickness. The

Material thickness

Note: Because of variables such as ram speed, ram pressure, and condition of dies, as well as the type of dies, test bends on scrap should be made to prove out the chart.

The chart will be very accurate when "bottoming" or "coining" with smaller internal bend radii.

"Air bending," especially with larger internal bend radii, will require some trial and error.

Press brake safety: When changing or setting up dies, always make sure the ram is at the bottom of its stroke.

Internal radius	020	025	031	040	050	062	080	090	093	119	125	187	250
1/64	034	040	050	067	076	090	116	130	134	168	176	258	344
1/32	042	048	058	068	082	098	122	138	140	176	182	266	350
3/64	046	054	064	072	088	102	128	144	146	182	188	272	356
1/16	054	062	070	080	096	110	136	152	154	188	196	278	364
3/32	068	074	084	094	110	124	150	164	168	202	208	292	378
1/8	082	088	098	108	124	138	162	178	180	216	222	326	390
3/16	108	116	124	134	150	164	190	206	208	242	250	332	448
1/4	136	142	152	162	176	190	216	232	234	270	276	360	469
3/8	188	196	206	214	232	244	270	286	288	322	330	412	499
1/2	242	250	258	268	284	288	324	340	342	356	384	466	552
1"	456	464	474	484	500	512	538	554	556	592	598	682	766

CHART 17-1 Bend Deduction Chart for 90° Bends

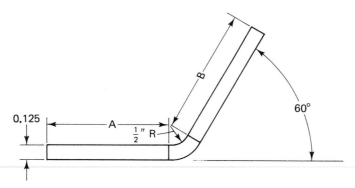

Figure 17-7 Bend
allowance formula.

formula, as its name indicates, was arrived at by trial and error and in thousands of shops has proven to be quite satisfactory.

The figures given in the bend deduction chart are arrived at by the application of the following additional formula: $2(R + T) \times$ the tangent of ½ the angle of bend, minus the bend allowance equals the bend deduction.

From the preceding explanations we see a difference between bend deduction and bend allowance. Originally developed for air frame fabrication, the bend allowance formula is for just 1 degree of bend angle and is illustrated in Figure 17-7. This is because it is easier to determine the flange lengths $A + B$ on the inside surface than on the outside surface if bends are other than either 90 or 45 degrees.

On the other hand, bend deduction charts utilize the enclosed angle, which is the supplement of the bent-up angle, the bent-up angle being the angle to which the part is actually bent. As indicated in Figure 17-8, the shear size is obtained by deducting the bend deduction number from the total of the outside mold line dimensions. A bend deduction number must be deducted for each bend to be made.

Rule: *To determine the shear size of a flat pattern, total the outside dimensions as given on the print for each flange. Multiply the required bend deduction figure from the chart by the number of bends. Deduct the total bend deduction from the total of all the flange dimensions.*

A flange is defined as being any flat surface or plane that results from a bending operation. In Figure 17-9, three bends form four separate flanges.

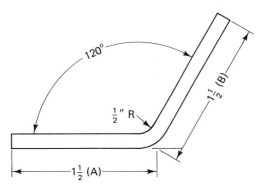

Bend deduction for 120° = 0.140
A + B = 3.000
3.000 − 0.140 = 2.860 (shear size)

Figure 17-8 Bend
deduction formula.

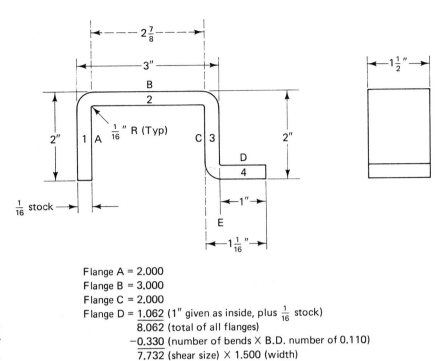

Flange A = 2.000
Flange B = 3.000
Flange C = 2.000
Flange D = 1.062 (1″ given as inside, plus $\frac{1}{16}$ stock)
         8.062 (total of all flanges)
       −0.330 (number of bends × B.D. number of 0.110)
         7.732 (shear size) × 1.500 (width)

Figure 17-9 Three
bends result in four
flanges.

The mechanic must be careful at this point to read the print accurately as to "inside" or "outside" dimensioning. Flange D in the example is shown to be an inside dimension. If the extension line, labeled E, were moved to the left, as represented by the dashed line, to include the stock thickness, it would then be read as an outside dimension. Similarly, if the flange labeled B in the example were dimensioned as indicated by the dashed extension lines, that would also be an inside dimension. In that instance two material thicknesses would have to be added so that it could be calculated as an outside dimension in using the bend deduction formula.

The dimension and extension lines on the blueprint must be accurately and clearly drawn to show this critical difference. So, too, the mechanic must accurately interpret the intent of the draftsperson. Why a dimension would be drawn one way or the other depends on the function of the part. If the 3-inch dimension was intended to allow the part in Figure 17-9 to fit into something, it would be drawn as shown, an "outside" dimension. If the part was meant to fit over another mating part, the same dimension would be drawn as an "inside" dimension. But regardless of how the print is dimensioned, the mechanic must always work with the outside dimensions to use the bend deduction chart and for the balance of the layout procedure. Whereas the completed bent-up part may have any number of inside or outside dimensions, the flat pattern can only have outside dimensions. The shear size for the part shown in the figure is 7.732 by 1.500.

**DETERMINING THE
BANK CORNER OF
THE FLAT PATTERN**

Before dimensioning of the flat pattern can begin, a starting point must be found. Does dimensioning start from the left side? the right side? the top? or the bottom? A well-drawn print will have most, if not all of its measurements starting from the same "corner." This corner denotes the adjacent zero edges from which all dimensioning of the flat pattern must begin. Figure 17-10 illustrates this critical determination. Accuracy is dependent on the layout being dimensioned exactly the same way the blueprint was originally drawn.

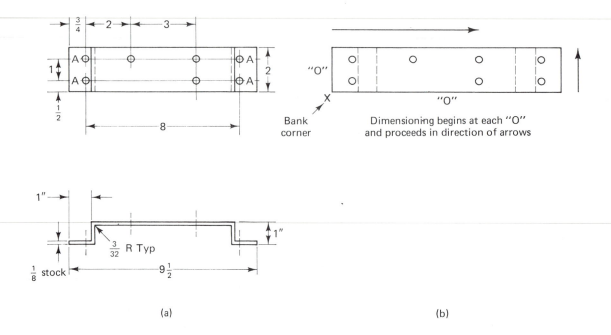

Figure 17-10   Bank corner determination: (a) print; (b) layout.

DIMENSIONING THE LAYOUT

Now that the bank corner and the 0 starting edges have been determined, the next step is to draw a single extension line from the details to a point beyond the perimeter of the layout. Single-line dimensioning by definition states that all dimensions begin from 0 or any assigned datum line and have the advantage of lending simplicity and clarity to the layout sketch.

Reading from the print and with pencil in hand, the mechanic now proceeds to dimension the layout.

Rule: To dimension the layout: Starting from 0, total all the individual outside dimensions leading up to the detail in question. Subtract a bend deduction for each bend passed on the way to the detail. Complete in each direction for all X and Y coordinate locations.

An example is given in Figure 17-11.

In Figure 17-12, the example that was used in determining the bank corner, Figure 17-10, can now be used to illustrate the application of the rule stated above. However, notice that the flat pattern has been rotated so that it would stand on its shorter 0 edge during the layout on the surface plate with the height gauge. There is no hard-and-fast rule, but common practice is to dimension the long way first, calling those dimensions the X coordinates and then designating the narrower direction the Y coordinates. On these examples the differences are obvious, but on layouts which are close to or actually square, this differentiation is critically important. On these two examples, notice that any fractional dimensions given are always converted to a decimal to enable quick and direct computation. Also, see that the bend lines are not dimensioned, as most precision bending would be done on a press brake (see Chapter 15) and would not be required. However, if the bending is to be done on the finger brake or if some detail happened to be located on the bend line, the dashed line that represents the bend should be dimensioned (see Chapter 15). Recall that the actual bend line falls halfway through the entire bend deduction. Thus, for the example given in Figure 17-11, the bend line dimension from 0 would be 1.195 (flange, 1.250 minus ½ of 0.110 equals 1.250 minus 0.055). In dimensioning the bend lines

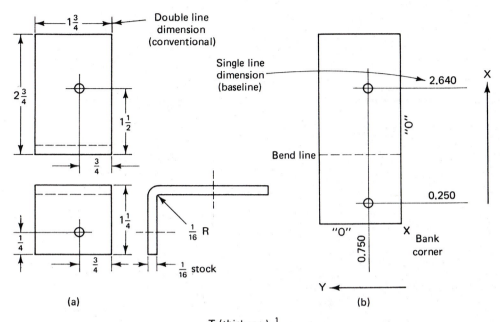

Figure 17-11 Flat pattern dimensioning: (a) print; (b) layout.

T (thickness) $\frac{1}{16}$

R (radius) $\frac{1}{16}$

BD (bend deduction) 0.110

SS (shear size) 3.890 × 1.750

on the example in Figure 17-12, you must follow through, from "0," each half, then each full bend in turn. The bend line labeled 1 would be 1.021 (1.000 plus 0.125 material thickness or total outside dimension of 1.125 minus 0.104). Bend line 2 is 1.813 (flange A, 1.125 plus flange B, 1.000,

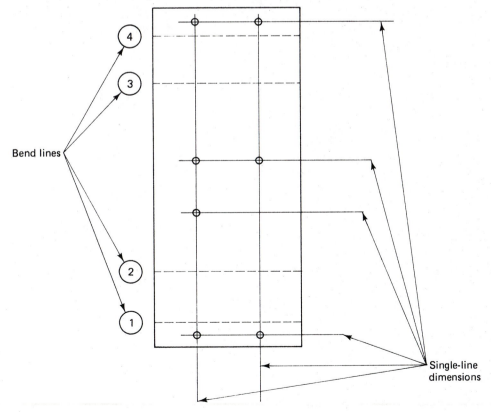

Figure 17-12 Another exercise in flat pattern dimensioning (see Fig. 17-10).

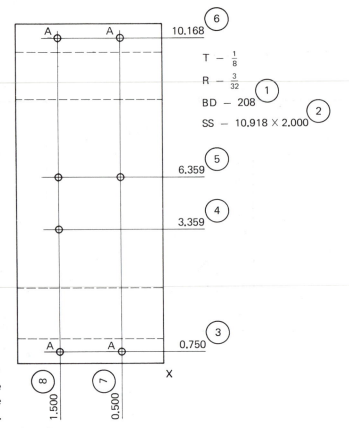

Figure 17-13 Complete dimensioning of the layout (see Fig. 17-12).

minus 1½ bend deductions, 0.312). To figure bend line 3, total flanges A, B, and C, then deduct 2½ bend deductions (bend line 3 = 9.105). Finally, for bend line 4 add up flanges A, B, C, and D from which 3½ bend deductions are subtracted (bend line 4 = 9.897).

To further illustrate and reinforce the rules for determining shear size and for dimensioning the layout, the flat pattern in Figure 17-12 will be completely dimensioned, except for the bend lines, which ordinarily would not be done but was just explained. Following this, each numbered dimension will be accompanied by the computations required (see Fig. 17-13).

DIMENSION 1: 0.208 (bend deduction). From the bend deduction chart and from the print, bending ⅛-inch-thick material over a ³⁄₃₂-inch radius requires this number.

DIMENSION 2: 10.918 × 2.000 (shear size)

From the print:		
	1.000	(flange)
	0.125	(material thickness to make an outside dimension)
	1.000	(flange height)
	7.500	(derived from 9½ overall length minus two 1-inch flanges)
	1.000	(second flange height)
	+ 1.125	(second outside dimension)
Total	11.750	
208 B.D. times four bends =	− 0.832	(total bend deduction subtracted)
	10.918	(length of piece to be sheared)
	2.000	(width of part from print, no bends involved)

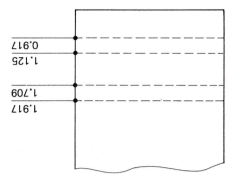

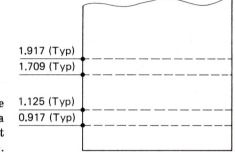

Figure 17-17 Outside mold lines scribed on a flat pattern layout template.

1.917 (Typ)
1.709 (Typ)
1.125 (Typ)
0.917 (Typ)

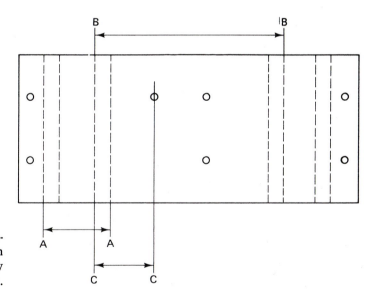

Figure 17-18 Measuring distances between mold lines to verify print dimensions.

tion. That location is 1.917. Subtracting one more bend deduction places a line at 1.709.

Note: The notation Typ (typical) on the print indicates that the same dimension exists for an identical set of details, while on a layout, it indicates that the calculated dimension is the same from the opposite edge.

    With the template or first piece so laid out with the outside dimension mold lines from the print scribed on the flat layout, it is now possible to check any or all print dimensions on the layout before any holes are punched or bends are made (see Fig. 17-18).

    Using a scale, the outside dimension between lines A and A is verified as 1 inch (from print, Fig. 17-10). The distance between lines B and B is as per print, 7½ inches. The measurement between C and C is also correct at 1¾ inches. Checking those dimensions determined as being typical can also verify the accuracy of the shear size.

DIMENSION 3: 0.750. Direct from print from bank edge "0." No bend line passed.

DIMENSION 4: 3.459.

From "0":   first flange 1.125 (outside)
              second flange 1.000 (as given on print)
Dimension from
  bend to first hole   1.750 (derived from given print dimensions, 1 inch minus ¾ inch equals ¼ inch to be subtracted from the 2-inch dimension given to hole)
                        + _____
          Total 3.875
                        − 0.416 two bend deductions (0.208 × 2)
                           3.459

DIMENSION 5: 6.459. From print; simple addition of 3 inches to dimension 4.

                3.459
             + 3.000
                6.459

DIMENSION 6: 10.168. Adding up individual dimensions as given on print or as derived from print.

From 0   1.125 (first flange, outside measurement)
                  1.000 (second flange height)
                  7.500 (third flange dimension derived from print)
                  1.000 (fourth flange, down other side)
                  0.375 (derived from print) from the fourth bend line to the hole is 0.250 which is an inside dimension; adding 0.125 material thickness equals 0.375
                + _____
          Total 11.000
Minus four B.D. − 0.832 (0.208 × 4)
                 10.168

DIMENSION 7: 0.500. Direct from print from bank edge 0. No bend line involved.

DIMENSION 8: 1.500. From print, simple addition of 1.000 to dimension 7.

                0.500
             + 1.000
                1.500

CHECKING THE LAYOUT The mechanic, especially functioning in a lead capacity, will have the responsibility for making layouts and templates that will be used for longer production runs. It is axiomatic that one is paid not so much for what one produces but for how much one is responsible for. What is now required are methods

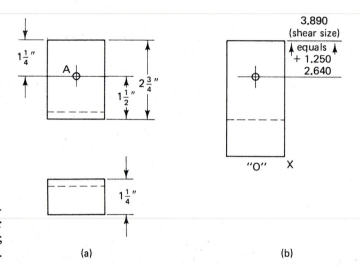

Figure 17-14 Verifying the layout and shear size: (1) print; (b) layout.

(a)   (b)

to be devised for checking the dimensioned layout for complete accuracy before committing it to production.

The word "devised" is the key to the concept of layout checking. There are no hard-and-fast rules, but rather the careful mechanic will try to find more than one way of coming up with the same layout dimension. For example, refer to the single bend part illustrated in Figure 17-14. The print indicates that the center of the hole labeled A is 1½ inches above the bend. If the overall flange height is 2¾ inches, the distance remaining to the top edge of the flange is 1¼ inches (2.750 − 1.500 = 1.250). Take this remainder (1.250) and add it to the calculated dimension from the bottom 0 edge of 2.640 on the layout. The resulting total is 3.890 and, as it should be, equal to the shear size. Thus, not only has the 2.640 dimension been double checked, but the shear size has also been verified. Referring back to the four-bend layout in Figure 17-13, the same method of double checking can be employed. The dimension of 10.168 was arrived at after several different computations were made, including the use of four-bend deductions. Not only would a misreading of the print be possible, but a simple mistake in either addition or subtraction would make the part worthless. The question the mechanic should ask is: Is the 10.168 correct? The print (Fig. 17-10) shows that the part is symmetrical as far as the two sets of holes labeled A are concerned. Being "symmetrical" means that if either a real or an imagined center line divided any two sets of details, they would be equal in dimensional location on both sides of that center line (see Fig. 17-15). In this case we know that the overall length of the part is 9½ inches (Fig. 17-10). We also see that the distance between the two sets of A holes is 8 inches, with the distance of the first set of holes being ¾ inch from the bank edge. Thus, if the total distance from the bank edge to the second set of holes is 8¾ inches, the balance needed to total 9½ inches is also ¾ inch. Therefore,

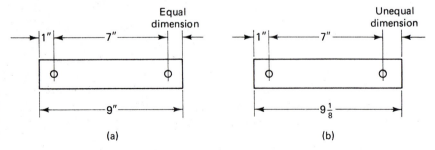

Figure 17-15 Examples of (a) a symmetrical and (b) an asymmetrical layout.

(a)   (b)

adding ¾ inch to the *CALCULATED DIMENSION* of 10.168 on the layout should equal the shear size first derived when starting the job (10.168 + 0.750 = 10.918).

As mentioned, mistakes in layout, even by experienced mechanics, are often in making simple computations. Upon analysis, each layout will present several opportunities for such double checking as explained. The place to find the mistake is in the template and first piece and not after 100 pieces have been sheared or 1000 punched holes are found to be 0.050 inch out of place.

USING THE HAND CALCULATOR

By the work done so far in layout, it is obvious that most if not all of the computations are merely a sequence of additions and subtractions. Depending solely on a calculator is not at all advisable when you consider the following. Suppose that in arriving at the 10.168 dimension a typical hand calculator was used. When adding the final ¾ inch it was found that it did not agree with the shear size. Where is the error? Simple additions and subtractions done on paper provide an accurate record for checking. If your work was accurate, the error could very well be on the print, as designers and drafters can also make mistakes. There are calculators with roll printouts, but it would still be more desirable to rely on a quick and agile mind than the fading batteries in a machine. Of course, in working with powers and roots and trigonometric functions involving long multiplications, the hand calculator is a great help.

MOLD LINE VERIFICATION

The checking and rechecking of calculated dimensions may still prove to be inadequate when contemplating the cost of revision or even scrapping after production has started. There is a method of not only proving that the calculated layout dimensions are correct but that the dimensional information given on the print is also correct and was correctly interpreted. The method involves placing the outside mold lines on the flat pattern. Figure 17-16 recalls the location and function of these lines.

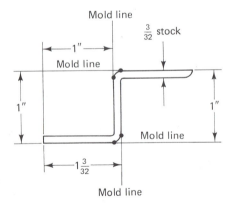

Figure 17-16 Location of the outside mold lines.

The dots indicate the actual location of these lines on the flat version of the bent-up part. Recall that the distance between them, around the external radius, represents the bend deduction.

With the height gauge, scribe the first outside mold line at 1.125 from the bank edge (see Fig. 17-17). This is usually done as a dashed line so as not to confuse it with a coordinate line. Next, subtract the bend deduction (0.208) and scribe that line at 0.917. The next mold line location is arrived at by adding the flanges 1.125 and 1.000 and subtracting one bend deduc-

TYPICAL LAYOUT PROBLEM The following exercise will not only demonstrate instances where details are actually located on bend lines but will also show the basic procedure for the layout of mitered corners. Figure 17-19 is a blueprint rendition and Figure 17-20 is the flat pattern layout for the same part.

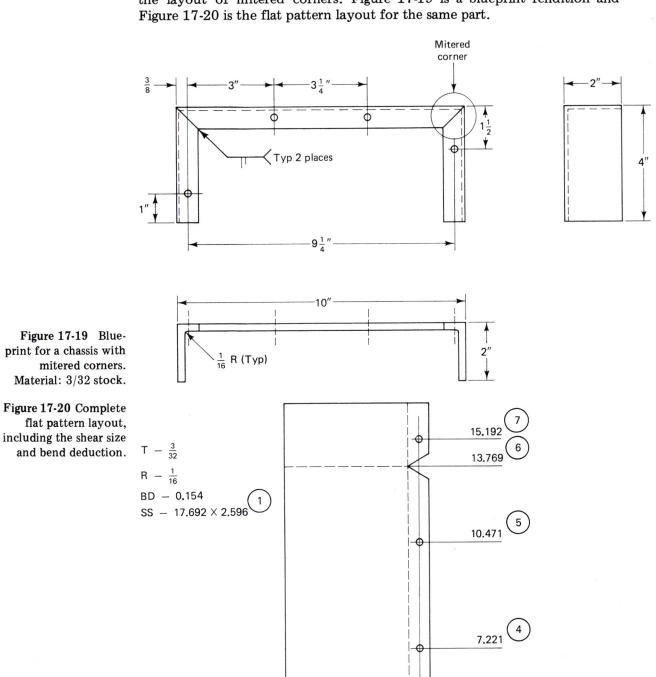

Figure 17-19 Blueprint for a chassis with mitered corners. Material: 3/32 stock.

Figure 17-20 Complete flat pattern layout, including the shear size and bend deduction.

The computations that are required for the layout as well as two additional computations that can be used as a double check are as follows:

DIMENSION 1: Shear size 17.692 × 2.596.

From print, add	4.000	(flange)
	10.000	(flange)
	+ 4.000	(flange)
	18.000	
Bend deduction (³⁄₃₂ thick, ¹⁄₁₆R) equals 0.154 × 2 =	− 0.308	
	17.692	

In other direction:	2.000	(flange)
	+ 0.750	(flange)
	2.750	
Bend deduction 0.154 × 1 =	− 0.154	
	2.596	

Complete shear size is 17.692 × 2.596.

DIMENSION 2: 1.000. Direct reading from print.

DIMENSION 3: 3.923. Bend line location for vee notch.

4.000	(flange)
− 0.077	(½ of bend deduction)
3.923	

DIMENSION 4: 7.221.

4.000	(flange)
+ 3.375	(hole location given plus ³⁄₈ inch as per print)
7.375	
− 0.154	(bend deduction)
7.221	

DIMENSION 5: 10.471.

7.221	(previous dimension)
+ 3.250	(from print)
10.471	

DIMENSION 6: 13.769. Bend line location for vee notch.

4.000	(flange)
+ 10.000	(flange)
14.000	
0.231	(1½ bend deductions)
13.769	

DIMENSION 7:   15.192.

```
      4.000   (flange)
     10.000   (flange)
   + 1.500    (from print)
     15.500
   - 0.308    (two bend deductions)
     15.192
```

DIMENSION 8:   1.923. Bend line location for depth of vee notch.

```
      2.000   (flange)
   - 0.077    (½ bend deduction)
      1.923
```

DIMENSION 9:   2.221.

```
      2.000   (flange)
   + 0.375    (from print)
      2.375
   - 0.154    (one bend deduction)
      2.221
```

To check: Take dimension 7, 15.192. Add remaining distance from the last hole to the end of the flange; 4.000 minus 1.500 equals 2.500. 17.692 is equal to shear size.

```
     15.192
   + 2.500
     17.692
```

Take dimension 9, 2.221. Add remaining distance from hole to edge of flange; 0.750 minus 0.375 equals 0.375. 2.596 is equal to shear size.

```
      2.221
   + 0.375
      2.596
```

Note: The outside mold lines could also be laid out on the part as previously described.

On this particular part, two additional points can be brought out to further clarify basic sheet metal fabrication methods.

First, in the actual making of the 90-degree notch required to form the mitered corner, all that is needed is an X and Y coordinate location for the point of the notcher described in Chapter 16. As the blade arrangement on the machine forms a 90-degree cutout, no other layout dimensioning is required. However, careful alignment with the cutting knives is necessary (see Fig. 17-21). The second point has to do with the use of bend reliefs, which was discussed in Chapter 15 but is worth reviewing here.

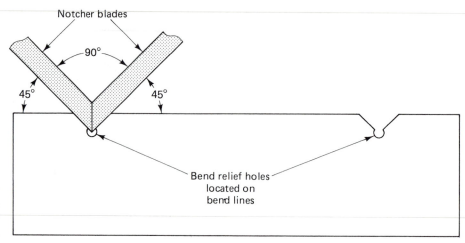

Figure 17-21 Alignment of the part with cutting blades for miter cutouts.

BEND RELIEFS   Bend relief holes are often called for in cases as just described and wherever two bent flanges form a 90-degree angle. Bend relief holes are located directly on the bend line on the layout. Their primary value is in eliminating the notch crack effect as the material is stretched and bent (see Fig. 17-22). The use of bend reliefs also allows for easier bending in providing a little extra room for any overbending needed to overcome a "spring-back" tendency.

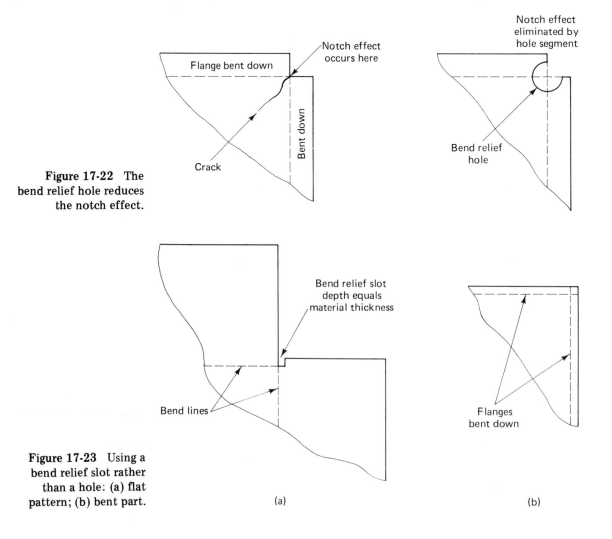

Figure 17-22 The bend relief hole reduces the notch effect.

Figure 17-23 Using a bend relief slot rather than a hole: (a) flat pattern; (b) bent part.

(a)

(b)

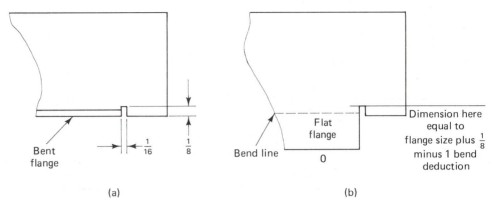

Figure 17-24 Bend relief slot that must be accurately dimensioned: (a) print view; (b) pattern layout.

The use of bend relief holes may not be expressly called out on the print and are used at the discretion of the mechanic. The size of such holes is related to the thickness of the material and the internal bend radius. If the bend radius is from "0" on up to the material thickness, the bend relief hole is twice the material thickness. For example, for $\frac{1}{16}$-inch material with up to a $\frac{1}{16}$-inch radius, a $\frac{1}{8}$-inch-diameter bend relief hole is required. Where the radius begins to exceed the material thickness and also depending on the ductility of the metal being bent, larger reliefs may be called for.

In some cases a bend relief slot rather than a hole may be better suited (see Fig. 17-23). If the bend relief slot is dimensioned on the print, it must be accurately executed (see Fig. 17-24).

NOTCHED CORNER CONSTRUCTION

Figure 17-25 illustrates several variations in the way a corner joint can be specified on a blueprint. In sketch (a) the location of the notch line and the bend line can be clearly seen to be a certain distance apart. However, in the same figure, other instances are shown where the dimensional implications for layout are not so apparent.

In order to bend adjoining flanges so that they form the desired corner, a notch cutout must be made in that corner of the flat layout. The notch line and the bend line must be of different dimension from the 0 bank edges to provide room for the flanges to be bent the full 90 degrees. This difference between the mathematical location of the bend line and the notch line may only be a few thousandths of an inch, but as material thickness and internal bend radii increase, this difference becomes significant.

Corner construction may be clearly specified on the print or may be left to the discretion of the mechanic as long as the overall dimensional requirements are satisfied. The type of corner then will be based on the method of joining that will be used, if any, and the bending sequence needed to complete the part.

To illustrate the dimensional implications in the transition from blueprint to layout, assume that the material for the parts in Figure 17-25 is $\frac{1}{16}$-inch thick and an internal bend radii of $\frac{1}{16}$ is used in each case. From the bend deduction chart, 0.110 (thousandths) is found to be the required bend deduction. Also, for the purpose of illustration, each of the flange sizes will be 1 inch (1.000).

Using the rule for flat pattern layout, the notch line for the part in sketch (a) is 1.445. The bend line location is 1.000 minus 0.055 or 0.945.

In sketch (b) the material is notched just past the bend line of each flange so as to form the typical "corner-to-corner" welded joint. The layout of sketch (b) clearly shows the close, but still different, notch and bend line dimensions.

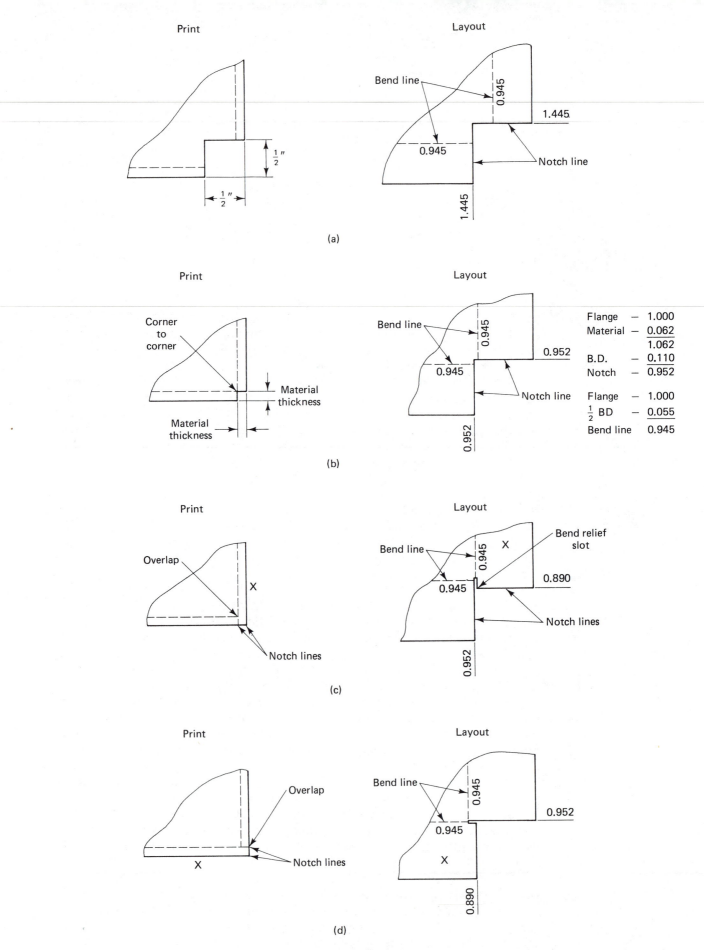

Figure 17-25 Laying out the notched corner.

Sketch (c) shows an overlapping corner joint. The print indicates that the notch line for flange X is not cut back a material thickness as in sketch (b). Thus the flat pattern dimension would be 1.000 minus a bend deduction or 0.890. However, as shown, the other flange would have to be notched exactly as in sketch (b) to allow it to fit inside flange X.

Sketch (d) shows the same overlapping configuration, but the new designation of flange X relocates the derived dimensions of the notch lines.

In determining a bending sequence for the part in either sketch (c) or (d), the flange labeled X would have to be bent first. This would allow the slight overbending often required to overcome any spring-back tendency of the material.

BOLT CIRCLE LAYOUTS   Sheet metal layouts will often require the incorporation of a series of holes laid out in a circle rather than on a basic X and Y location. Figure 17-26 shows such a situation together with a typical blueprint note.

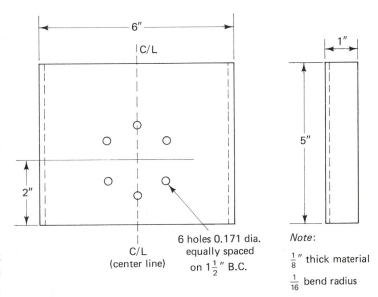

Figure 17-26 Blueprint drawing with a bolt circle requirement.

The bolt circle chart (Chart 17-2) makes possible the laying out of each individual hole on the basic X and Y coordinate location with perfect accuracy to within an actual 1 thousandth of an inch. Without the chart it would be necessary to construct a series of triangles and to make extensive use of trigonometry in figuring out the location of each hole. Moreover, the actual layout would require the use of a protractor, dividers, and essentially, only "eyeballed" scribed lines. Such methods would not meet the requirements of precision sheet metal fabrication.

Because Chart 17-2 uses logarithmic constants, any bolt circle diameter can be laid out, making the chart suitable for plate fabrication involving larger dimensions.

USING THE BOLT CIRCLE CHART   First, a flat pattern location for the theoretical or actual center of the bolt circle must be found (see Fig. 17-27). These dimensions are 3.890 and 2.000.

The appropriate single-line extensions are added in respect to the bank corner. For purposes of explanation only, the holes are labeled A, B, C, D, E, and F.

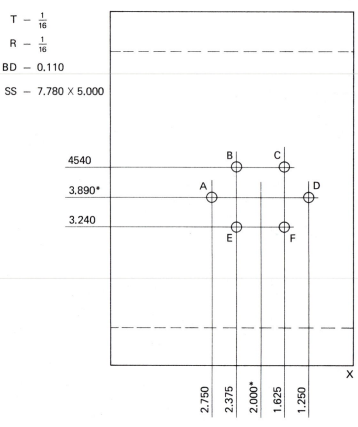

T — $\frac{1}{16}$

R — $\frac{1}{16}$

BD — 0.110

SS — 7.780 × 5.000

4540

3.890*

3.240

B C

A D

E F

X

2.750 2.375 2.000* 1.625 1.250

*Center location of
bolt circle pattern

Figure 17-27 Flat layout sketch of a part with the bolt circle hole pattern (Fig. 17-26, rotated 90°).

Chart 17-2 indicates the use of figure 3, the six-hole layout. The holes labeled A and D are located immediately as they fall on the line dimensioned as 3.890. The holes labeled B and C can be located by finding the value of A on the chart. To do this, multiply 0.433 (three-place decimal is accurate enough) by 1.500 (the diameter of the bolt circle). A is found to be 0.650. Working up from 3.890, holes B and C are at 4.540. The value A is again used, working down to locate holes E and F, so then subtract 0.650 from 3.890 (equals 3.240). This completes the X coordinates.

In figuring the Y coordinates, hole D falls on the radius of the specified 1.500-inch bolt circle. Thus its location is 2.000 minus 0.750 or 1.250. Hole A is similarly located (2.750). Holes F and C are determined by finding the value of B on the chart and adding it to 1.250 (1.625). Finding the value of C on the chart and adding that dimension to 1.625 will give the location of holes E and B (2.375).

Layouts such as this can be verified by setting the points of a pair of dividers to the 0.750 radius and scribing a 1½-inch circle on the laid-out pattern. The scribed circle should bisect each of the coordinate locations (see Fig. 17-28).

One final note: On this layout, see that the part is not symmetrical in respect to the flanges and the location of the bolt circle (see Fig. 17-29). While the center line location of the 6-inch dimension is symmetrical, the 2-inch dimension is not. The implication here is that if the part is not bent in the right direction, a mirror image of the print rendition, which may be in error, will result. In such situations an additional note can be made on the layout (see Fig. 17-30).

CONCLUSION The examples shown so far cover some of the more typical layout situations that are encountered. The method for determining shear size as well as for locating the bank corner and dimensioning the flat pattern are applicable to any and all precision sheet metal assignments. The reader need only apply

CHART 17-2 Bolt Circle Chart

TYPICAL BOLT CIRCLE PATTERNS

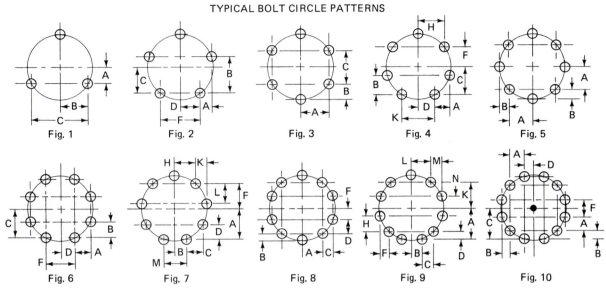

Fig. 1　　Fig. 2　　Fig. 3　　Fig. 4　　Fig. 5

Fig. 6　　Fig. 7　　Fig. 8　　Fig. 9　　Fig. 10

CONSTANTS USED FOR CALCULATING HOLE LOCATIONS
SPACED AROUND A CIRCLE

Fig. no.	No. of holes	Multiply value shown by diameter of circle being calculated									
		A	B	C	D	F	H	K	L	M	N
1	3	0.25000	0.43302	0.86603							
2	5	0.18164	0.55902	0.40451	0.29389	0.58779					
3	6	0.43302	0.25000	0.50000							
4	7	0.27052	0.33920	0.45049	0.21694	0.31175	0.39090	0.43388			
5	8	0.35355	0.14650	0.38263							
6	8	0.27059	0.27059	0.46194	0.19134	0.38268					
7	9	0.46985	0.17101	0.26200	0.21985	0.38302	0.32139	0.17101	0.29620	0.34202	
8	10	0.29389	0.09549	0.18164	0.25000	0.15451					
9	11	0.47975	0.14087	0.23701	0.15232	0.11704	0.25627	0.42063	0.27032	0.18449	0.21319
10	12	0.22415	0.12941	0.48297	0.12941	0.25882					

Note: In precision sheet metal applications it is only necessary to use a three-place decimal.

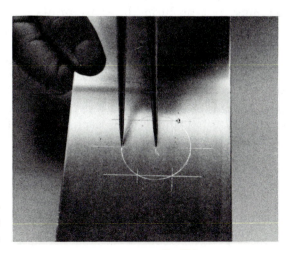

Figure 17-28 Verifying the bolt circle layout.

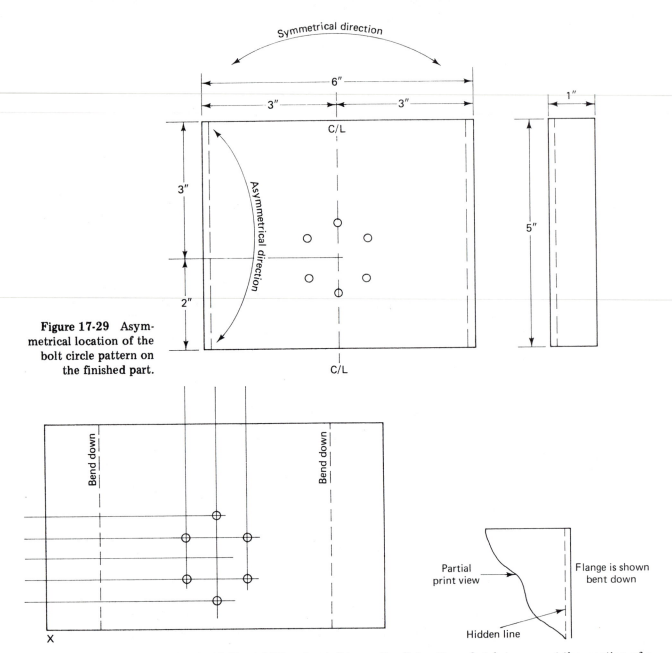

Figure 17-29 Asymmetrical location of the bolt circle pattern on the finished part.

Figure 17-30 Additional notation on the flat pattern sketch to prevent the creation of a "mirror image" of the given print view (see Fig. 17-29).

some additional common sense, logic, and employ basic mathematical competencies in order to go on to more complex and involved work. In doing so the reader must not be intimidated by prints that appear to be a maze of lines coupled with seemingly endless dimensional requirements.

The only difference between more detailed work and that which has been outlined here is simply a matter of time. A part with 100 holes and eight bends is going to take more time to lay out than a part with four holes and one bend.

At the end of this chapter there are two additional blueprint references, Figs. 17-31 and 17-33. Printed with each will be found the completely dimensioned flat patterns (Figs. 17-32 and 17-34). Fig. 17-35 is an actual photograph of the finished parts. Also will be found the completely dimensioned flat pattern for the electronic chassis shown in Figures 17-1 and 17-2. These are Fig. 17-36 and Fig. 17-37. The reader should attempt to develop and dimension a flat pattern working only from the blueprint of the part with its accompanying views, then reconcile the arrived-at dimensions with the correct layouts provided.

244

EXERCISE 1

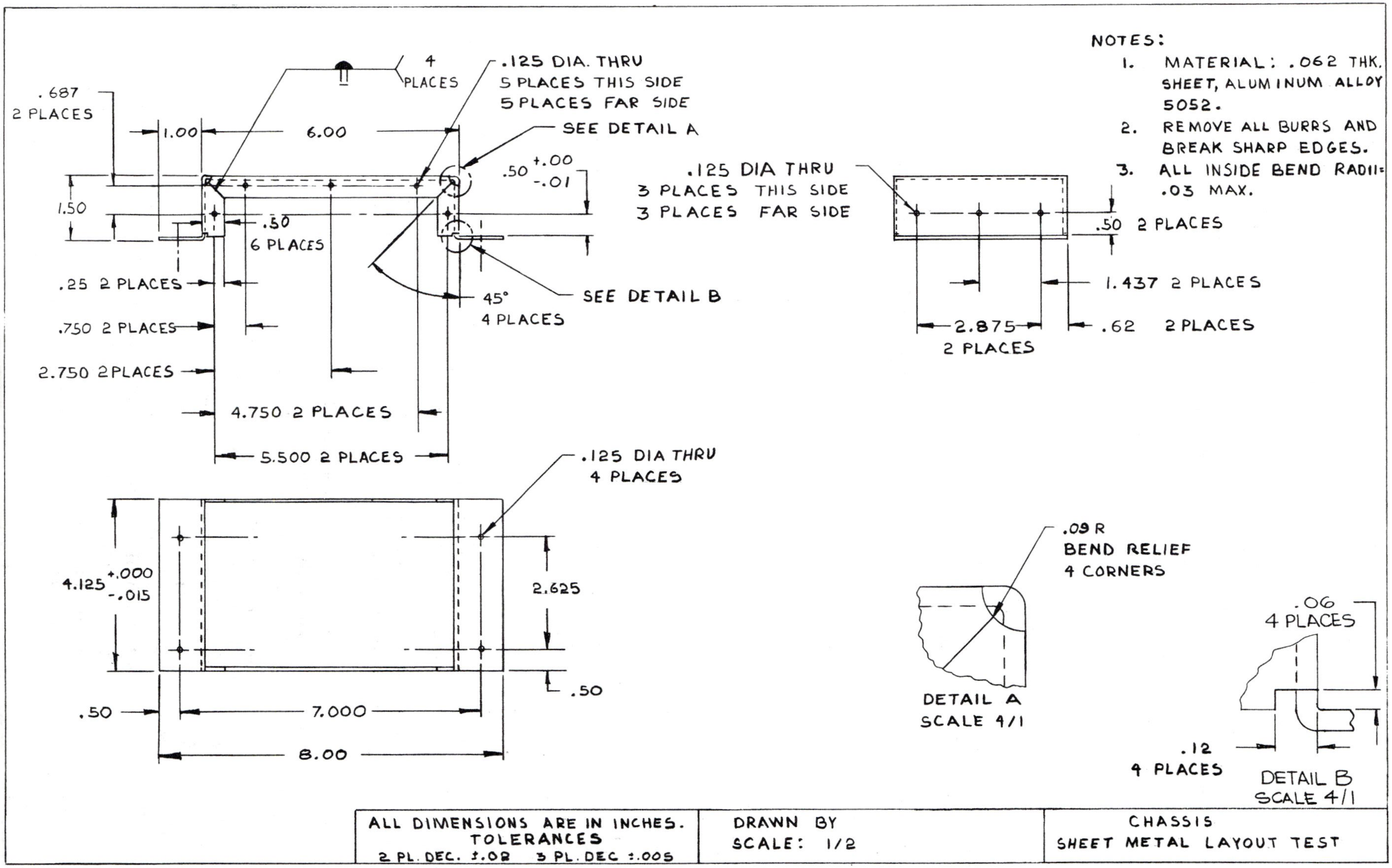

NOTES:
1. MATERIAL: .062 THK. SHEET, ALUMINUM ALLOY 5052.
2. REMOVE ALL BURRS AND BREAK SHARP EDGES.
3. ALL INSIDE BEND RADII .03 MAX.

.50
1.437 2 PLACES
.62   2 PLACES
.50 2 PLACES
2.875
2 PLACES

.125 DIA THRU
3 PLACES THIS SIDE
3 PLACES FAR SIDE
SEE DETAIL B

.125 DIA THRU
5 PLACES THIS SIDE
5 PLACES FAR SIDE
SEE DETAIL A

.50 +.00 -.01

45°
4 PLACES

4 PLACES

6.00

1.00

.687
2 PLACES

1.50

.50
6 PLACES

.25 2 PLACES
.750 2 PLACES
2.750 2 PLACES

4.750 2 PLACES
5.500 2 PLACES

.125 DIA THRU
4 PLACES

2.625

.50

7.000

8.00

4.125 +.000 -.015

.50

.09 R
BEND RELIEF
4 CORNERS

DETAIL A
SCALE 4/1

.06
4 PLACES

.12
4 PLACES

DETAIL B
SCALE 4/1

CHASSIS
SHEET METAL LAYOUT TEST

ALL DIMENSIONS ARE IN INCHES.
TOLERANCES
2 PL. DEC. ±.02   3 PL. DEC. ±.005

DRAWN BY
SCALE: 1/2

Figure 17-31 Layout Exercise #1.

245

Instructional notes:

1. The layout sketch need not be dimensionally accurate, only a fair representation.

2. Refer to text for the use of the term "Typ" on the layout.

3. Refer to text for use of bend reliefs.

T — 0.062

R — $\frac{1}{32}$

B.D. — 0.098

SS — 10.732 × 4.929

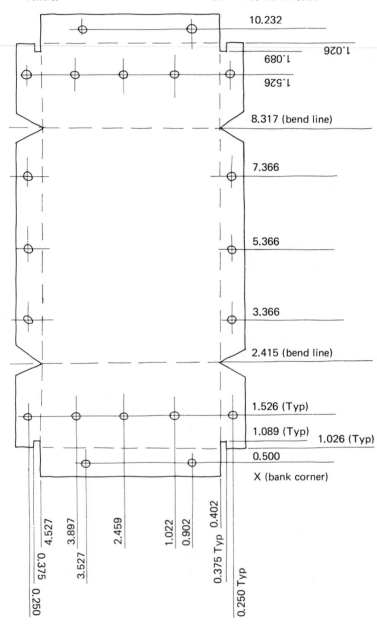

10.232

1.026

1.089

1.526

8.317 (bend line)

7.366

5.366

3.366

2.415 (bend line)

1.526 (Typ)

1.089 (Typ)   1.026 (Typ)

0.500

X (bank corner)

4.527

3.897

3.527

2.459

1.022

0.902

0.375 Typ   0.402

0.375 Typ

0.250

0.250 Typ

Figure 17-32 Flat pattern layout sketch for Exercise #1.

EXERCISE 2

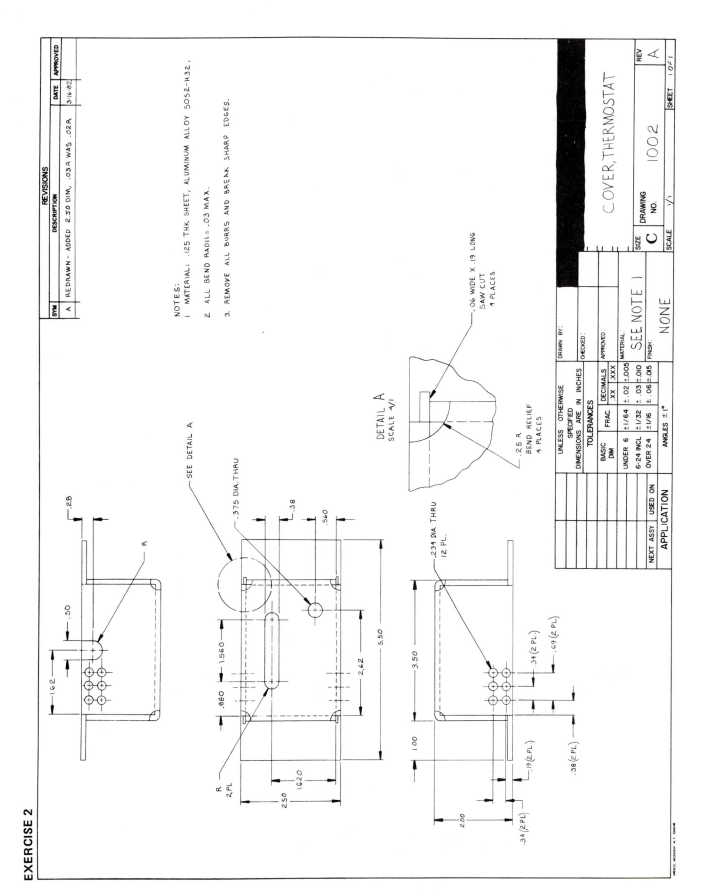

Figure 17-33 Layout Exercise #2.

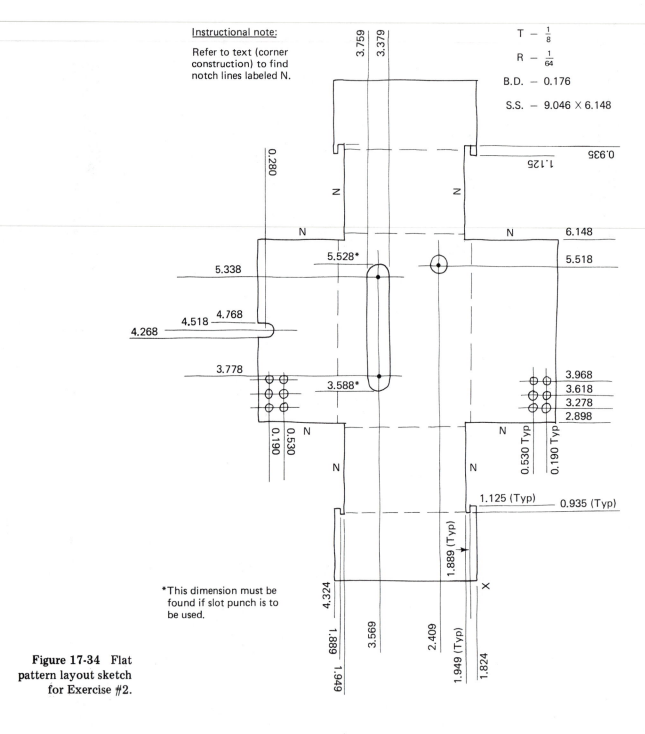

Figure 17-34 Flat pattern layout sketch for Exercise #2.

Figure 17-35 Completed items—Exercises #1 and #2.

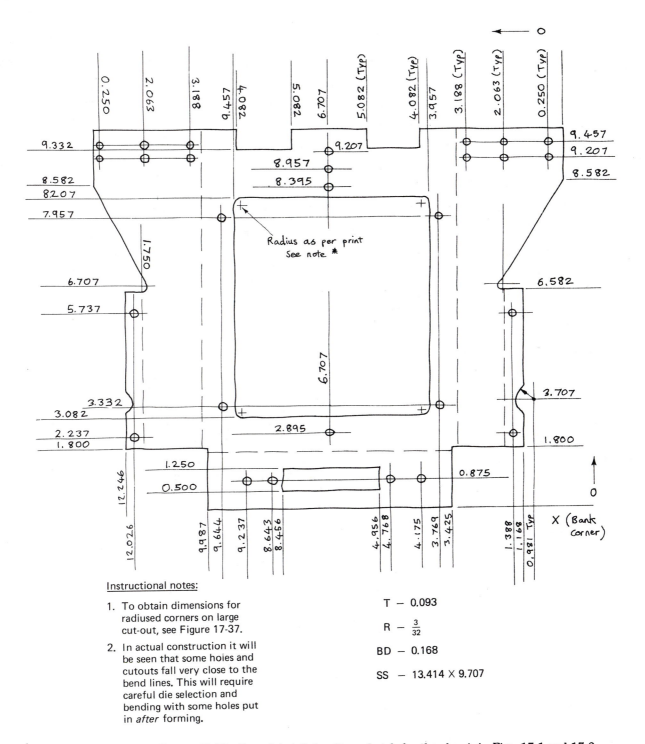

Instructional notes:

1. To obtain dimensions for radiused corners on large cut-out, see Figure 17-37.

2. In actual construction it will be seen that some holes and cutouts fall very close to the bend lines. This will require careful die selection and bending with some holes put in *after* forming.

T — 0.093

R — $\frac{3}{32}$

BD — 0.168

SS — 13.414 X 9.707

Figure 17-36 Completed flat pattern sketch for the chassis in Figs. 17-1 and 17-2.

249

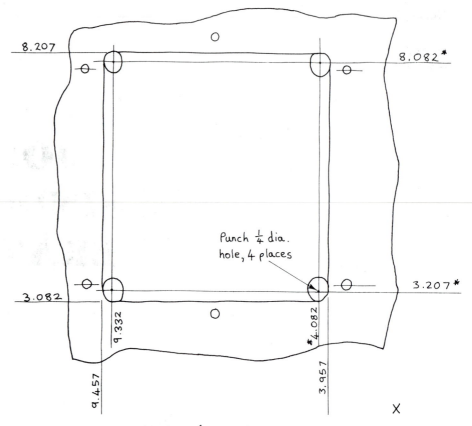

Figure 17-37 Layout
of radiused corners
(Fig. 17-36).

*Radius of $\frac{1}{8}$ is added or subtracted from
the appropriate layout dimension of the
cutout. A $\frac{1}{4}$ "-dia. hole is punched to
form the $\frac{1}{8}$ " radius at each corner. The
balance of the cutout can be nibbled out
with an appropriate rectangular slot punch.

Chapter 18

JOINING and FINISHING OPERATIONS

The fabrication of precision sheet metal assemblies must anticipate the method that will be employed to join and/or seal the mating edges and joints. The practicality of application as well as the limitations of any particular method should be considered during the initial planning stages of manufacture.

Considerations in the frabrication of the various joint types include not only machine capacities, but dimensional implications as well as additional time and material allowances. Figure 18-1 illustrates some standard sheet metal joints together with several variations.

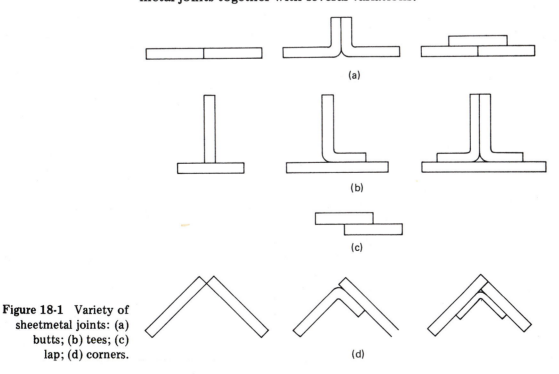

Figure 18-1 Variety of sheetmetal joints: (a) butts; (b) tees; (c) lap; (d) corners.

In order to intelligently select a joint design of one type or another, the fabricator must have a knowledge of the mechanics of the joining method selected.

FUSION WELDING
(Fig. 18-2)

As its name implies, fusion welding is the melting together of two mating edges. Generally, welding is considered where maximum strength is of primary importance. In precision sheet metal work, welding is most efficiently accomplished with the gas tungsten arc welding process (GTAW), or TIG as it is more commonly referred to. This process produces bright, clean welds with no flux and minimum distortion.

Oxyacetylene welding is applicable in sheet metal work but because of relatively low heat input the welding progresses much more slowly, causing excessive distortion and discoloration of the parts. It is very difficult to maintain dimensional accuracy under such conditions.

Figure 18-2 Fusion-welded joint.

Arc welding with stick electrodes usually proves too unstable when joining the thin sections encountered in sheet metal work. Problems of porosity as well as distortion are also evident. Arc welding also requires extensive slag removal and weld dressing.

The four primary concerns in fusion welding are:

1. Joint accessibility
2. Control of distortion
3. Dimensional stability
4. Weld dressing and cleanup

RESISTANCE
SPOT WELDING
(Fig. 18-3)

This process is highly mechanical in that it can make a large number of repetitive welds with basic limitations as to material thickness and again, joint accessibility. Joint type is limited to that of the "lap" type. Electrically generated heat and high-pressure squeezing of the mating parts produce a nugget of weld which can be from ⅛ to ⅜ inch in diameter depending on material thickness. There are no cleanup problems and distortion is virtually eliminated.

A variation of this process, known as resistance seam welding, is capable of making leaktight joints on tanks and containers.

Figure 18-3 Spot-welding operation.

BRAZING (Fig. 18-4) Brazing, unlike fusion welding, does not melt the parts being joined. They are joined by the addition of a filler material which bonds the metal together by either capillary action (silver filler alloys) or molecular cohesion (bronze filler alloys).

As illustrated, this brazed joint is accomplished with the basic oxyacetylene setup. Fluxes are required to clean the base metals and to improve the flow of the filler materials. Although the process is quick and inexpensive, it is severely limited in precision sheet metal work when done with a hand torch. An exception to this would be the silver alloy brazing method in which very small amounts of filler material are required. Distortion is still the main problem in any form of torch brazing.

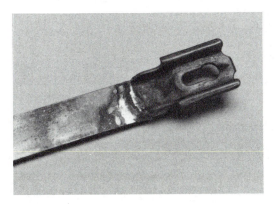

Figure 18-4 Brazed joint.

If the volume of production is enough to justify the outlay in equipment, repetitive joints can be efficiently brazed in gas-fired ovens (oven brazing) or by electrical induction heaters (induction brazing).

Another high-volume method, but also suited for single but complicated assemblies, is "dip brazing." Here the entire preassembled and prefluxed assembly is immersed in a bath of molten braze material. The braze flows only to the fluxed joint areas.

These batched brazing methods have the distinct advantage of controlling distortion to a great degree by evenly heating the work up to brazing temperature throughout its entire cross section. Also, the amount of filler material is controlled by the use of preformed rings and strips.

SOLDERING
(Fig. 18-5)

Soldering, using various combinations of tin and lead filler material, is much like a gluing process. The solder, by simple adhesion, holds the mating parts together; however, the strength of such joints is very low and should not at all be considered structural. Soldered joints should always be supplemented by a sort of mechanical configuration as shown in Figure 18-6.

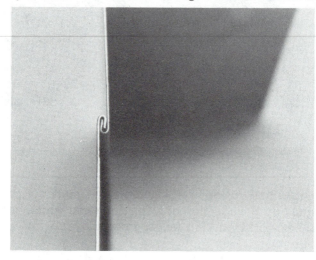

Figure 18-5 Joint designed for soldering. Note the mechanical connection.

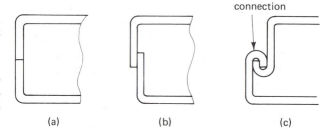

Figure 18-6 Joint designs appropriate for the joining method: (a) butt joint (welding); (b) lap joint (brazing); (c) grimped joint (solder).

(a) (b) Mechanical connection (c)

The primary advantages of soldering are in the excellent flow characteristics of the filler material, and there is practically no distortion because of the relatively low temperatures needed to melt the solder (300 to 400° F).

SCREWS

The use of machine screws and self-tapping screws is covered elsewhere in the text. However, in sheet metal assembly there are some additional considerations.

Where mating parts are simply to be bolted together, the tolerance of the clearance holes is much tighter. Whereas a ⅜-inch (0.375) bolt would require a $^{13}/_{32}$ (0.406) hole in plate fabrication, a typical sheet metal clearance would be $^{25}/_{64}$ (0.390) for the same ⅜-inch bolt.

For very close tolerance assembly, the use of dowel pins is recommended. Using both "press" and "slip"-fit hole sizes for the pins guarantees very close part alignment. For instance, in using a ¼-inch hardened dowel pin, the pin would be pressed into a 0.246-diameter hole (letter D drill). The slip-fit hole in the mating part would be 0.257 diameter (letter F drill).

Figure 18-7 Hardware for joining sheetmetal.

Another aspect is that both the soft and thinner materials used in sheet metal work are often not adequate for maintaining a tapped thread. In these cases, various types of supplementary hardware are used (see Fig. 18-7). These items require carefully sized and detailed holes for proper installation and are comprehensively covered in the literature available from the manufacturer.

RIVETING   Rivets are used to great advantage in all kinds of sheet metal fabrication. Rivets are practical for both long production runs as well as one- or two-piece prototype jobs.

The relative merits of riveting versus welding as a basic method of fabrication has been argued back and forth for years. Drawing conclusions is difficult, as there are a number of factors involved. Dissatisfaction with one method or another usually stems from inadequate planning in the design stage. However, without wishing to continue the argument, there are a number of advantages to riveted construction in precision work. First, no specialized skills are required in that the layout for, and the installation, of rivets can be made part of the fabrication scheme and not an additional operation as in the case of welding. In small quantities rivets can be installed with simple, inexpensive hand tools, while the installation of larger quantities can be easily mechanized. Tolerances are easily maintained and the problems of postoperation cleanup is for all practical purposes eliminated.

Commercial Rivets

Figure 18-8 illustrates a variety of rivet types that can be used for anything from securing belt buckles to sealing the back of a video game unit. Although

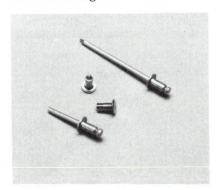

Figure 18-8 Typical aircraft rivets.

these do an adequate job, they are not considered structural from either the standpoint of original strength or longevity.

Aircraft Rivets

These rivets (see Fig. 18-9) and the methods and patterns of their installation represent permanent, high-strength, reliable assembly for both aircraft and various types of military hardware.

TYPES OF AIRCRAFT RIVETS.   There are a number of rivet types that are used in aircraft construction. They carry both generic and proprietary names such as Rivnuts, Cherry Rivets, Cherry Max Rivets, explosive rivets, Hi-shear, and Riv-pins. Each is designed for particular application and installation constraints.

Figure 18-9 Typical aircraft rivets.

Rivets acceptable for such use also carry a military specification number as a means of identification. Thus the specification box on the blueprint will list the required fastening hardware by these numerical designations, which, until learned, must be interpreted from the appropriate materials handbook or the manufacturer's literature.

The most widely used rivets are the types designated MS20426 and MS20470 (see Fig. 18-10). These are solid rivets used in all kinds of sheet metal fabrication. They are aluminum rivets, but the same basic type is available in both steels and brass alloys. Of course, as such, they bear different specification numbers.

The MS20426 and MS20470 rivets are supplied as either "hard" (2117 aluminum alloy) or "soft" (1100 aluminum alloy). Thus the rivet would be

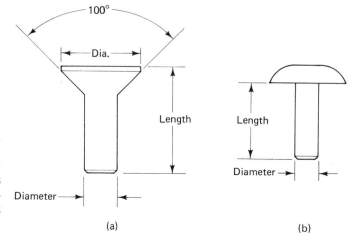

Figure 18-10 Common aircraft rivets with dimensional designations: (a) flathead rivet (MS20426); (b) universal head rivet (MS20470).

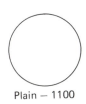

Plain — 1100

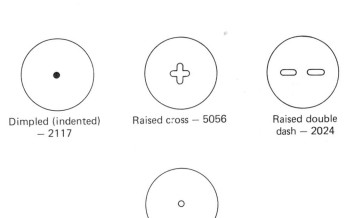

Dimpled (indented) — 2117   Raised cross — 5056   Raised double dash — 2024

Raised teat — 2017

Figure 18-11 Head markings to identify aluminum alloy type.

further designated as being either AD (hard) or A (soft). Those rivets that are hard are easily identified. The hardened rivets carry a center punch mark in the center of the head and most often supplied with an anodized finish. Soft rivets are usually supplied bright and shiny with no distinguishing markings. Figure 18-11 shows the identifying head markings on various types of aluminum rivets.

The size of the rivet is known by a dashed number following the type designation letter. The first digit gives the diameter in 32nds and the second digit gives the length in 16ths. For example, an MS20426 AD3-5 rivet is a flat-head, hard rivet, $\frac{3}{32}$ inch in diameter and $\frac{5}{16}$ inch long. An MS20470 A6-6 rivet is a soft, universal head rivet, $\frac{3}{16}$ inch in diameter and $\frac{3}{8}$ inch long.

Rivet Holes

A rivet hole can either be punched or drilled, but must be burr free. If the pieces to be riveted are drilled simultaneously, they should be separated and any drill burrs removed before the final assembly.

Rivet hole sizes should be just large enough to allow easy insertion of the rivet, but care should be taken to avoid oversize holes, which allow the rivet to buckle when squeezed. Typical rivet sizes, the recommended hole diameters, and if flat head rivets are used, the appropriate countersink diameters are included in the following table:

Rivet diameter (in.)	Hole size (in.)	Countersink diameter (in.)	Minimum sheet thickness (in.)
$\frac{1}{16}$	0.067 (No. 51 drill)	0.105	0.032
$\frac{3}{32}$	0.098 (No. 40 drill)	0.169	0.040
$\frac{1}{8}$	0.128 (No. 30 drill)	0.215	0.051
$\frac{5}{32}$	0.161 (No. 20 drill)	0.276	0.064
$\frac{3}{16}$	0.193 (No. 10 drill)	0.343	0.072
$\frac{1}{4}$	0.257 (F drill)	0.463	0.102

Figure 18-12 illustrates the recommendations of the chart.

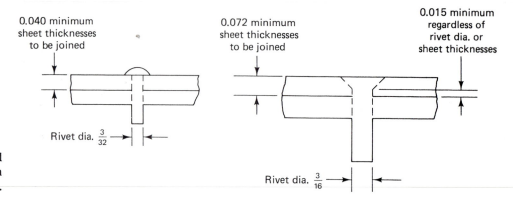

Figure 18-12 Typical rivet installation diagram.

Rivet Length

The rivet must be long enough so that enough of the shank protrudes through the materials being joined to allow proper driving. Driving or bucking of rivets is accomplished by either a pneumatic hammer, squeezing, or hammer blows to the upset end of the rivet (see Fig. 18-13). If a full head is required on the upset side, a properly sized "rivet set" is employed (see Fig. 18-14).

Figure 18-13 Bucking a rivet with a ball peen hammer to obtain an "upset" head.

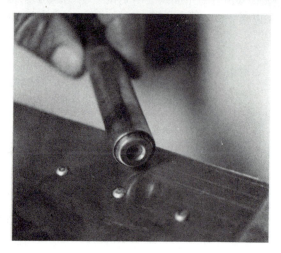

Figure 18-14 Using a rivet set to obtain a "full" head.

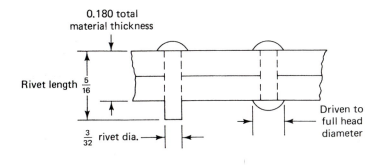
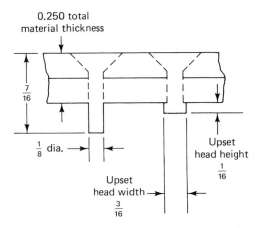

Notes:

1. Full head upsets are approximately equal to original head diameter and height.

2. Plain upset heads are approximately 1.5 X the original rivet diameter in width and 0.5 X the rivet diameter in height.

Figure 18-15 Proper rivet length for complete upsetting.

The basic rule for determining rivet length is 1.5 X rivet diameter, plus the material being assembled equals the rivet length. For example, if two pieces, each ⅛ inch thick, are to be riveted with ⅛-inch rivets, the rivet must be ¼ inch plus ⅛ X 1.5 or 0.437 of an inch long. This would be a −7 rivet, which is ⁷⁄₁₆ inch long (see Fig. 18-15). This length allows both a "full head" or a plain "upset head" to be driven to the recommended dimensions.

Riveted Assembly

Edge distances and rivet spacing are governed by the requirements of each design and by standards established by agencies such as the military or the FAA, but there are certain general rules which have been established. The minimum distance from an edge to the center line of the first row of rivets should be two and one-half times the rivet diameter. This is a minimum recommendation and may be increased if there is an expected fatigue factor on relatively rough cut edges. The minimum distance between rivets in any direction should be three times the rivet diameter. This is again a minimum and any maximum spacing allowable depends on the actual structure and design. These dimensions are illustrated in Figure 18-16.

Figure 18-17 demonstrates the use of Cleco fasteners used to hold the pieces of stock together as the rivets are being installed. These spring-loaded

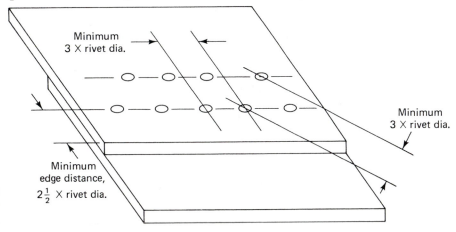

Figure 18-16 Generally recommended rivet pattern and edge distance spacing.

Figure 18-17 Using Cleco fasteners.

devices are available in sizes corresponding to the various rivet diameter sizes. Placed intermittently along the seam, they hold the predrilled holes in alignment to permit insertion of the rivets. Using specially designed pliers or guns, they are removed as the riveting proceeds.

CONCLUSION   Beyond the mechanical joining processes described, there are additional high-technology processes which are very exotic and sophisticated. These include laser and electron beam welding, the various plasma processes, friction and upset welding, and diffusion bonding. Although these methods can produce joints of exceptional quality and soundness, most deserve only a passing acknowledgment in a practical handbook such as this. These processes require extensive support systems having to do with precleaning, preassembly, and mechanization. They are enormously expensive in initial equipment outlay and are justified only by extremely high production rates or by heavy subsidization through other plant operations.

FINISHING   In precision sheet metal work finishing must be accomplished with great care and attention to detail. Components made of material only 40 or 50 thousandths thick can be ruined by careless sanding and deburring techniques.

Although many sheet metal parts are painted, many are finished with plated surfaces through various electrical and chemical processes. Whereas a coat of paint can mask many surface irregularities, these other finishes tend to show up residual grinding marks, file scratches, and any dents from careless handling.

While stainless sheets may have a protective paper coating, aluminum and mild steel surfaces are subject to surface wear and tear during manufacture. To mask these imperfections, two methods are used, either as a final operation or just before bending and forming. In the first method, the surface is grained in one direction across the entire width of the part. Flat parts are fed into a machine, where a continuous belt passes over them. These devices are known as "timesavers." Small parts that may already have been formed up can also be grained with belt sanders and wheels, as shown in Figure 18-18. Another device, the orbital sander (see Fig. 18-19), imparts a tightly swirled pattern that is very effective in hiding surface blemishes.

Deburring is the process of removing sharp edges caused by shearing, punching, or sawing. Figure 18-20 illustrates the use of an abrasive rubber

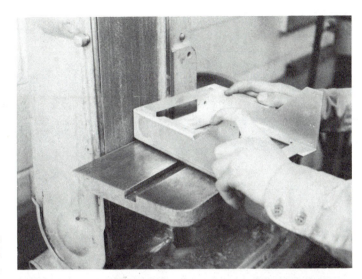

Figure 18-18 Belt sanding of finished parts.

Figure 18-19 Orbital sander in use.

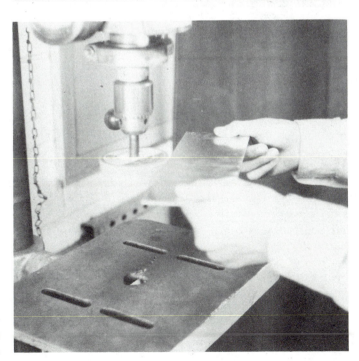

Figure 18-20 Deburring with a drill press attachment.

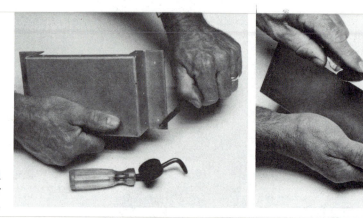

Figure 18-21 Hand
tools designed for
deburring operations.

wheel mounted in a drill press, and Figure 18-21 shows several hand tools used for getting into tight spots and inside corners.

   Various plating processes are done in plants which deal exclusively in those processes. One common process used on aluminum sheet metal parts is known as Irridite and can be accomplished in even a modest production facility. This is a chemical bath that imparts a greenish-yellow stain (although some Irridite coatings are clear) which inhibits the natural formation of oxides, which in turn can cause poor electrical grounding and other problems usually associated with electronic components. This process is also used as a primer for subsequent painting.

Chapter 19

TOOLS and EQUIPMENT USED

This section concentrates on the practical application and blending of traditional blacksmithing techniques and modern welding, heating, and flame-cutting operations. Pure traditional blacksmithing is an age-old art form but by modern standards has a very low production efficiency. The study of blacksmithing, however, can give metal fabricators, ironworkers, and welders a keen insight into the behavior of metals and a better understanding and appreciation of metalworking equipment. For this reason and the immense personal satisfaction that comes from making some of your own tools or creating pieces of ornamental ironwork, the study of blacksmithing is strongly encouraged. Many fine texts have been written on this subject and several are listed in Appendix 2.

The tools and equipment discussed in this chapter do not, by any means, represent a complete inventory of a fully equipped blacksmith shop. Instead, they represent the more basic and common items needed to perform the simple blacksmithing still widely used in the metal trades for tool and equipment repair and modification and the fabrication of ornamental ironwork.

THE FORGE Often, the methods used to heat steel for forging and forming operations will depend on the frequency of use and the size and number of pieces being worked. An oxyacetylene torch with a heating tip will work well for occasional work. However, if a large amount of heating is to be done, a forge will be needed. Gas and coal forges can be purchased commercially. Gas-fueled forges are cleaner and easier to use than the traditional coal forge; however, most are not made to handle large pieces.

For blacksmith work, the coal forge (see Fig. 19-1) is still the most versatile. Initially, much practice will be needed in the art of building and maintaining a proper forge fire. Although blacksmith coal can be purchased, most smiths make their own. Soft (bituminous) coal is the basic forge fuel. The sulfur content of the coal will adversely affect the steel being heated;

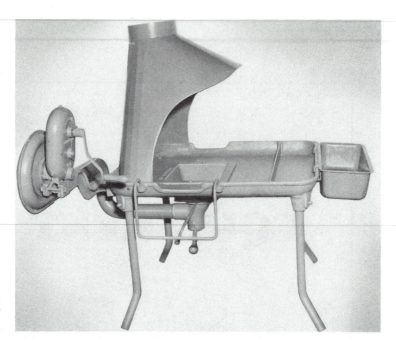

Figure 19-1 Coal forge. (Courtesy of Buffalo Forge Co.)

therefore, it must be removed. The first step in preparing the forge for lighting is to stand a firebrick or piece of wood in the center of the fire pot and mount dampened coal around it (see Fig. 19-2). Remove the brick and fill the open area left with wood shavings. Light the shavings and start the blower to accelerate the fire. When the shavings are well lit, add a small amount of coal on top, It is at this stage that the heat from the fire will start to partially burn the mound of dampened coal around it. This partial heating will burn off the unwanted gases and transform the coal into coke. Do not add any green coal directly to the fire but rake in the partially burned coke surrounding it. Dampening the mound of coal will help control the size of the fire. The depth of the fire should be generous. A shallow fire has the tendency to allow too much oxygen to be blown through it, causing overoxidation of the metal being heated. Any clinkers (fused coal ash) formed as the forge is used must be removed or they will severely restrict the heat output.

If a coal forge is not readily available or the purchase cost prohibitive, one can be easily constructed from ¼-inch steel plate (see Fig. 19-3). The fire

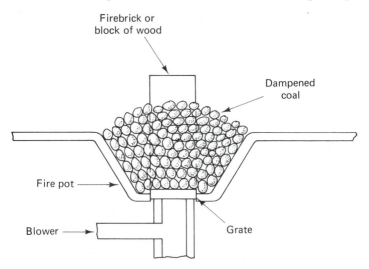

Figure 19-2 Starting the forge fire.

Figure 19-3 Home-
made coal forge.

pot should be about 6 inches deep with a grate made of steel at least ⅜-inch thick (see Fig. 19-4). The fire pot can also be lined with firebrick or retort cement to increase the life of the forge. The air blast must be adjustable in order to control the intensity of the fire. A heavy-duty impeller-type electric fan controlled by an ordinary household dimmer switch works quite nicely (see Fig. 19-5).

The hood and wind screen can be made from 16-gauge sheet metal with a collar on top to accept 4-inch stove pipe. A word of caution: Coal gas is toxic. If the forge is being used indoors, it must be properly vented.

Figure 19-4 Forge
firepot.

Figure 19-5   Forge blower assembly.

THE ANVIL   A good anvil is an indispensable piece of equipment (see Fig. 19-6). It is made of cast steel with a hardened face and size-classified by weight. For general iron shop work, anvils between 100- and 200- pounds are ideal.

Each part of the anvil is designed for a specific purpose. The hardened face is the surface on which all of the flat hammering is done. The square hardy hole accepts a wide range of cutting and forming tools. The pritchel or round hole is used for hot-punching holes. The cutting block, which is usually not a hardened surface, is the section of the anvil on which pieces of stock are chisel-cut and the horn is used for bending and forming curves.

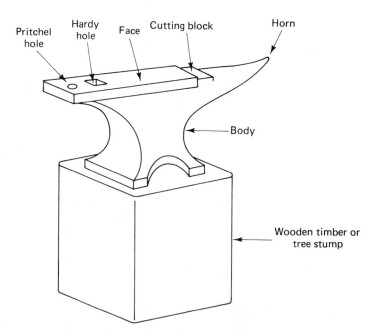

Figure 19-6   Anvil.

THE VISE   Vises used in blacksmith work tend to take a tremendous amount of physical stress; therefore, only those of heavy-duty quality should be considered. A blacksmith vise (see Fig. 19-7) is specifically designed for this type of work, but a bench or machinist's vise (see Fig. 19-8) of suitable size will work equally as well. The vise jaws should be about 5 inches in length with a 6-inch opening capacity.

Figure 19-7 Black-
smith vise.

Figure 19-8 Machinist
vise.

THE QUENCH TANK   A readily available supply of water for dampening coal and quenching forge work is an important item in blacksmith work. The quench tank should have a wide opening at the top and at least a 20-gallon capacity. This can be constructed from mild-steel plate or a cut-down 55-gallon drum (see Fig. 19-9). Set the tank on a stand in order to raise it to a comfortable working height.

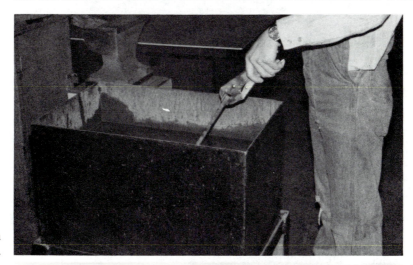

Figure 19-9 Quench
tank.

THE OXYACETYLENE OUTFIT

The availability of an oxyacetylene welding and cutting outfit (see Fig. 19-10) is often desirable. This equipment not only has the advantage of being very portable but provides a quick source of heat for forming and bending operations and a fast, efficient method for cutting steel stock. The outfit should consist of a torch with a selection of welding tips, a heating tip, and a cutting attachment or blowpipe. A basic knowledge of the use of oxyacetylene equipment is imperative.

Figure 19-10 Oxyacetylene outfit.

THE ARC WELDER

An arc welding machine, like the oxyacetylene outfit, can be an extremely valuable tool. If welding needs are limited, a small inexpensive transformer (see Fig. 19-11) will serve quite nicely. Machines designed for continuous operation will be considerably larger and more expensive. The authors

Figure 19-11 Arc welder.

recommend at least a basic knowledge of arc welding for those involved in ironwork and steel fabrication. *Note*: If instruction is needed in the area of arc welding or oxyacetylene cutting and welding, see the readings in Appendix 2.

HAND TOOLS The hand tools required to do basic blacksmith work include a variety of hammers, tongs, and pliers. The styles of hammers used are the ball peen, sledge, and cross peen (see Fig. 19-12). The recommended size for ball and cross peen hammers are between 16 and 48 ounces. The sledge-hammer should weigh about 10 pounds.

Figure 19-12 Assorted hammers.

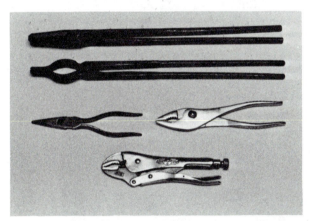

Figure 19-13 Tongs and pliers.

The assortment of tongs and pliers needed to handle and form hot metal is shown in Figure 19-13. These include flat jaw tongs, curved lip tongs, heavy-duty needle nose pliers, heavy-duty combination pliers, and Vise-Grip pliers.

SUGGESTED ADDITIONAL EQUIPMENT Power tools such as hacksaws and band saws, hydraulic ironworkers, and shears, discussed in Chapter 8, are all tremendous worksavers and great to have at one's disposal. However, for those working on a limited budget, there are smaller, less expensive tools that will work quite well for a limited production or prototype operation. A hand-operated hydraulic open-end shear (see Fig. 19-14) will easily cut bar stock up to ½ inch in thickness. Small portable band saws (see Fig. 19-15) use blades which are approximately 5½ feet in length and can cut stock up to 6 inches in diameter. Hand punches (see

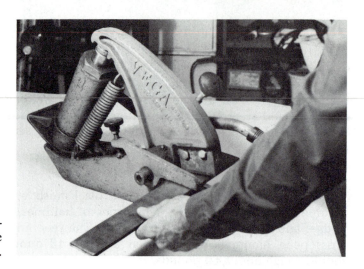

Figure 19-14 Hand-operated hydraulic shear.

Figure 19-15 Small band saw.

Figure 19-16 Hand punch.

Figure 19-17 Bench grinder. (Courtesy of Black and Decker.)

Fig. 19-16), discussed in Chapters 8 through 16, are ideal for punching and notching material to ⅛-inch thickness. Two types of grinding tools are also suggested, a 4-inch hand grinder (see Fig. 13-7) and a bench grinder (see Fig. 19-17). Mount a medium and a fine grit wheel on the bench grinder for dressing off and finishing cutting tools.

A final note of caution: Blacksmithing involves work with very hot metal. Always be aware of the potentional burn hazards.

Chapter 20

DESIGN and LAYOUT

Successful ornamental ironwork design is based on two factors, strength and eye appeal. Strength will always be the primary concern when safety or security is involved, such as with fire escapes, hand railings, or security window guards and gates. However, eye appeal should never be overlooked even on the most functional jobs. With some careful consideration and planning, the institutional look can be easily avoided. When the work is strictly ornamental, as with the candle holder shown in Figure 20-1, a smooth,

Figure 20-1 Decorative candle holder.

uniform, eye-pleasing design will be the priority. Steel used for such jobs will usually more than exceed the strength required for the normal use and abuse that the piece will be subjected to.

Designing a job utilizing the basic blacksmithing and welding techniques is not all that difficult. A traditional ironwork design will usually consist of a series or combination of twists and scrolls. Contemporary designs utilize straight or curved pieces of basic structural shapes, particularly tubing and pipe (see Fig. 20-2). Choice of design will be determined by job specification or personal preference.

The first and most important rule of thumb for developing a design is not to get yourself in over your head. The complexity of design must be limited by skill and equipment available. Intricate designs of the type shown in Figure 20-3 require a high level of skill and should only be under-

Figure 20-2 Contemporary hand rail.

Figure 20-3 Intricate ironwork design.

taken by those capable of doing such work. By following the suggestions discussed in this chapter, fabricators having a basic knowledge of welding and simple blacksmithing will be able to create a successful design.

RAILINGS   The basic railing construction is shown in the cross section in Figure 20-4. End posts should be made of 1-inch square stock. The top rail can be flat stock, half oval or top rail molding, depending on design considerations or personal preference. Recommended picket size is ½- or ⅝-inch square stock, with ½ inch being the most common choice. For best overall appearance, pickets should be spaced no farther than 6 inches apart. There is almost an infinite number of design variations utilizing twists and scrolls which can be employed. Several suggestions are shown in Figure 20-5. Whatever pattern is used, uniformity will be the key to success. When laying out the design, make sure that the pattern or patterns chosen can be equally spaced throughout the entire job. Making a scale sketch of the layout is strongly suggested.

Regardless of railing height or length, the method of layout and assembly will be basically the same. A standard residential railing will be between 32 and 36 inches high. Commercial handrails are usually 42 inches high. For the purpose of demonstration, we will use the 32-inch-high railing shown in Figure 20-6.

The first step should be a detail sketch to determine design and the number of pickets required. After this is accomplished, fabricate all of the

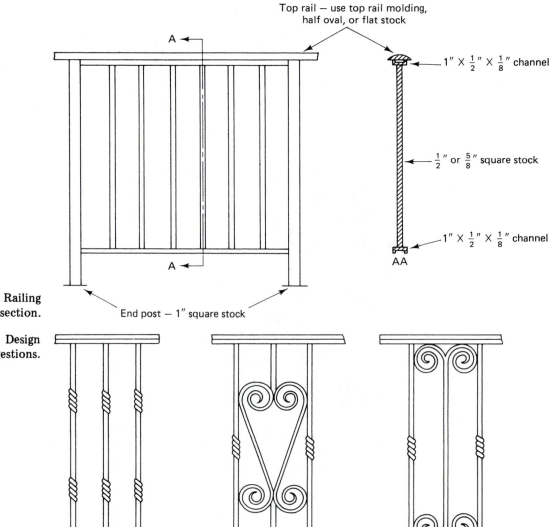

Top rail — use top rail molding, half oval, or flat stock

$1'' \times \frac{1}{2}'' \times \frac{1}{8}''$ channel

$\frac{1}{2}''$ or $\frac{5}{8}''$ square stock

$1'' \times \frac{1}{2}'' \times \frac{1}{8}''$ channel

AA

End post — 1″ square stock

Figure 20-4 Railing cross section.

Figure 20-5 Design suggestions.

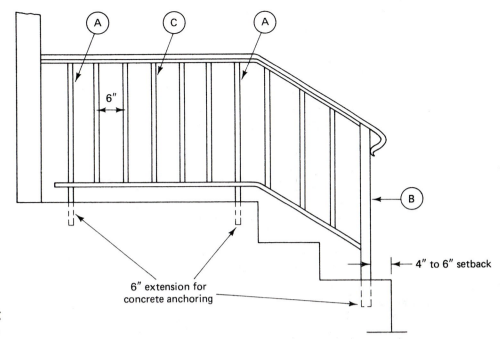

Figure 20-6 Railing layout.

pickets (C) to a length of 28 inches. If the railing is to be surface mounted, make pickets (A) 32 inches long and end post (B) 35 inches long. The end post will be longer because of its setback on the bottom step. If the rail is to be set in concrete, allow an additional 6 inches on the pickets and the post.

The angle for a standard stairway is approximately 34 to 35 degrees. In some instances this may vary and should be checked prior to layout.

After all the pickets are fabricated, cut two pieces of 1-inch channel to length and lay out the location of each picket. Next, punch a square hole at each location point. The holes should be $\frac{1}{32}$ inch larger than the picket square stock ($\frac{17}{32}$ for $\frac{1}{2}$-inch square stock and $\frac{21}{32}$ for $\frac{5}{8}$-inch stock). If a bend must be made to accommodate a stairway, remember that the bottom channel must be bent flanges down and the top channel flanges up and picket holes punched $7\frac{1}{4}$ inches apart for a 6-inch spacing (see Fig. 20-7).

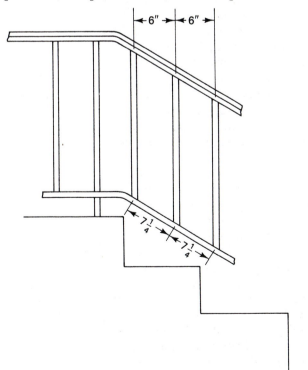

Figure 20-7 Layout for pickets on an incline. (This is an approximate figure. The $7\frac{1}{4}$-inch measurement will vary with the stairway angle.)

275

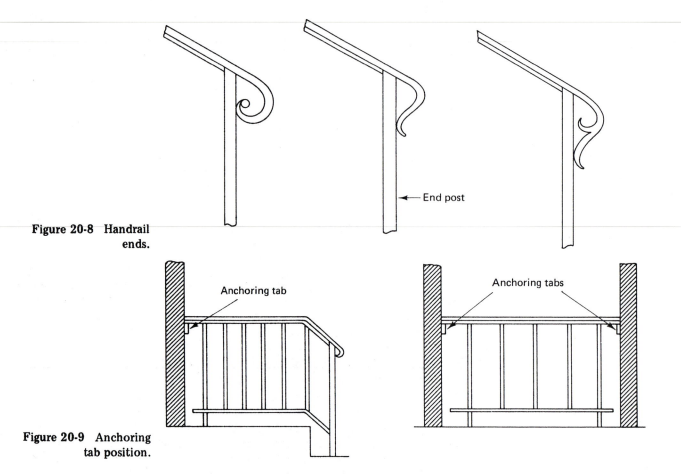

Figure 20-8 Handrail ends.

← End post

Anchoring tab

Anchoring tabs

Figure 20-9 Anchoring tab position.

Set all of the pickets in place so that each end protrudes approximately ⅛ inch through the holes in the channels. Square up and clamp the assembly. All of the welding can be done inside the channel so that none will be visible on the completed railing. The final step is the fabrication of the top rail. The top rail should be cut between 12 and 18 inches oversize if a decorative end is to be made. Several suggestions are shown in Figure 20-8 (construction of these decorative ends is covered in Chapter 21). This should be done first, then the top rail can be set in place and cut to finished length. Stitch-weld the top rail to the top channel.

Anchoring tabs should be welded to the top channel when contact is made with a wall or column (see Fig. 20-9).

GATES   The design and layout for a gate is similar to that for railings. However, the material used must be proportional to the size of the job. Because gates are constantly opened and closed, additional strength factors must be considered. If the gate is relatively small in size such as the type shown in Figure 20-10, the material used for railings would be adequate. For a larger undertaking of the type shown in Figure 20-11, material size must be substantially increased. Using Figure 20-11 as an example, the main frame of the gate (A) would be made of ½-inch by 2-inch flat stock; the cross bars (B) are ⅜-inch by 2-inch flat stock; all vertical bars (C) should be ⅝-inch or ¾-inch square stock and scrolls (D) should be formed from ¼-inch by 1-inch flat bar.

Several additional design suggestions are illustrated in Figure 20-12. Regardless of the design selected, keep in mind that the gate must be constructed so that the entire assembly is tied together. This can be accomplished by

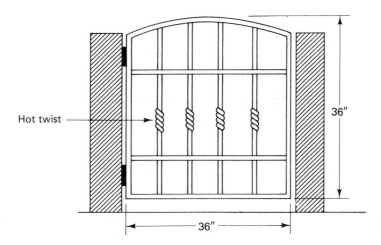

Figure 20-10 Small gate.

Hot twist

36″

36″

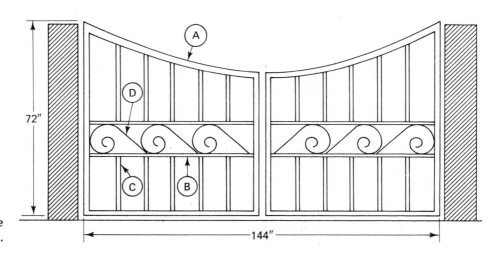

Figure 20-11 Large gate.

A

D

72″

C

B

144″

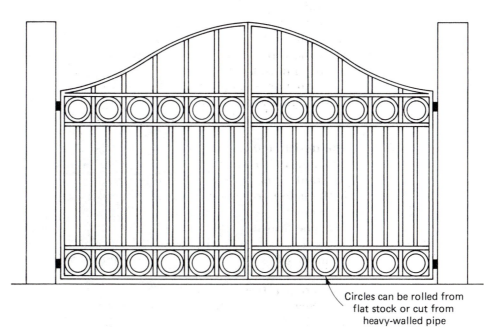

Figure 20-12 Gate design suggestions: (a) large gate; (b) small gates.

Circles can be rolled from flat stock or cut from heavy-walled pipe

(a)

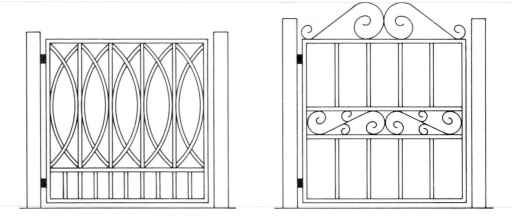

Figure 20-12 (Cont.)   (b)

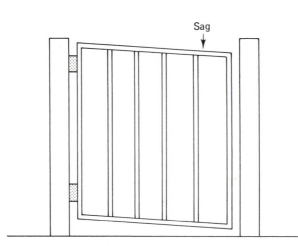

Figure 20-13 Laterally
unsupported gate.

utilizing cross bars, diagonal bracing, or connecting scroll work. If this is not done, the gate will have a tendency to sag under its own weight (see Fig. 20-13).

The layout of large gates, particularly those having curved surfaces, can be made much easier by making a full-size layout with chalk or soapstone on a large layout table or concrete floor (see Fig. 20-14). For demonstration purposes we will again use the design in Figure 20-11.

Figure 20-14 Gate
layout on the floor.

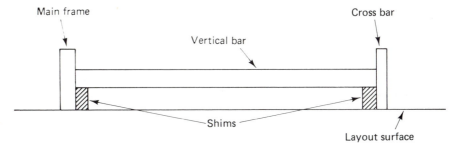

Figure 20-15 Centering vertical bars.

Using the layout lines as a template, the top bars of the main frame can be formed and cut to length. After this is completed, the entire main frame and cross bars can be cut, squared up, and tacked together. Do not weld completely until all of the component parts are tacked in place. Because the main frame and cross bars are 2 inches wide and the vertical bars are ¾ inch wide, several ⅝-inch shims must be made up to center the vertical bars (see Fig. 20-15). Place the shims on the layout surface directly under each vertical bar position, place the bar on top of them, and tack weld. Next, make up a scroll template (see Chap. 21) using the layout diagram as a guide. Form all of the scrolls and weld them in place.

HINGES AND LOCKS

Gate hinges that work most efficiently and cause the least amount of trouble are usually those of the simplest design, such as the pin hinges shown in Figure 20-16. The flat plate pin hinge is the easiest to make. As always, the size of the hinge must be proportional to the size of the gate. For the small gate, ⅜-inch by 1-inch flat stock and ½-inch round stock will be sufficient.

Figure 20-16 Simple pin hinges.

For a large gate, ¾-inch by 2-inch flat stock and ¾-inch to 1-inch round stock will be needed. Regardless of size, fabrication is similar. The first factor to consider is adequate hinge length to allow gate clearance. If the hinges are shorter than one-half the width of the gate frame, the gate will not open fully (see Fig. 20-17) but will jam against the mounting surface. The distance between the gate and the mounting surface should be at least 1½ times the gate thickness (see Fig. 20-18).

The actual construction of the hinge is quite simple. Cut the flat stock pieces to length and lay out each piece for drilling (see Fig. 20-19). Drill holes 1/32 inch larger in diameter than the round stock being used for the pins. Cut the pins ¾ inch longer than twice the plate thickness (see Fig. 20-20). Next, set the pin into one of the plates so that it protrudes approx-

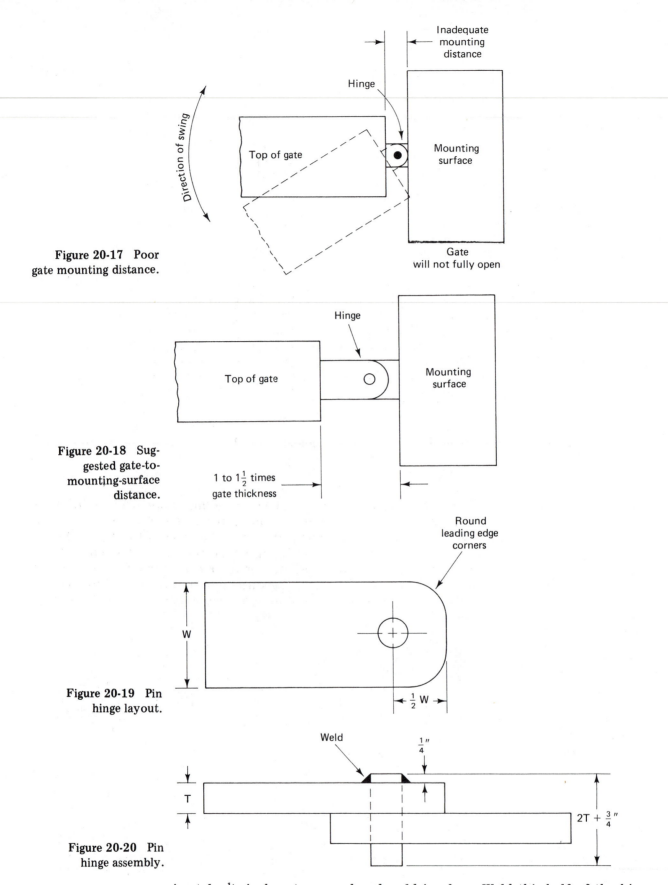

Figure 20-17 Poor gate mounting distance.

Figure 20-18 Suggested gate-to-mounting-surface distance.

Figure 20-19 Pin hinge layout.

Figure 20-20 Pin hinge assembly.

imately ¼ inch out one end and weld in place. Weld this half of the hinge onto the gate. The other half of the hinge gets welded to a mounting plate and attached to the mounting surface. If the gate is to be mounted on new masonry, this half of the hinge can be made extra long and mortared in place.

The other variation of pin hinge shown in Figure 20-21 utilizes heavy wall pipe, tubing, or bored round stock instead of flat plate. Hinges of this

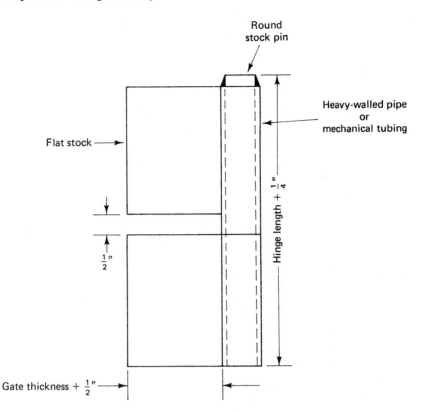

Figure 20-21 Pin hinge variation.

type should only be used on gates which are going to open in one direction only or where close fit between gate and mounting surface is desired. As with the hinges discussed previously, the inside diameter of the pipe or bored round stock used should be $\frac{1}{32}$ inch larger than the pin. Hinge length for a small gate should be about 3 inches. For a large gate, an 8-inch length is recommended. Suggested material thicknesses are the same as those discussed previously. Use the layout procedure in Figure 20-22 as a guide. The $\frac{1}{2}$-

Figure 20-22 Hinge layout: (a) top half; (b) bottom half.

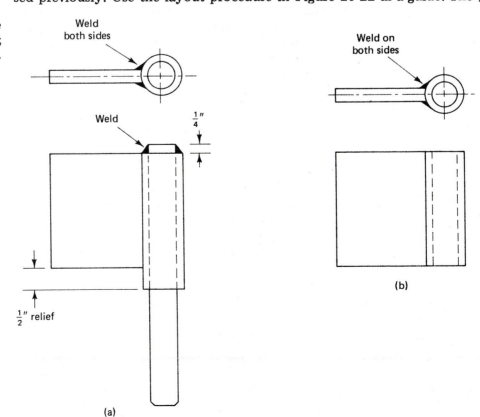

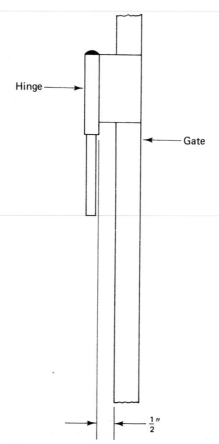

Figure 20-23   Hinge
offset.

inch relief will prevent the hinges from binding in the fully closed position. The hinge half with the pin should be welded onto the gate and the other half onto the mounting plate. Each should be welded so that the round portion of the hinge extends approximately ½ inch beyond the end of the gate (see Fig. 20-23). Hinge pins should be kept well greased.

Very heavy gates may require a ground-mounted pin hinge and caster wheel (see Fig. 20-24). Casters make the opening of large gates easier and help prevent sagging.

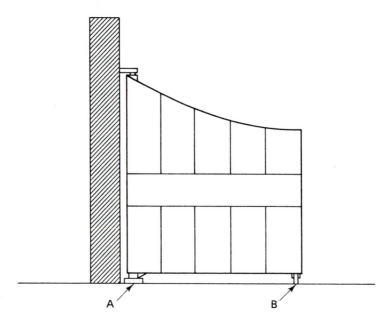

Figure 20-24   Ground-
mounted pin hinge and
caster.

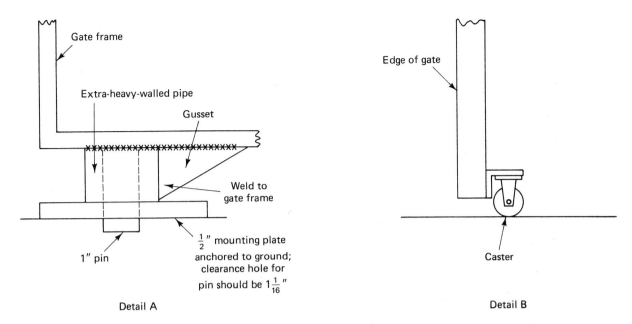

Detail A

Detail B

Figure 20-24 (Cont.)

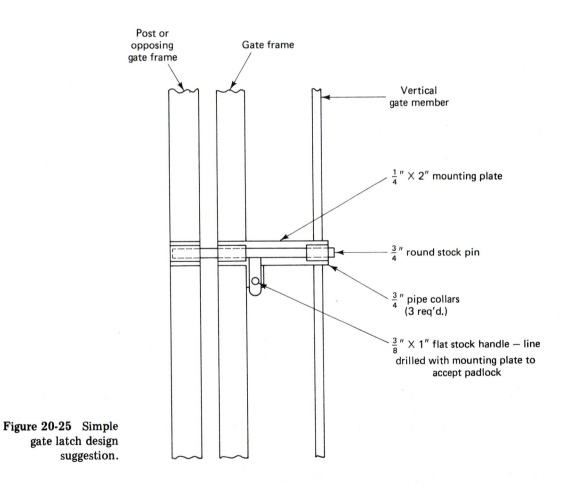

Figure 20-25 Simple gate latch design suggestion.

Like hinges, gate latches and locks should be kept as simple as possible. Latches of this type, shown in Figure 20-25, can easily be constructed and secured with a padlock. If a key lock is desired, a section of the gate can be boxed with 1/8- or 1/4-inch plate and a commercially manufactured dead bolt

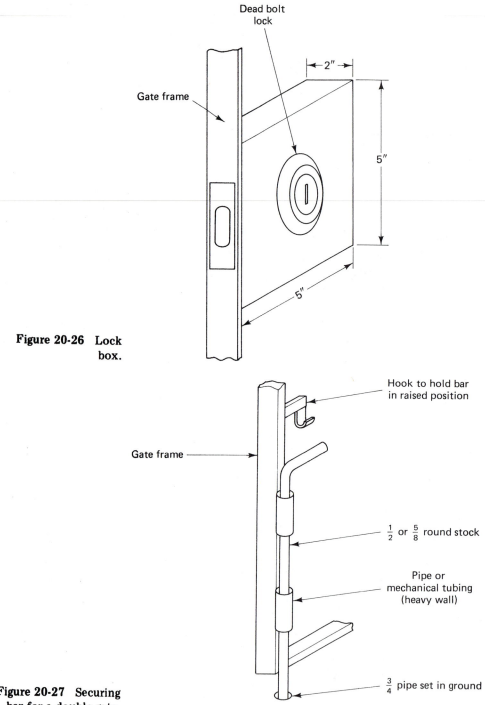

Figure 20-26   Lock box.

Figure 20-27   Securing bar for a double gate.

can be installed (see Fig. 20-26). Follow directions for the specific lock used for recommended clearance holes. With double gates, one side must be secured to the ground when in the closed position (see Fig. 20-27).

SECURITY DOORS   A security door is nothing more than a variation of a gate. Important design factors to consider are never spacing vertical bars more than 6 inches apart and having enough lateral support, either with scroll work or cross bars, to prevent the bars from being pried apart. Material used for vertical bars

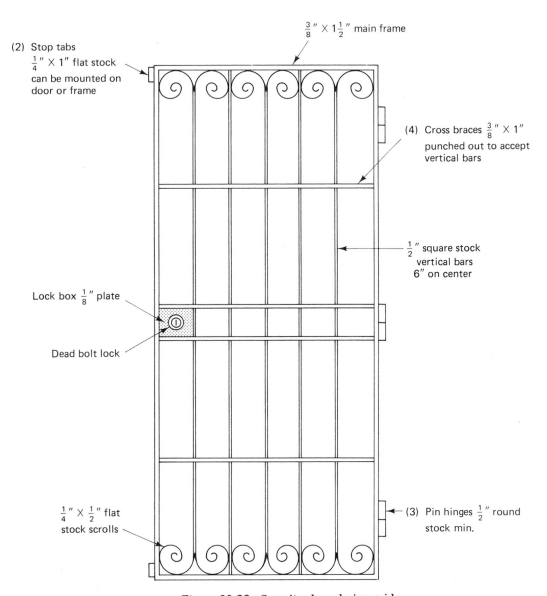

(2) Stop tabs $\frac{1}{4}$" × 1" flat stock can be mounted on door or frame

$\frac{3}{8}$" × 1$\frac{1}{2}$" main frame

(4) Cross braces $\frac{3}{8}$" × 1" punched out to accept vertical bars

$\frac{1}{2}$" square stock vertical bars 6" on center

Lock box $\frac{1}{8}$" plate

Dead bolt lock

$\frac{1}{4}$" × $\frac{1}{2}$" flat stock scrolls

(3) Pin hinges $\frac{1}{2}$" round stock min.

Figure 20-28 Security door design guide.

should never be less than ½ inch thick. The door illustrated in Figure 20-28 can be used as a design guide. Construction and layout methods discussed in the section on railings can be readily used.

The type shown in Figure 20-29 is made to fit inside a steel frame which was mounted over an existing door frame. For installations such as this, the mounting frame can be constructed of angle iron at least $\frac{3}{16}$ inch thick. If the installation is in close proximity to an existing door, care must be taken to make sure that the security door will clear any existing door handle when in the closed position. Utilizing an angle-iron frame will automatically provide surfaces for hinging and mounting. Pin hinges may be used on security doors but must be of sufficient length so that the door cannot be lifted off the hinges while in the closed position.

Doors made to fit an opening where no existing door is present can be mounted using the methods discussed for gates. Figure 20-30 shows several design suggestions.

The locking device used can either be a padlock or double-set dead

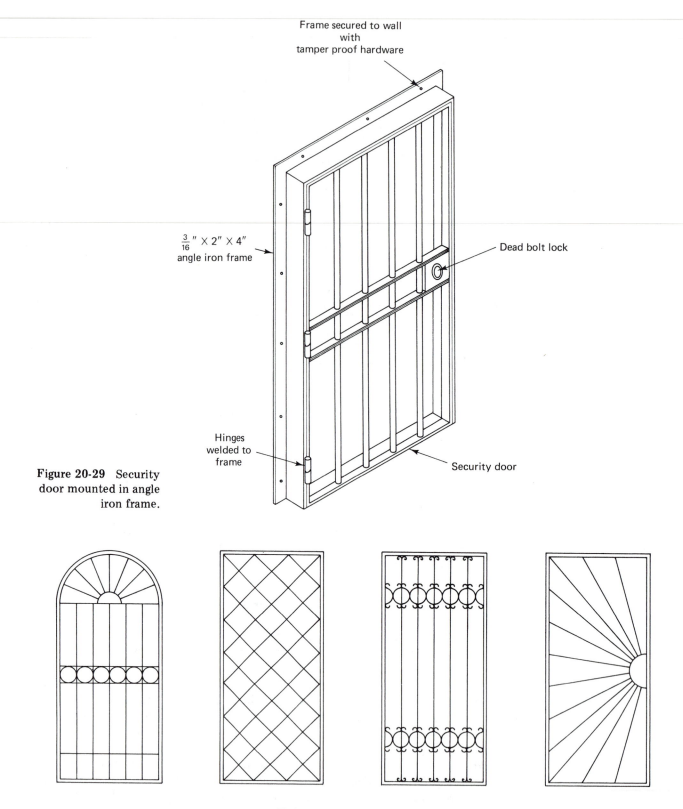

Frame secured to wall
with
tamper proof hardware

$\frac{3}{16}$ " × 2" × 4"
angle iron frame

Dead bolt lock

Hinges
welded to
frame

Security door

Figure 20-29 Security door mounted in angle iron frame.

Figure 20-30 Additional door design suggestions.

bolt lock. A section of the door can be boxed in, as with the suggestion for gates previously discussed, or set right into the door frame if square tubing is used in the construction (see Fig. 20-31).

Figure 20-31 Dead
bolt lock mounted in
a door frame.

WINDOW GUARDS   A successful window guard design should give the appearance of security and
aesthetic beauty without an institutional prison look. Several suggestions are
illustrated in Figure 20-32. Keep in mind that vertical bars (at least ½ inch in
diameter) should be spaced no more than 6 inches on center and given
enough lateral support to prevent them from being pried apart. Two other
design factors unique to window guards must be carefully considered. The
first of these is adequate stand-off space between window and guard to
allow for opening and cleaning. Except for special instances, a stand-off of
4 inches will suffice (see Fig. 20-33).

The second and most important factor is mounting location. Improper
mounting will render the sturdiest window guard useless. This is particularly
true on wood frame structures. Try to lay out the guard so that the mounting
points fall directly over the main frame studs of the window opening. The
guard can then be secured with 5/16- or 3/8-inch by 3-inch-long lag or tamperproof one-way bolts. If this is impractical to do and the mounting points are

Figure 20-32 Window guard designs.

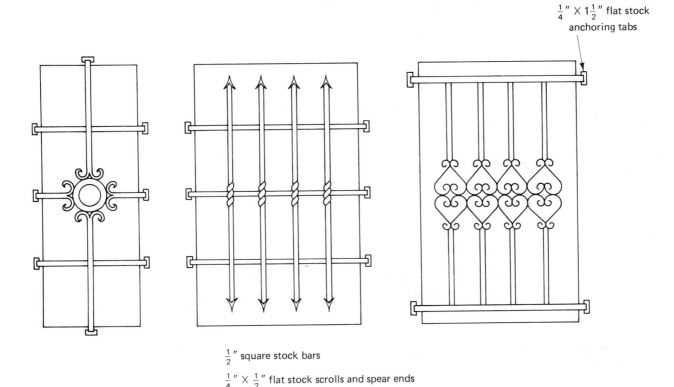

$\frac{1}{4}$ " × 1$\frac{1}{2}$ " flat stock
anchoring tabs

$\frac{1}{2}$ " square stock bars

$\frac{1}{4}$ " × $\frac{1}{2}$ " flat stock scrolls and spear ends

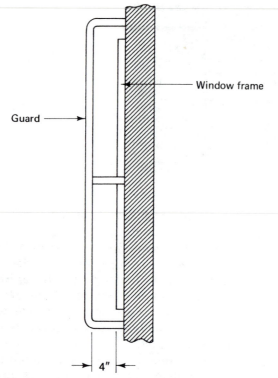

Figure 20-33 Window guard standoff.

Guard

Window frame

4"

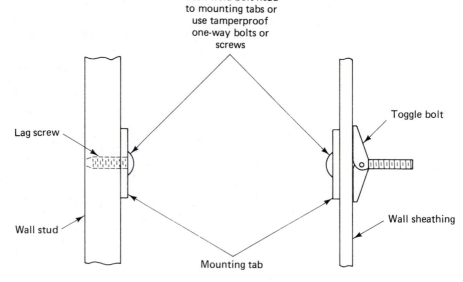

Tack weld bolt head to mounting tabs or use tamperproof one-way bolts or screws

Lag screw

Toggle bolt

Wall stud

Wall sheathing

Mounting tab

Figure 20-34 Lag and toggle bolt mountings.

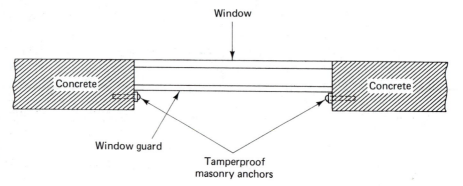

Window

Concrete

Concrete

Figure 20-35 Window guard mounting on concrete.

Window guard

Tamperproof masonry anchors

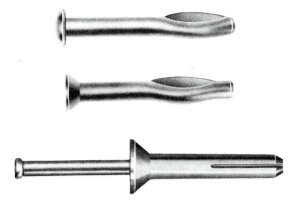

over sheathing, toggle bolts can be used (see Fig. 20-34). If at all possible, when designing window guards for a masonry surface such as a basement window, have the guard fit into the window opening to allow side mounting (see Fig. 20-35). This method of mounting is the most tamperproof. If a flush mount is required, use tamperproof masonry anchors of the type shown in Figure 20-36. A word of caution: These are high-strength permanent fastenings. Make sure that everything is in its proper place before they are set. A wide assortment of anchors and anchoring shields are commercially available. Check with local hardware or masonry suppliers for availability and recommendations.

SPIRAL STAIRCASES

Spiral staircases (see Fig. 20-37) made for a standard height of 8 feet will require 13 steps and make one complete revolution (the thirteenth step will wind up directly over the first). The spiral can be either clockwise or counterclockwise depending on location and personal preference. The center column, which is made of 3½- or 4-inch pipe, should extend 36 inches above the top of the last step (see Fig. 20-38). Therefore, an 8-foot rise would require a center column 11 feet long.

The major portion of construction can be done two ways: Each step unit can be welded directly to the column or each step can be welded onto a 4-inch pipe collar which can then be positioned on the 3½-inch pipe column and welded or bolted in place (see Fig. 20-39). The latter method will have to be used if the final staircase assembly has to be done in an area where welding would be impractical. For the purpose of demonstration we will lay out the steps with collars.

First, the center column must be assembled and layout lines struck. In this case, an 11-foot length of 3½-inch black pipe has to be capped and ground smooth on one end and have a 10-inch-diameter floor mounting plate welded on the other (see Fig. 20-40). Next, divide and mark the circumference of the pipe into 12 equal sections and lay out on each section line a mark to indicate the top of each step (see Fig. 20-41). The rise for each step will be approximately 7⅜ inches. Center punch each location to avoid having to do the layout over if lines are accidentally rubbed off.

Layout and fabrication of the individual step units will be the next procedure. Steps should be at least 24 inches wide. Use Figure 20-42 as a fabrication guide. The top of the step can be made in several different ways. It can be formed by bending ⅛-inch plate or diamond plate and welding the end cap on, or made of ¼- by 1½-inch flat stock with tabs welded as shown in Figure 20-43 to accept a wooden stair tread. All steps must be fabricated in

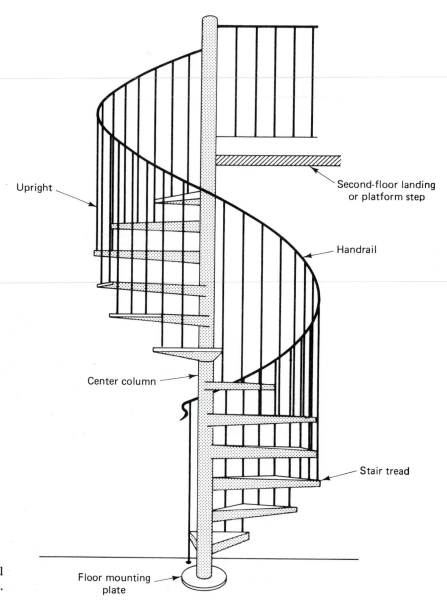

Upright

Second-floor landing
or platform step

Handrail

Center column

Stair tread

Figure 20-37 Spiral
staircase.

Floor mounting
plate

Figure 20-38 Column
extension above the
last step.

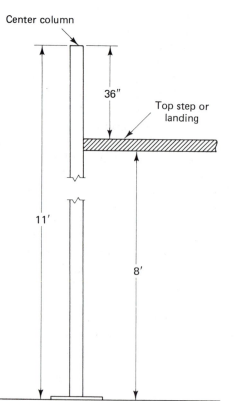

Center column

36"

Top step or
landing

11'

8'

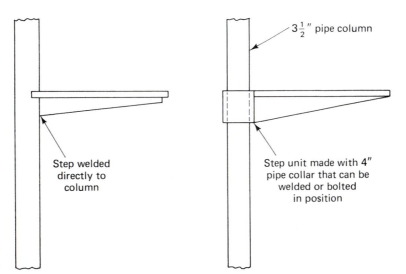

$3\frac{1}{2}''$ pipe column

Step welded
directly to
column

Step unit made with 4″
pipe collar that can be
welded or bolted
in position

Figure 20-39 Attaching steps to the column.

this fashion. If there is no provision for an upper-level landing, the thirteenth step must be made square (see Fig. 20-44).

When the steps are completed, plumb the center column in the upright position. Make sure that the column is properly secured so that it will neither fall or move. It may seem cumbersome, but this procedure will make locating steps and the layout of handrails much easier.

Slide each step unit onto the column, line them up on their respective marks, and tack weld in position. Check that each step is evenly spaced and that all have the same rise.

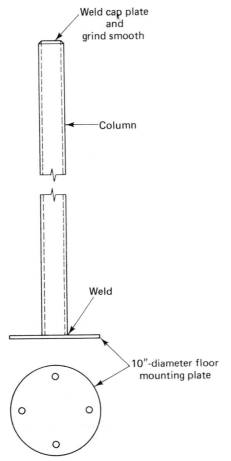

Weld cap plate
and
grind smooth

Column

Weld

10″-diameter floor
mounting plate

Figure 20-40 Center column fabrication.

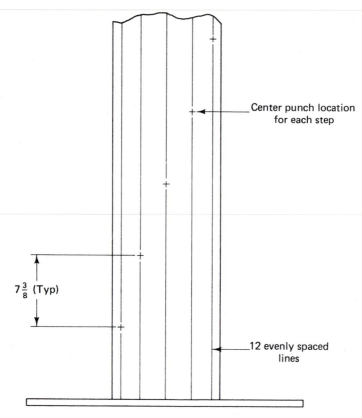

Figure 20-41 Layout for step location (approximate measurement).

Next comes the most difficult part of the layout, the handrail. The first step is to set the uprights for the handrail on each step (see Fig. 20-45). Use ½- or ⅝-inch round stock for the uprights. On solid-steel steps, weld the uprights to the top of the step. If the step was made to accept a wooden tread, weld the upright to the outside edge of the step and gusset (see Fig. 20-46). The top of the upright should measure 32 inches above the top of the step. Check to make sure that each is plumb.

The handrail itself is made of ¾-inch black pipe. To simplify fabrica-

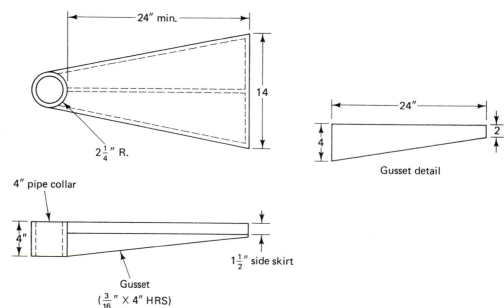

Figure 20-42 Step layout guide.

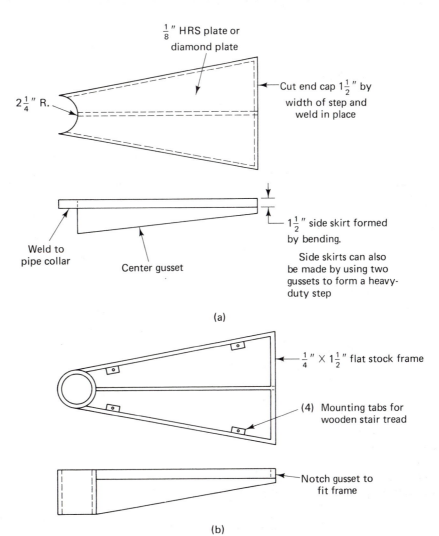

$\frac{1}{8}$ " HRS plate or diamond plate

Cut end cap $1\frac{1}{2}$ " by width of step and weld in place

$2\frac{1}{4}$ " R.

Weld to pipe collar

Center gusset

$1\frac{1}{2}$ " side skirt formed by bending.

Side skirts can also be made by using two gussets to form a heavy-duty step

(a)

$\frac{1}{4}$ " × $1\frac{1}{2}$ " flat stock frame

(4) Mounting tabs for wooden stair tread

Notch gusset to fit frame

(b)

Figure 20-43 Step design guide: (a) solid steel step, (b) frame step made to accept wooden tread.

Figure 20-44 Top-step layout.

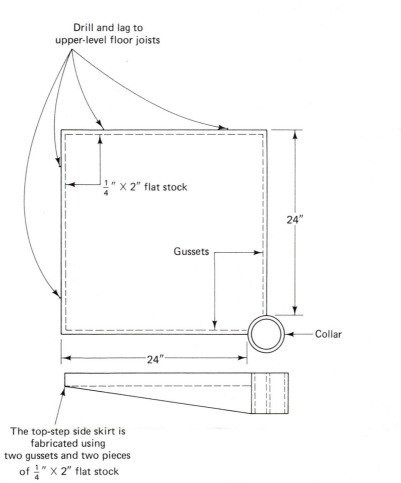

Drill and lag to upper-level floor joists

$\frac{1}{4}$ " × 2" flat stock

Gussets

24"

Collar

24"

The top-step side skirt is fabricated using two gussets and two pieces of $\frac{1}{4}$ " × 2" flat stock

293

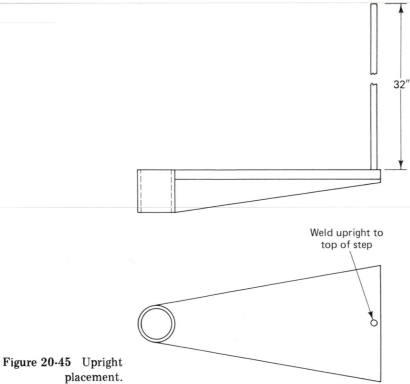

Figure 20-45 Upright placement.

tion, it can be made in sections. A bending jig of the type shown in Figure 20-47 will be needed to bend each section. These jigs are fairly easy to construct. Weld pieces of steel onto a short piece of 6- or 8-inch pipe in what resembles one quarter of a wagon wheel. Next, measure the distance from

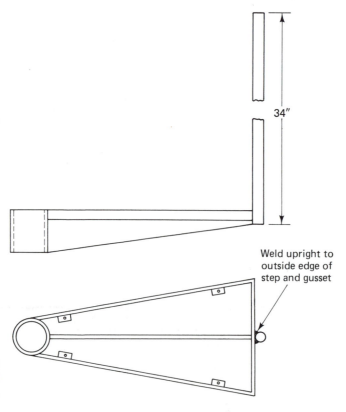

Figure 20-46 Upright placement for framed steps.

Figure 20-47 Handrail bending jig.

the center of the step collar to the inside of the upright, in this case approximately 25½ inches. Mark this distance on the bending jig and weld on the vertical legs of the jig. The last step in preparing the jig is to weld a piece of 1-inch angle or channel to the vertical legs at the same angle as the rise of the steps. With the use of a heating torch, the handrail sections can now be formed. In the ends of each section weld a plug about 1 inch long to aid in the alignment of each section (see Fig. 20-48). During the assembly, tack each completed section to the uprights. It may be necessary to adjust the curve for proper alignment and contour. This can be done using a modified heavy-duty clamp similar to that shown in Figure 20-49. When the entire railing is assembled, weld it solidly to each upright, weld up all joining seams, cap the ends, and grind smooth. Figure 20-50 illustrates several alternative handrail designs. Additional uprights can be added to produce a close upright pattern (see Fig. 20-51). These additional members can be fabricated and installed after the final handrail assembly.

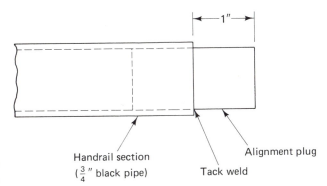

|←— 1″ —→|

Handrail section
($\frac{3}{4}$″ black pipe)

Tack weld

Alignment plug

Figure 20-48 Handrail alignment plug.

Figure 20-49 Handrail bending clamp.

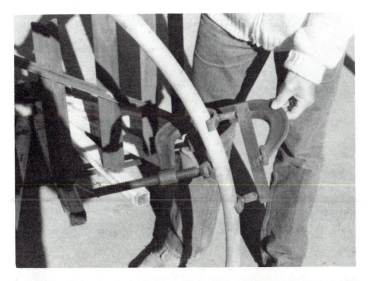

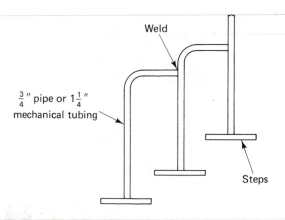

Weld

$\frac{3}{4}''$ pipe or $1\frac{1}{4}''$
mechanical tubing

Steps

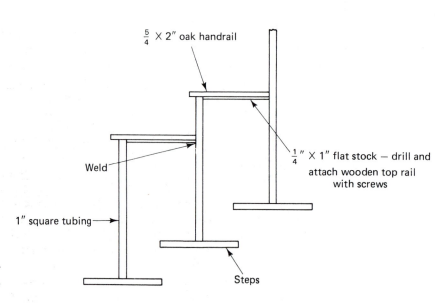

$\frac{5}{4}$ × 2″ oak handrail

Weld

$\frac{1}{4}''$ × 1″ flat stock — drill and
attach wooden top rail
with screws

1″ square tubing

Steps

Figure 20-50 Alternate handrail designs.

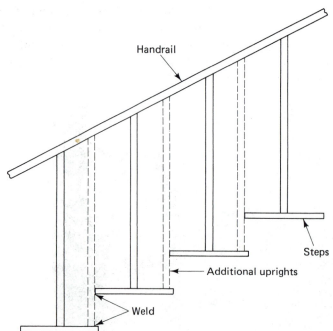

Handrail

Steps

Additional uprights

Weld

Figure 20-51 Additional uprights.

Chapter 21

BASIC TECHNIQUES

The two skills which must be developed in order to perform even the simplest smithing operations are heat control and correct use of the hammer. As stated in Chapter 19, the heat can be supplied either by forge or by heating torch. The choice of heating method should be determined by the size and number of pieces being worked, as well as the amount of heat required. For example, if one or two small pieces have to be formed, the amount of time and heat that would be needed hardly warrants the time and trouble to start up the coal forge. Often, small jobs can be worked more easily and quickly with a heating torch. Depending on the type of forming operation, working mild steel will require pieces to be heated to either a red or a yellow heat. Heat requirements will be discussed with each of the forming operations.

To make hammering more comfortable and efficient, the anvil must be set at the proper height. The rule of thumb is to have the face of the anvil touching your knuckles when your arm is hanging straight at your side (see Fig. 21-1). The anvil should also be mounted on a heavy timber or log section, not on a steel table.

Figure 21-1 Anvil at knuckle height.

TAPERING This technique is used to reduce the cross section of a piece of steel to produce a flattened end, straight taper, or point (see Fig. 21-2). To form a flattened end, heat approximately 2 inches of the workpiece (in this case ½-inch square stock) to a dark yellow color, place on the anvil, and strike with the hammer at a slight angle (see Fig. 21-3). Use moderately forceful blows. After striking several blows, turn the piece over and hammer the opposite side. This rotating back and forth should be continued throughout the operation. Reheat the workpiece when it cools to a dark red.

Always bring the hammer down so that the head strikes the work squarely (see Fig. 21-4). Using the edge of the hammer will cause sharp dents which are difficult to remove. Also keep in mind that uneven hammer

Figure 21-2 (*From top to bottom*) Flattened, tapered, and pointed ends.

Figure 21-3 Forming a flattened end.

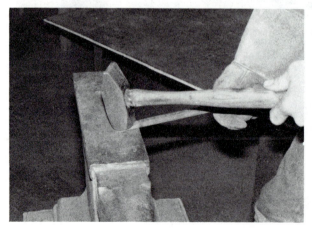

Figure 21-4 Square hammer blows.

Figure 21-5 Unevenly formed end.

Figure 21-6 Finished flat end.

blows will cause the flattened area to form unevenly. Figure 21-5 shows such an effect. In this particular case more force was exerted on the right side, causing excessive stretching. In less severe cases this condition can be corrected by applying more hammer force on the left side to compensate.

As you reach the desired shape, hammer blows should be lighter in force and more rapid. This will produce a smooth, uniform finished surface (see Fig. 21-6). Additional finishing can be done by filing.

Straight tapers are made using basically the same technique except that the spooning effect of flattening must be eliminated. This is done by periodically laying the workpiece on its side during the tapering operation to hammer out any spooning in the material in order to maintain a uniform width (see Fig. 21-7). This must be done frequently. Trying to eliminate excessive spooning will cause the steel to fold and ruin the job.

Figure 21-7 Keeping a taper straight.

Figure 21-8 Forming a tapered point.

Drawing the end of a piece of steel to a point requires constant turning during the hammering operation to ensure that all sides taper uniformly. Maintaining correct heat will make the job quite easy. Try not to let the work area get any cooler than light cherry red. To start the point, heat about 1½ inches of the end of the workpiece. Do not try to draw a long point in one single operation. You must start at the end and work back gradually.

Hammer a point on the workpiece by striking hammer blows at an angle while rotating the work 90 degrees after every two hits (see Fig. 21-8). Hammer each side uniformly until the desired point is drawn. If a longer tapered point is required, increase the length of the heated area and repeat the drawing operation.

UPSETTING   Upsetting is a method by which a portion of the workpiece is increased in cross-sectional thickness (see Fig. 21-9). This is accomplished by heating the area to a yellow heat, standing the workpiece up on end on the anvil, and

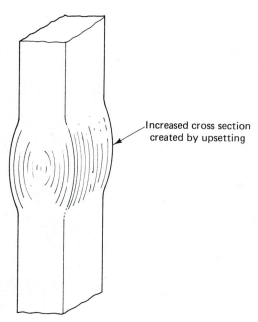

Increased cross section created by upsetting

Figure 21-9 Upsetting.

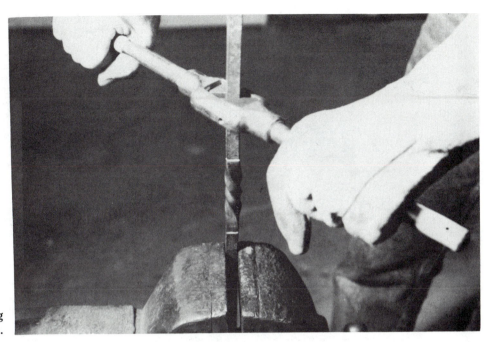

Figure 21-17 Forming
the hot twist.

Figure 21-18 Twisting
machine.

21-18 is made from a junked automobile standard transmission. When a transmission is selected, lock it into first or reverse gear for the greatest mechanical advantage. The base can be made from two pieces of angle or a piece of 6-inch channel. The dies used to hold the square stock should be approximately $\frac{1}{32}$ inch larger than the material being twisted and perfectly in line with one another so that the workpiece will remain straight during the twisting operation. The machine must be securely mounted to a workbench or stand and will easily cold-twist square stock up to $\frac{1}{2}$ inch. An example of the resulting twist is shown in Figure 21-19.

A different variation of the hot twist is the upset basket twist shown in Figure 21-20. They are made from four pieces of square or round stock welded into a section of square stock. For demonstration, we will make a 4-inch basket twist using $\frac{1}{2}$- and $\frac{1}{4}$-inch square stock. To make a 4-inch twist, cut four pieces of $\frac{1}{4}$-inch square stock 6 inches long and tape them tightly together. Next, weld them between two pieces of $\frac{1}{2}$-inch square stock. Heat the welds to a cherry red and hammer flat to give the appearance of one smooth piece (see Fig. 21-21). The length of the assembly at this

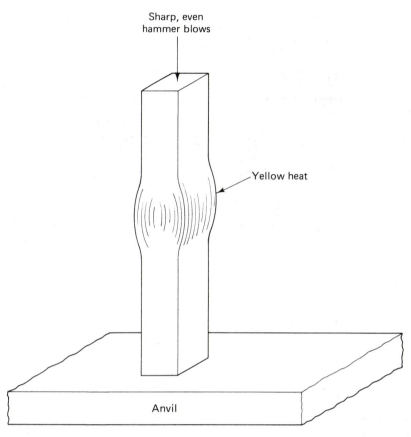

Figure 21-10 Upset
technique.

striking the other end with sharp hammer blows (see Fig. 21-10). This looks and sounds easy but is one of the most difficult techniques to master. The problem comes from the fact that the workpiece will more easily bend than compress. After several hammer blows, stop and hammer out any bends in the work area. This must be done frequently during the upsetting operation. The expansion of the area cross section happens gradually and the work must constantly be reheated. The yellow heat must be maintained to achieve the desired result.

The most common application of the upsetting process is in making sharp right-angle bends in square or round stock. The $\frac{1}{2}$-inch square stock in Figure 21-11 was heated and bent at a sharp right angle. Notice that the bending had the effect of badly stretching the metal around the outside edge, thereby reducing its cross-sectional thickness and strength. If the work

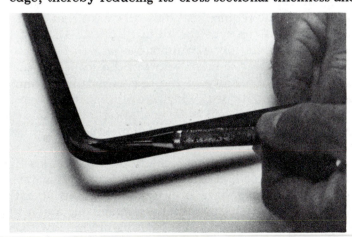

Figure 21-11 Right-
angle bend with a
reduced cross section.

Hammer to concentrate
the bulge on one side of
the workpiece

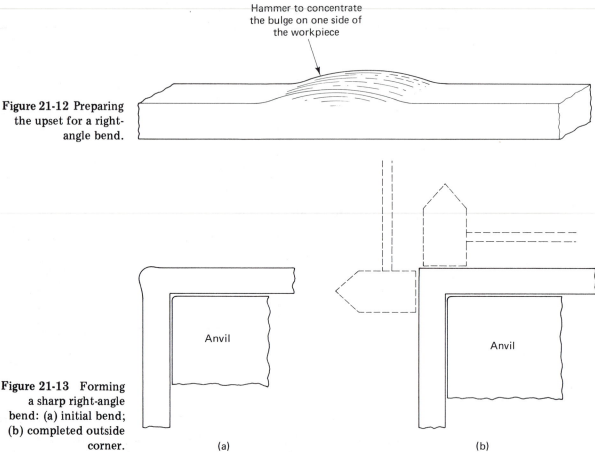

Figure 21-12 Preparing
the upset for a right-
angle bend.

Figure 21-13 Forming
a sharp right-angle
bend: (a) initial bend;
(b) completed outside
corner.

(a)   (b)

Figure 21-14 90°
twist.

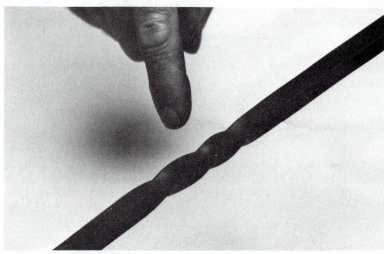

Figure 21-15 Hot
twist.

Figure 21-16 Twist
area marked with
soapstone.

area is upset prior to bending, the upset area can then be hammered and formed so that the bulge is concentrated on the side of the workpiece (see Fig. 21-12). The piece can then be reheated and bent to a sharp right angle. The extra material in the upset bulge can be hammered to form a sharp out-side corner (see Fig. 21-13). The bend will now have uniform cross-sectional thickness and strength.

TWISTING Twists can be formed both hot or cold depending on material thickness and intricacy required. The twist shown in Figure 21-14 is a simple 90-degree turn and can easily be done cold using a vise and adjustable wrench. Twists of this type would require heat only on workpieces of heavy thicknesses.

Twists of the type shown in Figure 21-15 must be done hot. The first step in the operation is to mark the area to be twisted with soapstone (see Fig. 21-16). Heat the area between the soapstone marks to a uniform light cherry red. Uniformity of the heat is very important if a consistently even twist is to be obtained. When the workpiece is heated, secure one end in a vise and the other end with a large tap handle or two adjustable wrenches (see Fig. 21-17). Turn the handle until the desired twist is obtained. In this case the 4-inch-long twist on ½-inch square stock required one complete revolution. Increasing the revolutions will produce tighter twists. After the twist is completed, remove loose scale with a wire brush and correct any bending that may have occurred during the operation. Twists done this way will have a tighter, more uniform and decorative appearance.

A simple hand-operated twisting machine of the type shown in Figure

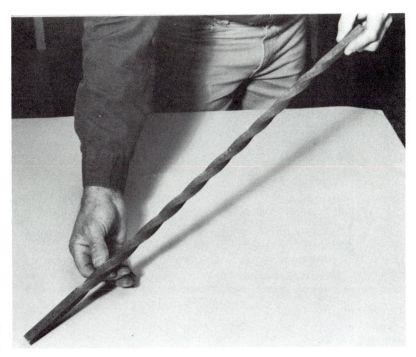

Figure 21-19 Finished machine twist.

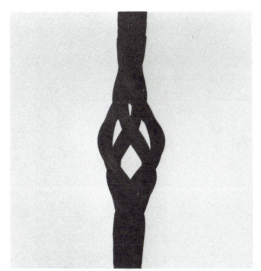

Figure 21-20 Upset basket twist.

Figure 21-21 Initial welding of twist components.

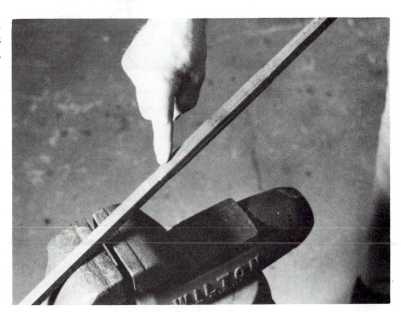

305

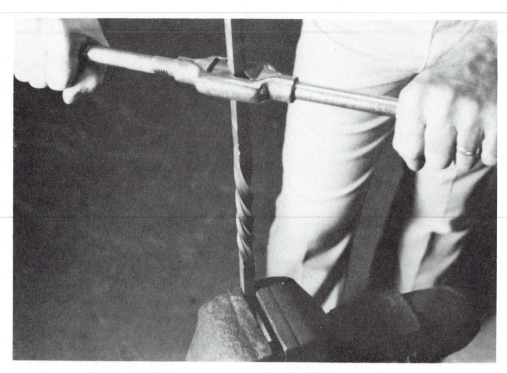

Figure 21-22 Making the initial twist.

Figure 21-23 Forming the upset.

point should be 2 inches longer than the desired finished size. Uniformly heat the welded section and twist one full revolution (see Fig. 21-22). Quickly, before the twist cools, strike the top of the bar with a hammer. This will upset the twist, forcing it to open and form the basket (see Fig. 21-23). Continue tapping with the hammer until the desired shape is achieved.

SCROLL MAKING   The fastest and easiest method of making scrolls is by using a commercially manufactured scroller (see Fig. 21-24). However, these tools are designed

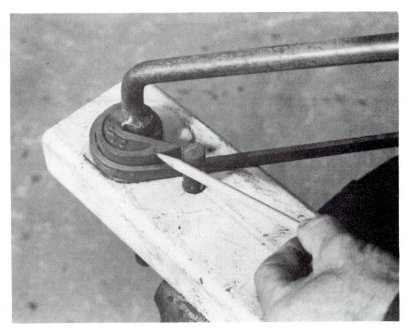

Figure 21-24 Scroller head.

only to bend scrolls of selected diameters from material cut square on the ends. This limitation may render them all but useless for custom work.

When designing a scroll layout, try to avoid the unfinished look of a square-cut end. Several other alternatives are illustrated in Figure 21-25. The tapered end is the easiest to form. The scroll material is simply drawn to a straight taper prior to bending. The rolled end is a variation of the tapered end. For this design the end of the stock must be straight-tapered to a thinner cross section. The piece is then reheated to yellow heat and hammered lightly but rapidly (see Fig. 21-26). This hammering action will cause the end of the workpiece to roll tightly. Bolt ends are formed by welding a piece of round stock to the end of the scroll material as shown in Figure 21-27. After the weld is completed, it should be hand filed to a smooth curve to give the appearance of one piece. The half-penny design is formed by heating the workpiece to yellow heat, holding it on edge and flattening (see Fig. 21-28). The flattened end can then be filed to the desired shape.

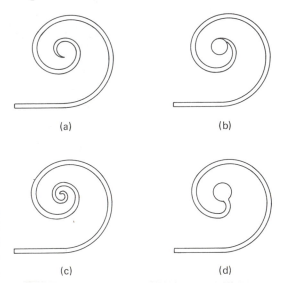

(a)

(b)

Figure 21-25 Scroll designs: (a) tapered end; (b) bolt end; (c) rolled end; (d) half-penny end.

(c)

(d)

Figure 21-26 Rolled end being formed.

Figure 21-27 Scroll bolt end.

Figure 21-28 Forming a half-penny end.

After the desired end has been shaped, the scroll itself can be formed with bending forks (see Fig. 21-29). Draw the desired scroll shape on a table-top or piece of wood. This can be used as a guide during the bending operation. If a quantity of similar scrolls has to be formed, a bending jig should be made. Take a piece of steel bar (at least ¼ inch by 1 inch) and bend it into the desired scroll shape. After the shape is formed, clamp the end of it securely in a vise and strike it on the side with a hammer in order to produce

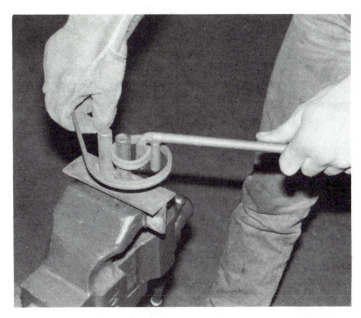

Figure 21-29 Forming a scroll with a bending fork.

a spiral (see Fig. 21-30). This can now be welded to a piece of plate and the scroll material clamped in place and bent (see Fig. 21-31). Keep in mind that in cold bending of scrolls, the finished product will always be slightly larger than the jig. If this condition is unacceptable, the jig should be made undersized or the scrolls bent hot. After removing scrolls from the bending jig, they must be hammered flat. The inside end of the scroll may also have to be hand-formed because very often the jig will leave a flat spot at the beginning of the bend.

Decorative hand railing ends of the type shown in Figure 21-32 are formed in basically the same way as a scroll. As discussed previously, drawing the desired shape on the worktable top or piece of wood will serve as a reference guide.

The bolt end design (Fig. 21-32a) is produced by welding a piece of ½-inch round stock to the end of the railing material and filing or disk sanding a smooth curve prior to bending (see Fig. 21-33). The scroll ends (Fig. 21-32b and c) are made by first tapering the railing stock as shown in Figure 21-34. End (c) is made of two pieces. Each must be tapered prior to bending.

Figure 21-30 Forming the spiral for a scroll bending jig.

Figure 21-31 Completed scroll jig.

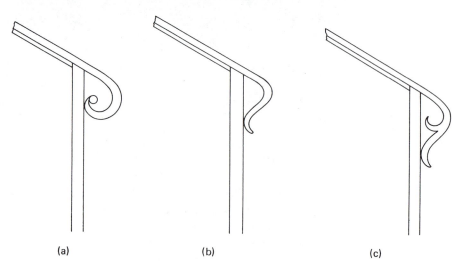

Figure 21-32 Decorative handrail ends.

(a)   (b)   (c)

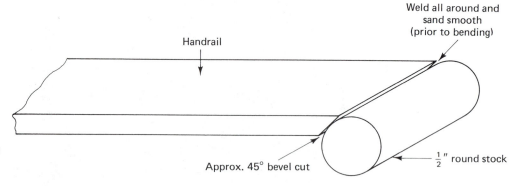

Handrail

Weld all around and sand smooth (prior to bending)

Approx. 45° bevel cut

$\frac{1}{2}$ " round stock

Figure 21-33 Layout of a bolt-end handrail.

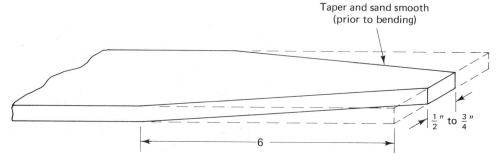

Taper and sand smooth (prior to bending)

6

$\frac{1}{2}$ " to $\frac{3}{4}$ "

Figure 21-34 Handrail tapered ends.

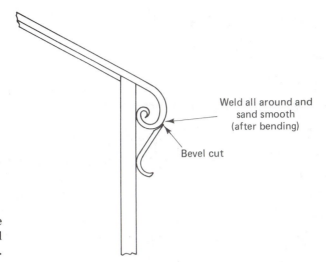

Figure 21-35 Double scroll end handrail layout.

When the forming of both pieces is complete, the joining edge (see Fig. 21-35) should be cut on a bevel so that after welding, the completed end can be more easily filed to a smooth curve. The quickest way to perform these tapering operations is with a cutting torch.

Because heavier metal is used for hand rails, the forming of the scroll end is more easily done hot. Try to avoid any sharp hammer blows during this operation, as they will easily dent the hot workpiece and cause an unsightly finish. Do most of the forming with bending forks. When the hammer must be used, strike lightly.

An alternative to using bending forks is the use of a bending jig. The type shown in Figure 21-36 was made of assorted pieces of scrap pipe and bar stock. Choice of material for the center pin is determined by the desired bend radius. For example, if a ½-inch bend radius is required, the center pin would be made of 1-inch round stock. If larger diameters are required, pipe or heavy wall mechanical tubing with the appropriate outside diameter can be used. To form the exact radius of the bending jig, the workpiece should

Figure 21-36 Bending jig for hot forming handrail ends.

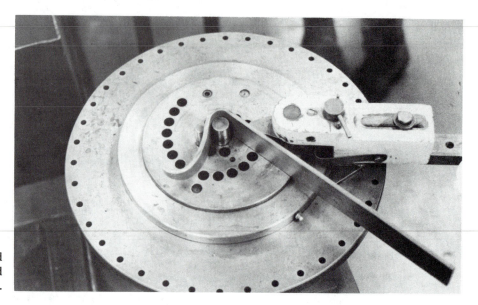

Figure 21-37 Cold forming a handrail end on a bending machine.

be heated to a cherry red in the bend area and formed hot. Accurate cold bending of material most often used in ornamental ironwork can only be done in a hydraulic bender or a mechanical forming machine of the type shown in Figure 21-37.

DECORATIVE STRAP HINGES

The hinge shown in Figure 21-38 can be formed one of two ways. The easiest method involves tracing the desired pattern on the workpiece and flame cutting the design (see Fig. 21-39). The cut piece can be easily ground or filed to the desired shape. The second method involves forming the spear shaped end with a hammer and anvil (see Fig. 21-40). A yellow heat should be maintained for easy forming. This method will work quite well on relatively light material (in this case ¼-inch by 1-inch stock) but will be very time consuming on larger designs.

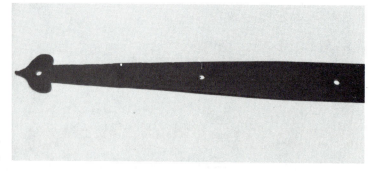

Figure 21-38 Decorative strap hinge.

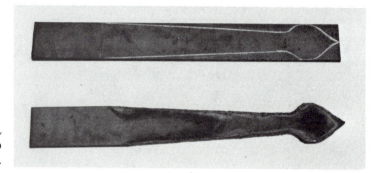

Figure 21-39 Layout and cutting of a strap hinge.

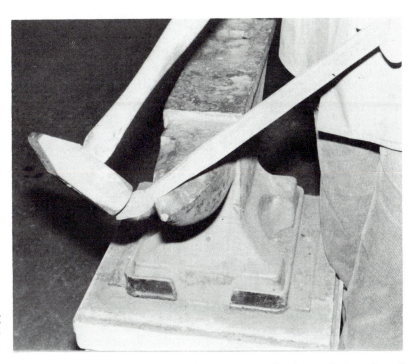

Figure 21-40 Forming a decorative strap hinge end on the anvil.

The hinge section itself can be made by roll forming the ends of the workpieces or using pieces of small-diameter pipe or structural tubing. Figure 21-41 shows two hinge design suggestions.

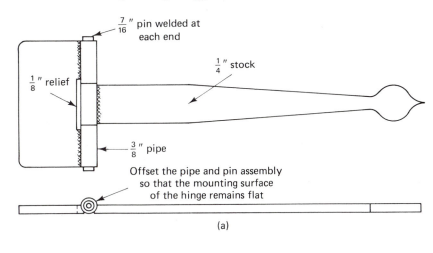

$\frac{7}{16}$" pin welded at each end

$\frac{1}{4}$" stock

$\frac{1}{8}$" relief

$\frac{3}{8}$" pipe

Offset the pipe and pin assembly so that the mounting surface of the hinge remains flat

(a)

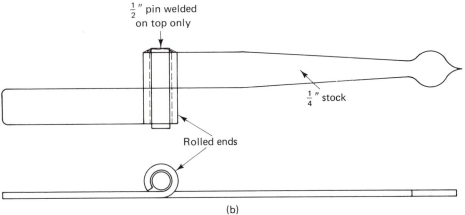

$\frac{1}{2}$" pin welded on top only

$\frac{1}{4}$" stock

Rolled ends

Figure 21-41 Hinge designs.

(b)

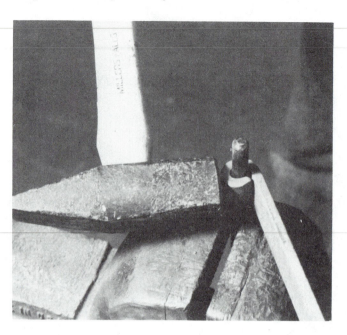

Figure 21-42 Forming
a rolled hinge end.

The ⅛-inch relief cut in part (a) will prevent the hinge from binding. The rolled ends in part (b) are formed around a bending jig as shown in Figure 21-42. Remember to maintain a yellow heat during the forming operation.

For additional information on blacksmithing and ornamental ironwork, see the readings in Appendix 2.

Chapter 22

ANNEALING, HARDENING, and TEMPERING

The discussion of heat-treating methods in this chapter will be confined to those processes most commonly done by forge or heating torch to medium- and high-carbon steels. Mild steels having a carbon content lower than 0.30% are not generally considered heat treatable, but they can be case hardened or hardsurfaced. These techniques are discussed later in the chapter. Methods used on the various alloys, particularly the nonferrous types, are discussed in Chapter 5.

The ability to alter steel hardness is extremely important to metal workers and fabricators, particularly those working in small shops. Often, tool alteration or modification will be necessary to get the job done. The following hardening and tempering processes can be used only on steel having at least a 0.30% carbon content.

ANNEALING This is a process by which steel is made soft, and internal stresses caused by forging or working are removed. This will often have to be done to hardened steel in order to have it formed, drilled, or machined. The process is accomplished by heating the workpiece to a cherry red, approximately 1500° to 1600°F, and cooling it slowly. The cooling process can be slowed down by surrounding the heated workpiece with material having a low thermal conductivity such as dry ashes or sand. The use of powdered asbestos is not recommended because of the potential health hazard. The annealing process usually takes several hours.

HARDENING Hardening is the process by which steel is heated and rapidly quenched, producing a hard and brittle part. As with annealing, the workpiece is first heated to a cherry red (approximately 1500° to 1600°F), but then quenched rapidly in room-temperature water or oil. An oil quench will produce sufficient hardness for most practical applications. On many steels, a rapid water quench may cause the workpiece to crack.

When the workpiece is put into the quench, move it vigorously in a circular motion (Fig. 22-1). If the heated workpiece is held in one spot in the quench tank, steam or gas pockets will develop and slow the cooling. Keep the heated area completely submerged until cooling is completed. The technique of flame hardening can be employed if, because of location or size, the workpiece cannot be heated and quenched in the aforementioned manner. Its greatest advantage, however, is in the ability to harden a surface rather than an entire cross section (see Fig. 22-2). This is done by working your way along the workpiece, heating the desired surface to a dull cherry red with a torch, and quenching it with a water hose (see Fig. 22-3). Both torch and hose are moved simultaneously along the length of the work to produce a continuous heating and quenching effect.

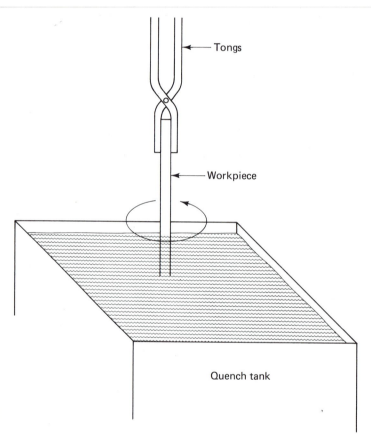

Figure 22-1 Quenching in a circular motion.

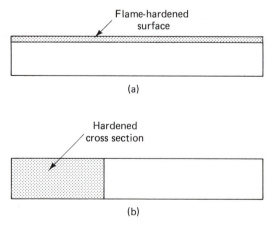

Figure 22-2 Flame-hardening effect. (a) Only the surface is hardened. The remainder of the cross section stays ductile. (b) Conventional heating and quenching methods heat treat the entire cross section.

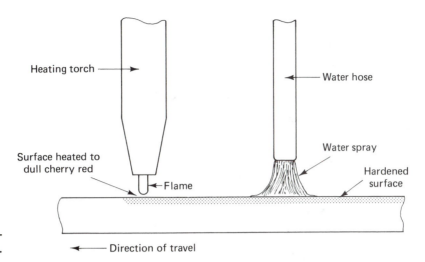

Heating torch

Water hose

Water spray

Surface heated to
dull cherry red

Hardened
surface

Flame

Figure 22-3 Flame-
hardening technique.

Direction of travel

TEMPERING   Tempering or drawing is a method used to relieve internal stresses of fully hardened steel in order to increase its toughness and ductility. Steel in the fully hardened state is too hard and brittle for most applications. Different degrees of hardness can be achieved by utilizing various tempering temperatures (see Chart 22-1). The higher the temperature, the softer the steel will become. The temperature used is therefore determined by the ductility and strength characteristic required. The color that the steel will turn during the drawing operation is used to determine the desired temperature. If the workpiece is sanded to a bright clean finish, the color spectrum caused by increasing heat will be highly visible. Before any tempering can be done, the workpiece must be in the fully hardened state. After this is accomplished, the area to be tempered must be sanded to a bright shiny finish. This is imperative if accurate tempering is to be done. The color spectrum will not be visible on a scaley surface. The part can now be heated until the desired color is reached and quenched in oil. A variety of oils are recommended for this use (mineral oil, olive oil, light machine oil); however, light motor oil is the least expensive and will work quite well. The oil should be used at room temperature.

An example of the tempering process is shown in Figure 22-4. Notice that the prehardened and polished center punch tip is being heated indirectly (the flame is being concentrated on the opposite end). As the heat travels

CHART 22-1   Tempering Chart

Color	Approximate temperature (°F)	Applications
Blue	570	Screwdriver tips, wrenches, springs, pliers
Dark purple	550	Knife blades, cold chisels
Light purple	530	Scribes, center punches
Dark straw	480	Punches, dies, pry bars
Straw	460	Hammer faces, reamers
Light straw	440	Drills, milling cutters
Very light straw	420	Lathe cutting tools, bearing scrapers

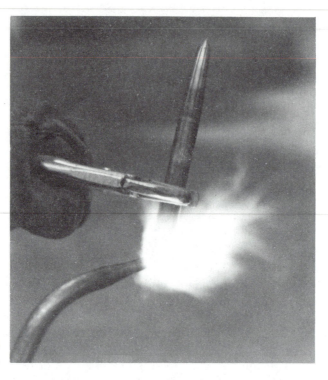

Figure 22-4
Tempering.

up the workpiece, the tip will start to turn colors. When the tip reaches the desired color, in this case light purple, it should be quenched in oil. Only quench the tip end (see Fig. 22-5). The striking end will now cool slowly and start to anneal. This will prevent the striking end of the punch from cracking during use. Remember to move the tip in a circular motion during quenching.

A readily available supply of the medium- and high-carbon steel needed to make simple tools and pieces of equipment can be found in your local junkyard. Items such as leaf and coil springs, files, power hacksaw blades, and axle shafts can be used successfully. Figure 22-6 shows a variety of tools made from junk. The bearing scraper was formed from a three-sided file. Most of the rough forming was done hot and then finished by grinding. The completed scraper was hardened and then tempered (light straw).

Figure 22-5 Quench-
ing the tempered end
in oil.

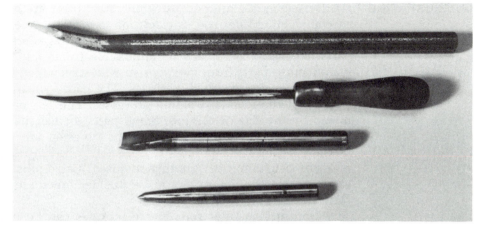

Figure 22-6 Hand-made tools. (*From top to bottom*) Pry bar, bearing scraper, chisel, and punch.

The chisel, pry bar, and center punch were made from a small-diameter axle shaft. Each was hot formed with a hammer and anvil and ground to a finish. Upon completion, all were hardened and tempered using Chart 22-1 as a guide. In each case the tempering heat was applied indirectly as shown previously, and only the working end of each of the tools was quenched.

CASE HARDENING   This is a process used to surface harden a thin outer layer of a piece of steel while allowing the inner core to remain soft and ductile. This method is used primarily on low-carbon steel. As stated previously, low-carbon steel is not considered heat treatable because its carbon content is not sufficient to be drastically affected by heating and quenching. What the case-hardening process does is add carbon to the metal surface by means of a carburizing agent. The material most commonly used for this purpose is Kasenite. This granular black powder, consisting of almost pure carbon, is the agent recommended most because it is noncombustible and nontoxic.

The following case-hardening procedure is suggested:

1. Heat the workpiece uniformly to a cherry red (approximately 1650°F).
2. Dip and roll the heated piece into the Kasenite powder.
3. Reheat the part until it returns to dull red. The case-hardening compound will start to bubble and form a crust.
4. Repeat step 2 and reheat until the dull red color is reestablished.
5. Quench the workpiece rapidly in cold water. Move the part vigorously in a circular motion while quenching.

Always wear tinted safety glasses and work in a well-ventilated area when case hardening. The carburizing compound produces a bright glare and quite a lot of smoke.

A less effective alternative method of case hardening can be done with an oxyacetylene torch using the following procedure:

1. Heat the part to a uniform cherry red using a neutral flame.
2. Shut off the oxygen valve completely. The flame of pure acetylene will produce a heavy carbon soot.
3. Let the soot of the flame coat the heated area.
4. Turn the oxygen valve back on to form a neutral flame and reheat the workpiece to a cherry red.
5. Repeat steps 3 and 4 three more times and quench the part rapidly in cold water.

HARDSURFACING   Hardsurfacing is a method by which steel parts are coated or layered with a special welding filler rod or electrode to increase its corrosion, wear, and impact resistance. The process's greatest advantages are in the repair of worn parts expensive to replace or impossible to get and in giving the ability to manufacture parts from inexpensive mild steel which can then be surfaced to produce the desired characteristics. The hardsurfacing method can be done by any of the manual welding processes. The process used is usually determined by the size of the job. Small parts such as shear blades, punches, and dies would best be done by the gas tungsten arc (TIG) or oxyacetylene method because the process can be controlled more carefully with a minimum of machining or grinding required. Large jobs such as those done on earth-moving equipment would be shielded metal arc (stick) or gas metal arc (MIG) welded.

Hardsurface filler rods and electrodes can be broadly classed in four groups: ferrous-based alloys, tungsten cobalt, tungsten carbide, and copper alloy. The ferrous-based alloys (nickel, chromium, molybdenum, manganese) are added singularly or in combination to the welding rods to produce a surface with high corrosion and impact resistance. Tungsten cobalt rods are used when high abrasion resistance and red hardness (the ability to maintain hardness at high temperatures) are desired. The tungsten carbide alloy is employed when severe abrasion resistance is imperative. The copper-alloy filler rods, particularly silicon bronze, have good corrosion resistance and are easy to apply with the oxyacetylene and TIG process.

When hardsurfacing with the oxyacetylene torch, weld with a carburizing flame (excessive acetylene). This will add carbon to the weld deposit and increase hardness.

Most hardsurfacing applications require a skilled welder. For this reason, coupled with the fact that hardsurfacing electrodes can cost as much as $20 a pound, those inexperienced in this area should consult local welding suppliers for job recommendations.

THERMAL   Thermal spraying can also be used to surface mild-steel parts. The process
SPRAYING   utilizes an electric arc, oxy-fuel flame, or plasma arc to melt and propel the coating material and bond it to the work surface. The coatings can either be hard or soft, metallic or nonmetallic (ceramic), and produce a variety of surface characteristics, such as abrasive wear, heat, and saltwater corrosion resistance. The process is quite often used to build up worn surfaces to allow for remachining. Because of the specialized equipment required, the average fabrication shop will seldom have thermal spraying capabilities. If a special surfacing problem presents itself, more detailed information can be obtained from local welding distributors or companies specializing in the process.

Appendix 1

GLOSSARY

AISI: American Iron and Steel Institute.

Anneal: To make soft or to remove temper.

ASTM: American Society for Testing and Materials.

Back-shear: A secondary operation to obtain a final and more accurate dimension.

Bank edge: The edge of a blank piece from which all dimensions must begin.

Burr: A sharp residual edge. The result of sawing, punching, shearing, etc.

Case harden: To harden only the surface of a metal object to a certain depth.

Cast iron: An alloy consisting mainly of iron, silicon, and carbon. Very hard and brittle, with low tensile strength but high compressive strength.

Chassis: A metal structure that will carry a variety of electrical and electronic components.

Cold working: Bending, twisting, or drawing of metal at conventional temperatures. Also called strain hardening.

Coordinates: A set of lines, the intersection of which marks the location of a detail, such as a hole, cutout, etc.

Deoxidizer: An agent that attracts and utilizes oxygen.

Ductility: The ability of a material to deform without fracturing.

Elongation: Usually expressed as a percentage. The amount a material will stretch or yield before a fracture occurs.

Extruded: To form metal by forcing it through a variety of shaped dies.

Ferrous: An alloy whose principal ingredient is iron.

Fillet weld: An inside corner weld joining two pieces whose surfaces are approximately 90 degrees to each other.

Fishplate: A plate that overlaps a welded or bolted joint and is used to increase cross-sectional thickness and strength.

Flame cutting: Cutting that utilizes the flame of an oxy-fuel torch and high-pressure stream of oxygen.

Flange: Any flat surface that results from a bending operation. A rim or projection for attaching purposes.

Flipping: The reorientation of the original starting points (zero edges) by turning over or rotation of the part.

Flux: A chemical agent that removes surface contaminents which would interfere with welding, brazing, or soldering.

Forging: Forming of metal by repeated hammer blows.

Galvanic action: The process by which a metal begins to break down when exposed to a particular environment or atmosphere.

Graduation: The markings on any type of measuring device.

Groove weld: The welding of two pieces of metal whose joining edges are beveled in order to increase weld penetration.

Hardness: In metallurgical terms, the ability to resist penetration.

Hardsurfacing: Hardening steel surfaces by means of special welding filler rods or electrodes (also called hardfacing).

Heating torch: An oxy-fuel torch tip specifically designed for heating operations (also called a rosebud tip).

Heat treatment: A method of imparting mechanical properties to metal by various thermal exposures.

Hypotenuse: The longest side of a triangle, opposite the 90-degree right angle.

Induction heating: Heating with the use of electric coils or prods.

Inert-gas welding: A method of fusion welding that eliminates the need for a flux by enveloping the weld in an inert-gas atmosphere.

In-house: To resort to one's own facilities rather than purchasing from the outside.

Job shop: A smaller shop which takes in a variety of limited work from larger firms.

Kerf: The gap left by material removed in a cutting operation.

Layout dye: A blue marking dye used on metal surfaces to facilitate accurate layout.

Lead person: A person who either makes or double checks layouts, templates, and machine setups. Usually carries out orders of a department foreman.

Loupe (jeweler's): A small magnifying glass, usually providing two or three times magnification.

Malleable: The ability of a metal to be easily formed by a hammering and forging.

MAPP gas: A synthetic hydrocarbon fuel gas (methyl acetylene propadiene).

Mechanic: A person who is capable of performing all the operations within a trade area and can work with a minimum of supervision.

Mensuration: The act of measuring.

Mild steel: Steel with a minimum carbon content.

Milling: A machine process wherein a cutting tool is applied to the work, which can be moved both horizontally and vertically.

Miter: A 90-degree corner formed by two members each cut to 45 degrees.

Nominal: The exact dimension required without any consideration for deviation.

Nonferrous: An alloy containing no iron or only trace amounts.

Notch effect: A crack caused by an insufficient radius of an inside corner.

Numerical control: A method of manufacture wherein the coordinate location of details are programmed into a machine for automatic execution.

Oxides: A compound of oxygen combined with another element(s).

Pilot hole: A small-diameter hole made to facilitate easier drilling with large-diameter bits or other devices.

Plumb: A term used to indicate if a line or surface is exactly vertical.

Primer: An undercoating or base for subsequent painting.

Prototype: The first of its kind or the making of only a few of a certain kind.

Quenching: Rapid cooling by immersion in a liquid.

Radii: More than one radius.

Radius: A segment of a line from the center of a circle to an outer point. A segment of a circle as defined by a stated radius dimension.

Ram: The part of a machine that cycles and holds the tool which acts on the work.

SAE: Society of Automotive Engineers.

Scriber: A sharp pointed or edged device for scratch marking metal.

Shear strength: The resistance a metal offers to any shearing action (approximately 80% of tensile strength).

Shim: A thin metal piece used to make up very small dimensional differences.

Soapstone: A marking device which leaves a nonpowdering line.

Stick welding: A common shop term for shielded metal arc welding which utilizes a flux-coated electrode.

Strain harden: *See* Cold working.

Tack welding: Short welds used to hold parts in alignment.

Tapering: Reducing the cross section of a piece of metal by heating and hammering (also referred to as drawing out).

Tapping: The process of producing internal threads.

Temper: A degree of hardness induced by either heat treatment or cold working.

Template: A master pattern from which actual parts of duplicate settings can be made. Usually made of a more durable material than subsequent reproductions.

Tensile strength: The strength of material when resisting a force that tends to stretch it.

Tolerance: The amount of deviation allowed for a dimension.

Tool steel: Steel alloyed with various elements to impart specific characteristics needed for hard and repeated use, usually under high-heat conditions.

Torque tightening: The tightening of nuts and bolts to a specified torque using a torque wrench (usually measured in foot-pounds).

Toughness: The ability of a metal to resist tearing, such as in punching and shearing operations.

Triangulation: Method of determining a location by means of bearings from two known and fixed points.

Turning: A machine process in which the work is rotated against an adjustable but essentially fixed cutting tool.

Ultimate strength: The point at which a fracture occurs under a tensile force.

Upsetting: A process by which a steel bar is heated and compressed by hammer blows to increase cross-sectional thickness.

Vernier: A scale used to indicate finer divisions of a larger scale. May either be in fractions, hundredths, or thousandths of an inch.

Weld penetration: The depth of fusion in the base metal as measured from its surface.

Wrought: Worked into shape by mechanical means.

Yield strength: The point at which a material begins to change shape or deform.

Appendix 2

REFERENCE READING LIST

Brady, G.S. *Materials Handbook*. New York: McGraw-Hill, 1971.

Carr, R.H., and R.L. O'Con. *Welding Practices and Procedures*. Englewood Cliffs, N.J.: Prentice-Hall, 1983.

Giesecke, F., A. Mitchell, H. Spencer, and I. Hill. *Technical Drawing*. New York: Macmillan, 1967.

Steel Construction Manual. New York: American Institute of Steel Construction, 1953.

Streeter, D. *Professional Smithing*. New York: Scribner's, 1980.

Tronaas, E.M. *Mathematics for Technicians*. Englewood Cliffs, N.J.: Prentice-Hall, 1971.

Van Leuven, E.P. *General Trade Mathematics*. New York: McGraw-Hill, 1952.

Weygers, A.G. *The Modern Blacksmith*. New York: Van Nostrand Reinhold, 1974.

Appendix 3

DATA SECTION

Fraction, Decimal, and Millimeter Conversion Chart

Decimals to Millimeters				Fractions to Decimals to Millimeters					
Decimal	mm	Decimal	mm	Fraction	Decimal	mm	Fraction	Decimal	mm
0.001	0.0254	0.500	12.7000	1/64	0.0156	0.3969	33/64	0.5156	13.0969
0.002	0.0508	0.510	12.9540	1/32	0.0312	0.7938	17/32	0.5312	13.4938
0.003	0.0762	0.520	13.2080	3/64	0.0469	1.1906	35/64	0.5469	13.8906
0.004	0.1016	0.530	13.4620						
0.005	0.1270	0.540	13.7160						
0.006	0.1524	0.550	13.9700	1/16	0.0625	1.5875	9/16	0.5625	14.2875
0.007	0.1778	0.560	14.2240						
0.008	0.2032	0.570	14.4780						
0.009	0.2286	0.580	14.7320	5/64	0.0781	1.9844	37/64	0.5781	14.6844
		0.590	14.9860	3/32	0.0938	2.3812	19/32	0.5938	15.0812
0.010	0.2540			7/64	0.1094	2.7781	39/64	0.6094	15.4781
0.020	0.5080								
0.030	0.7620								
0.040	1.0160	0.600	15.2400	1/8	0.1250	3.1750	5/8	0.6250	15.8750
0.050	1.2700	0.610	15.4940						
0.060	1.5240	0.620	15.7480						
0.070	1.7780	0.630	16.0020	9/64	0.1406	3.5719	41/64	0.6406	16.2719
0.080	2.0320	0.640	16.2560	5/32	0.1562	3.9688	21/32	0.6562	16.6688
0.090	2.2860	0.650	16.5100	11/64	0.1719	4.3656	43/64	0.6719	17.0656
0.100	2.5400	0.660	16.7640						
0.110	2.7940	0.670	17.0180						
0.120	3.0480	0.680	17.2720	3/16	0.1875	4.7625	11/16	0.6875	17.4625
0.130	3.3020	0.690	17.5260						
0.140	3.5560								
0.150	3.8100			13/64	0.2031	5.1594	45/64	0.7031	17.8594
0.160	4.0640	0.700	17.7800	7/32	0.2188	5.5562	23/32	0.7188	18.2562
0.170	4.3180	0.710	18.0340	15/64	0.2344	5.9531	47/64	0.7344	18.6531
0.180	4.5720	0.720	18.2880						
0.190	4.8260	0.730	18.5420						
0.200	5.0800	0.740	18.7960	1/4	0.2500	6.3500	3/4	0.7500	19.0500
0.210	5.3340	0.750	19.0500						
0.220	5.5880	0.760	19.3040	17/64	0.2656	6.7469	49/64	0.7656	19.4469
0.230	5.8420	0.770	19.5580	9/32	0.2812	7.1438	25/32	0.7812	19.8438
0.240	6.0960	0.780	19.8120	19/64	0.2969	7.5406	51/64	0.7969	20.2406
0.250	6.3500	0.790	20.0660						
0.260	6.6040								
0.270	6.8580			5/16	0.3125	7.9375	13/16	0.8125	20.6375
0.280	7.1120	0.800	20.3200						
0.290	7.3660	0.810	20.5740						
		0.820	20.8280	21/64	0.3281	8.3344	53/64	0.8281	21.0344
0.300	7.6200	0.830	21.0820	11/32	0.3438	8.7312	27/32	0.8438	21.4312
0.310	7.8740	0.840	21.3360	23/64	0.3594	9.1281	55/64	0.8594	21.8281
0.320	8.1280	0.850	21.5900						
0.330	8.3820	0.860	21.8440						
0.340	8.6360	0.870	22.0980	3/8	0.3750	9.5250	7/8	0.8750	22.2250
0.350	8.8900	0.880	22.3520						
0.360	9.1440	0.890	22.6060						
0.370	9.3980			25/64	0.3906	9.9219	57/64	0.8906	22.6219
0.380	9.6520			13/32	0.4062	10.3188	29/32	0.9062	23.0188
0.390	9.9060			27/64	0.4219	10.7156	59/64	0.9219	23.4156
		0.900	22.8600						
0.400	10.1600	0.910	23.1140						
0.410	10.4140	0.920	23.3680	7/16	0.4375	11.1125	15/16	0.9375	23.8125
0.420	10.6680	0.930	23.6220						
0.430	10.9220	0.940	23.8760						
0.440	11.1760	0.950	24.1300	29/64	0.4531	11.5094	61/64	0.9531	24.2094
0.450	11.4300	0.960	24.3840	15/32	0.4688	11.9062	31/32	0.9688	24.6062
0.460	11.6840	0.970	24.6380	31/64	0.4844	12.3031	63/64	0.9844	25.0031
0.470	11.9380	0.980	24.8920						
0.480	12.1920	0.990	25.1460						
0.490	12.4460	1.000	25.4000	1/2	0.5000	12.7000	1	1.0000	25.4000

Roots and Powers

n	n^2	$\sqrt{n}$	$\sqrt{10n}$	n^3	$\sqrt[3]{n}$	$\sqrt[3]{10n}$	$\sqrt[3]{100n}$	$1/n$
1.0	1.0000	1.0000	3.1623	1.0000	1.0000	2.1544	4.6416	1.0000
1.1	1.2100	1.0488	3.3166	1.3310	1.0323	2.2240	4.7914	.9091
1.2	1.4400	1.0954	3.4641	1.7280	1.0627	2.2894	4.9324	.8333
1.3	1.6900	1.1402	3.6056	2.1970	1.0914	2.3513	5.0658	.7692
1.4	1.9600	1.1832	3.7417	2.7440	1.1187	2.4101	5.1925	.7143
1.5	2.2500	1.2247	3.8730	3.3750	1.1447	2.4662	5.3133	.6667
1.6	2.5600	1.2649	4.0000	4.0960	1.1696	2.5198	5.4288	.6250
1.7	2.8900	1.3038	4.1231	4.9130	1.1935	2.5713	5.5397	.5882
1.8	3.2400	1.3416	4.2426	5.8320	1.2164	2.6207	5.6462	.5556
1.9	3.6100	1.3784	4.3589	6.8590	1.2386	2.6684	5.7489	.5263
2.0	4.0000	1.4142	4.4721	8.0000	1.2599	2.7144	5.8480	.5000
2.1	4.4100	1.4491	4.5826	9.2610	1.2806	2.7589	5.9439	.4762
2.2	4.8400	1.4832	4.6904	10.6480	1.3006	2.8020	6.0368	.4545
2.3	5.2900	1.5166	4.7958	12.1670	1.3200	2.8439	6.1269	.4348
2.4	5.7600	1.5492	4.8990	13.8240	1.3389	2.8845	6.2145	.4167
2.5	6.2500	1.5811	5.0000	15.6250	1.3572	2.9240	6.2996	.4000
2.6	6.7600	1.6125	5.0990	17.5760	1.3751	2.9625	6.3825	.3846
2.7	7.2900	1.6432	5.1962	19.6830	1.3925	3.0000	6.4633	.3704
2.8	7.8400	1.6733	5.2915	21.9520	1.4095	3.0366	6.5421	.3571
2.9	8.4100	1.7029	5.3852	24.3890	1.4260	3.0723	6.6191	.3448
3.0	9.0000	1.7321	5.4772	27.0000	1.4422	3.1072	6.6943	.3333
3.1	9.6100	1.7607	5.5678	29.7910	1.4581	3.1414	6.7679	.3226
3.2	10.2400	1.7889	5.6569	32.7680	1.4736	3.1748	6.8399	.3125
3.3	10.8900	1.8166	5.7446	35.9370	1.4888	3.2075	6.9104	.3030
3.4	11.5600	1.8439	5.8310	39.3040	1.5037	3.2396	6.9795	.2941
3.5	12.2500	1.8708	5.9161	42.8750	1.5183	3.2711	7.0473	.2857
3.6	12.9600	1.8974	6.0000	46.6560	1.5326	3.3019	7.1138	.2778
3.7	13.6900	1.9235	6.0828	50.6530	1.5467	3.3322	7.1791	.2703
3.8	14.4400	1.9494	6.1644	54.8720	1.5605	3.3620	7.2432	.2632
3.9	15.2100	1.9748	6.2450	59.3190	1.5741	3.3912	7.3061	.2564
4.0	16.0000	2.0000	6.3246	64.0000	1.5874	3.4200	7.3681	.2500
4.1	16.8100	2.0248	6.4031	68.9210	1.6005	3.4482	7.4290	.2439
4.2	17.6400	2.0494	6.4807	74.0880	1.6134	3.4760	7.4889	.2381
4.3	18.4900	2.0736	6.5574	79.5070	1.6261	3.5034	7.5478	.2326
4.4	19.3600	2.0976	6.6333	85.1840	1.6386	3.5303	7.6059	.2273
4.5	20.2500	2.1213	6.7082	91.1250	1.6510	3.5569	7.6631	.2222
4.6	21.1600	2.1448	6.7823	97.3360	1.6631	3.5830	7.7194	.2174
4.7	22.0900	2.1679	6.8557	103.823	1.6751	3.6088	7.7750	.2128
4.8	23.0400	2.1909	6.9282	110.592	1.6869	3.6342	7.8297	.2083
4.9	24.0100	2.2136	7.0000	117.649	1.6985	3.6593	7.8837	.2041
5.0	25.0000	2.2361	7.0711	125.000	1.7100	3.6840	7.9370	.2000
5.1	26.0100	2.2583	7.1414	132.651	1.7213	3.7084	7.9896	.1961
5.2	27.0400	2.2804	7.2111	140.608	1.7325	3.7325	8.0415	.1923
5.3	28.0900	2.3022	7.2801	148.877	1.7435	3.7563	8.0927	.1887
5.4	29.1600	2.3238	7.3485	157.464	1.7544	3.7798	8.1433	.1852

Source: *E.M. Tronaas*, Mathematics for Technicians. *Englewood Cliffs, N.J.: Prentice-Hall, 1971.*

Roots and Powers (*Continued*)

n	n^2	$\sqrt{n}$	$\sqrt{10n}$	n^3	$\sqrt[3]{n}$	$\sqrt[3]{10n}$	$\sqrt[3]{100n}$	$1/n$
5.5	30.2500	2.3452	7.4162	166.375	1.7652	3.8030	8.1932	.1818
5.6	31.3600	2.3664	7.4833	175.616	1.7758	3.8259	8.2426	.1786
5.7	32.4900	2.3875	7.5498	185.193	1.7863	3.8485	8.2913	.1754
5.8	33.6400	2.4083	7.6158	195.112	1.7967	3.8709	8.3396	.1724
5.9	34.8100	2.4290	7.6811	205.379	1.8070	3.8930	8.3872	.1695
6.0	36.0000	2.4495	7.7460	216.000	1.8171	3.9149	8.4343	.1667
6.1	37.2100	2.4698	7.8102	226.981	1.8272	3.9365	8.4809	.1639
6.2	38.4400	2.4900	7.8740	238.328	1.8371	3.9579	8.5270	.1613
6.3	39.6900	2.5100	7.9372	250.047	1.8469	3.9791	8.5726	.1587
6.4	40.9600	2.5298	8.0000	262.144	1.8566	4.0000	8.6177	.1563
6.5	42.2500	2.5495	8.0623	274.625	1.8663	4.0207	8.6624	.1538
6.6	43.5600	2.5690	8.1240	287.496	1.8758	4.0412	8.7066	.1515
6.7	44.8900	2.5884	8.1854	300.763	1.8852	4.0615	8.7503	.1493
6.8	46.2400	2.6077	8.2462	314.432	1.8945	4.0817	8.7937	.1471
6.9	47.6100	2.6268	8.3066	328.509	1.9038	4.1016	8.8366	.1449
7.0	49.0000	2.6458	8.3666	343.000	1.9129	4.1213	8.8790	.1429
7.1	50.4100	2.6646	8.4261	357.911	1.9220	4.1408	8.9211	.1408
7.2	51.8400	2.6833	8.4853	373.248	1.9310	4.1602	8.9628	.1389
7.3	53.2900	2.7019	8.5440	389.017	1.9399	4.1793	9.0041	.1370
7.4	54.7600	2.7203	8.6023	405.224	1.9487	4.1983	9.0450	.1351
7.5	56.2500	2.7386	8.6603	421.875	1.9574	4.2172	9.0856	.1333
7.6	57.7600	2.7568	8.7178	438.976	1.9661	4.2358	9.1258	.1316
7.7	59.2900	2.7749	8.7750	456.533	1.9747	4.2543	9.1657	.1299
7.8	60.8400	2.7928	8.8318	474.552	1.9832	4.2727	9.2052	.1282
7.9	62.4100	2.8107	8.8882	493.039	1.9916	4.2908	9.2443	.1266
8.0	64.0000	2.8284	8.9443	512.000	2.0000	4.3089	9.2832	.1250
8.1	65.6100	2.8460	9.0000	531.441	2.0083	4.3267	9.3217	.1235
8.2	67.2400	2.8636	9.0554	551.368	2.0165	4.3445	9.3599	.1220
8.3	68.8900	2.8810	9.1104	571.787	2.0247	4.3621	9.3978	.1205
8.4	70.5600	2.8983	9.1652	592.704	2.0328	4.3795	9.4354	.1190
8.5	72.2500	2.9155	9.2195	614.125	2.0408	4.3968	9.4727	.1176
8.6	73.9600	2.9326	9.2736	636.056	2.0488	4.4140	9.5097	.1163
8.7	75.6900	2.9496	9.3274	658.503	2.0567	4.4310	9.5464	.1149
8.8	77.4400	2.9665	9.3808	681.472	2.0646	4.4480	9.5828	.1136
8.9	79.2100	2.9833	9.4340	704.969	2.0723	4.4647	9.6190	.1124
9.0	81.0000	3.0000	9.4868	729.000	2.0801	4.4814	9.6549	.1111
9.1	82.8100	3.0166	9.5394	753.571	2.0878	4.4979	9.6905	.1099
9.2	84.6400	3.0332	9.5917	778.688	2.0954	4.5144	9.7259	.1087
9.3	86.4900	3.0496	9.6436	804.357	2.1029	4.5307	9.7610	.1075
9.4	88.3600	3.0659	9.6954	830.584	2.1105	4.5468	9.7959	.1064
9.5	90.2500	3.0822	9.7468	857.375	2.1179	4.5629	9.8305	.1053
9.6	92.1600	3.0984	9.7980	884.736	2.1253	4.5789	9.8648	.1042
9.7	94.0900	3.1145	9.8489	912.673	2.1327	4.5947	9.8990	.1031
9.8	96.0400	3.1305	9.8995	941.192	2.1400	4.6104	9.9329	.1020
9.9	98.0100	3.1464	9.9499	970.299	2.1472	4.6261	9.9666	.1010
10.0	100.000	3.1623	10.000	1000.00	2.1544	4.6416	10.0000	.1000

Natural Trigonometric Functions

Degrees	Radians	Sin	Cos	Tan	Cot	Sec	Csc		
0° 00′	.0000	.0000	1.0000	.0000	——	1.000	——	1.5708	90° 00′
10	029	029	000	029	343.8	000	343.8	679	50
20	058	058	000	058	171.9	000	171.9	650	40
30	.0087	.0087	1.0000	.0087	114.6	1.000	114.6	1.5621	30
40	116	116	.9999	116	85.94	000	85.95	592	20
50	145	145	999	145	68.75	000	68.76	563	10
1° 00′	.0175	.0175	.9998	.0175	57.29	1.000	57.30	1.5533	89° 00′
10	204	204	998	204	49.10	000	49.11	504	50
20	233	233	997	233	42.96	000	42.98	475	40
30	.0262	.0262	.9997	.0262	38.19	1.000	38.20	1.5446	30
40	291	291	996	291	34.37	000	34.38	417	20
50	320	320	995	320	31.24	001	31.26	388	10
2° 00′	.0349	.0349	.9994	.0349	28.64	1.001	28.65	1.5359	88° 00′
10	378	378	993	378	26.43	001	26.45	330	50
20	407	407	992	407	24.54	001	24.56	301	40
30	.0436	.0436	.9990	.0437	22.90	1.001	22.93	1.5272	30
40	465	465	989	466	21.47	001	21.49	243	20
50	495	494	988	495	20.21	001	20.23	213	10
3° 00′	.0524	.0523	.9986	.0524	19.08	1.001	19.11	1.5184	87° 00′
10	553	552	985	553	18.07	002	18.10	155	50
20	582	581	983	582	17.17	002	17.20	126	40
30	.0611	.0610	.9981	.0612	16.35	1.002	16.38	1.5097	30
40	640	640	980	641	15.60	002	15.64	068	20
50	669	669	978	670	14.92	002	14.96	039	10
4° 00′	.0698	.0698	.9976	.0699	14.30	1.002	14.34	1.5010	86° 00′
10	727	727	974	729	13.73	003	13.76	981	50
20	756	756	971	758	13.20	003	13.23	952	40
30	.0785	.0785	.9969	.0787	12.71	1.003	12.75	1.4923	30
40	814	814	967	816	12.25	003	12.29	893	20
50	844	843	964	846	11.83	004	11.87	864	10
5° 00′	.0873	.0872	.9962	.0875	11.43	1.004	11.47	1.4835	85° 00′
10	902	901	959	904	11.06	004	11.10	806	50
20	931	929	957	934	10.71	004	10.76	777	40
30	.0960	.0958	.9954	.0963	10.39	1.005	10.43	1.4748	30
40	989	987	951	992	10.08	005	10.13	719	20
50	.1018	.1016	948	.1022	9.788	005	9.839	690	10
6° 00′	.1047	.1045	.9945	.1051	9.514	1.006	9.567	1.4661	84° 00′
10	076	074	942	080	9.255	006	9.309	632	50
20	105	103	939	110	9.010	006	9.065	603	40
30	.1134	.1132	.9936	.1139	8.777	1.006	8.834	1.4573	30
40	164	161	932	169	8.556	007	8.614	544	20
50	193	190	929	198	8.345	007	8.405	515	10
7° 00′	.1222	.1219	.9925	.1228	8.144	1.008	8.206	1.4486	83° 00′
10	251	248	922	257	7.953	008	8.016	457	50
20	280	276	918	287	7.770	008	7.834	428	40
30	.1309	.1305	.9914	.1317	7.596	1.009	7.661	1.4399	30
40	338	334	911	346	7.429	009	7.496	370	20
50	367	363	907	376	7.269	009	7.337	341	10
8° 00′	.1396	.1392	.9903	.1405	7.115	1.010	7.185	1.4312	82° 00′
10	425	421	899	435	6.968	010	7.040	283	50
20	454	449	894	465	6.827	011	6.900	254	40
30	.1484	.1478	.9890	.1495	6.691	1.011	6.765	1.4224	30
40	513	507	886	524	6.561	012	6.636	195	20
50	542	536	881	554	6.435	012	6.512	166	10
9° 00′	.1571	.1564	.9877	.1584	6.314	1.012	6.392	1.4137	81°00′
		Cos	Sin	Cot	Tan	Csc	Sec	Radians	Degrees

Source: *R. Placek*, Technical Mathematics with Calculus. *Englewood Cliffs, N.J.: Prentice-Hall, 1968.*

Natural Trigonometric Functions (*Continued*)

Degrees	Radians	Sin	Cos	Tan	Cot	Sec	Csc		
9° 00'	.1571	.1564	.9877	.1584	6.314	1.012	6.392	1.4137	81° 00'
10	600	593	872	614	197	013	277	108	50
20	629	622	868	644	084	013	166	079	40
30	.1658	.1650	.9863	.1673	5.976	1.014	6.059	1.4050	30
40	687	679	858	703	871	014	5.955	1.4021	20
50	716	708	853	733	769	015	855	992	10
10° 00'	.1745	.1736	.9848	.1763	5.671	1.015	5.759	1.3963	80° 00'
10	774	765	843	793	576	016	665	934	50
20	804	794	838	823	485	016	575	904	40
30	.1833	.1822	.9833	.1853	5.396	1.017	5.487	1.3875	30
40	862	851	827	883	309	018	403	846	20
50	891	880	822	914	226	018	320	817	10
11° 00'	.1920	.1908	.9816	.1944	5.145	1.019	5.241	1.3788	79° 00'
10	949	937	811	974	066	019	164	759	50
20	978	965	805	.2004	4.989	020	089	730	40
30	.2007	.1994	.9799	.2035	4.915	1.020	5.016	1.3701	30
40	036	.2022	793	065	843	021	4.945	672	20
50	065	051	787	095	773	022	876	643	10
12° 00'	.2094	.2079	.9781	.2126	4.705	1.022	4.810	1.3614	78° 00'
10	123	108	775	156	638	023	745	584	50
20	153	136	769	186	574	024	682	555	40
30	.2182	.2164	.9763	.2217	4.511	1.024	4.620	1.3526	30
40	211	193	757	247	449	025	560	497	20
50	240	221	750	278	390	026	502	468	10
13° 00'	.2269	.2250	.9744	.2309	4.331	1.026	4.445	1.3439	77° 00'
10	298	278	737	339	275	027	390	410	50
20	327	306	730	370	219	028	336	381	40
30	.2356	.2334	.9724	.2401	4.165	1.028	4.284	1.3352	30
40	385	363	717	432	113	029	232	323	20
50	414	391	710	462	061	030	182	294	10
14° 00'	.2443	.2419	.9703	.2493	4.011	1.031	4.134	1.3265	76° 00'
10	473	447	696	524	3.962	031	086	235	50
20	502	476	689	555	914	032	039	206	40
30	.2531	.2504	.9681	.2586	3.867	1.033	3.994	1.3177	30
40	560	532	674	617	821	034	950	148	20
50	589	560	667	648	776	034	906	119	10
15° 00'	.2618	.2588	.9659	.2679	3.732	1.035	3.864	1.3090	75° 00'
10	647	616	652	711	689	036	822	061	50
20	676	644	644	742	647	037	782	032	40
30	.2705	.2672	.9636	.2773	3.606	1.038	3.742	1.3003	30
40	734	700	628	805	566	039	703	974	20
50	763	728	621	836	526	039	665	945	10
16° 00'	.2793	.2756	.9613	.2867	3.487	1.040	3.628	1.2915	74° 00'
10	822	784	605	899	450	041	592	886	50
20	851	812	596	931	412	042	556	857	40
30	.2880	.2840	.9588	.2962	3.376	1.043	3.521	1.2828	30
40	909	868	580	994	340	044	487	799	20
50	938	896	572	.3026	305	045	453	770	10
17° 00'	.2967	.2924	.9563	.3057	3.271	1.046	3.420	1.2741	73° 00'
10	996	952	555	089	237	047	388	712	50
20	.3025	979	546	121	204	048	356	683	40
30	.3054	.3007	.9537	.3153	3.172	1.049	3.326	1.2654	30
40	083	035	528	185	140	049	295	625	20
50	113	062	520	217	108	050	265	595	10
18° 00'	.3142	.3090	.9511	.3249	3.078	1.051	3.236	1.2566	72° 00'
		Cos	Sin	Cot	Tan	Csc	Sec	Radians	Degrees

Natural Trigonometric Functions (*Continued*)

Degrees	Radians	Sin	Cos	Tan	Cot	Sec	Csc		
18° 00′	.3142	.3090	.9511	.3249	3.078	1.051	3.236	1.2566	72° 00′
10	171	118	502	281	047	052	207	537	50
20	200	145	492	314	018	053	179	508	40
30	.3229	.3173	.9483	.3346	2.989	1.054	3.152	1.2479	30
40	258	201	474	378	960	056	124	450	20
50	287	228	465	411	932	057	098	421	10
19° 00′	.3316	.3256	.9455	.3443	2.904	1.058	3.072	1.2392	71° 00′
10	345	283	446	476	877	059	046	363	50
20	374	311	436	508	850	060	021	334	40
30	.3403	.3338	.9426	.3541	2.824	1.061	2.996	1.2305	30
40	432	365	417	574	798	062	971	275	20
50	462	393	407	607	773	063	947	246	10
20° 00′	.3491	.3420	.9397	.3640	2.747	1.064	2.924	1.2217	70° 00′
10	520	448	387	673	723	065	901	188	50
20	549	475	377	706	699	066	878	159	40
30	.3578	.3502	.9367	.3739	2.675	1.068	2.855	1.2130	30
40	607	529	356	772	651	069	833	101	20
50	636	557	346	805	628	070	812	072	10
21° 00′	.3665	.3584	.9336	.3839	2.605	1.071	2.790	1.2043	69° 00′
10	694	611	325	872	583	072	769	1.2014	50
20	723	638	315	906	560	074	749	985	40
30	.3752	.3665	.9304	.3939	2.539	1.075	2.729	1.1956	30
40	782	692	293	973	517	076	709	926	20
50	811	719	283	.4006	496	077	689	897	10
22° 00′	.3840	.3746	.9272	.4040	2.475	1.079	2.669	1.1868	68° 00′
10	869	773	261	074	455	080	650	839	50
20	898	800	250	108	434	081	632	810	40
30	.3927	.3827	.9239	.4142	2.414	1.082	2.613	1.1781	30
40	956	854	228	176	394	084	595	752	20
50	985	881	216	210	375	085	577	723	10
23° 00′	.4014	.3907	.9205	.4245	2.356	1.086	2.559	1.1694	67° 00′
10	043	934	194	279	337	088	542	665	50
20	072	961	182	314	318	089	525	636	40
30	.4102	.3987	.9171	.4348	2.300	1.090	2.508	1.1606	30
40	131	.4014	159	383	282	092	491	577	20
50	160	041	147	417	264	093	475	548	10
24° 00′	.4189	.4067	.9135	.4452	2.246	1.095	2.459	1.1519	66° 00′
10	218	094	124	487	229	096	443	490	50
20	247	120	112	522	211	097	427	461	40
30	.4276	.4147	.9100	.4557	2.194	1.099	2.411	1.1432	30
40	305	173	088	592	177	100	396	403	20
50	334	200	075	628	161	102	381	374	10
25° 00′	.4363	.4226	.9063	.4663	2.145	1.103	2.366	1.1345	65° 00′
10	392	253	051	699	128	105	352	316	50
20	422	279	038	734	112	106	337	286	40
30	.4451	.4305	.9026	.4770	2.097	1.108	2.323	1.1257	30
40	480	331	013	806	081	109	309	228	20
50	509	358	001	841	066	111	295	199	10
26° 00′	.4538	.4384	.8988	.4877	2.050	1.113	2.281	1.1170	64° 00′
10	567	410	975	913	035	114	268	141	50
20	596	436	962	950	020	116	254	112	40
30	.4625	.4462	.8949	.4986	2.006	1.117	2.241	1.1083	30
40	654	488	936	.5022	1.991	119	228	054	20
50	683	514	923	059	977	121	215	1.1025	10
27° 00′	.4712	.4540	.8910	.5095	1.963	1.122	2.203	1.0996	63° 00′
		Cos	Sin	Cot	Tan	Csc	Sec	Radians	Degrees

Natural Trigonometric Functions (*Continued*)

Degrees	Radians	Sin	Cos	Tan	Cot	Sec	Csc		
27° 00′	.4712	.4540	.8910	.5095	1.963	1.122	2.203	1.0996	63° 00′
10	741	566	897	132	949	124	190	966	50
20	771	592	884	169	935	126	178	937	40
30	.4800	.4617	.8870	.5206	1.921	1.127	2.166	1.0908	30
40	829	643	857	243	907	129	154	879	20
50	858	669	843	280	894	131	142	850	10
28° 00′	.4887	.4695	.8829	.5317	1.881	1.133	2.130	1.0821	62° 00′
10	916	720	816	354	868	134	118	792	50
20	945	746	802	392	855	136	107	763	40
30	.4974	.4772	.8788	.5430	1.842	1.138	2.096	1.0734	30
40	.5003	797	774	467	829	140	085	705	20
50	032	823	760	505	816	142	074	676	10
29° 00′	.5061	.4848	.8746	.5543	1.804	1.143	2.063	1.0647	61° 00′
10	091	874	732	581	792	145	052	617	50
20	120	899	718	619	780	147	041	588	40
30	.5149	.4924	.8704	.5658	1.767	1.149	2.031	1.0559	30
40	178	950	689	696	756	151	020	530	20
50	207	975	675	735	744	153	010	501	10
30° 00′	.5236	.5000	.8660	.5774	1.732	1.155	2.000	1.0472	60° 00′
10	265	025	646	812	720	157	1.990	443	50
20	294	050	631	851	709	159	980	414	40
30	.5323	.5075	.8616	.5890	1.698	1.161	1.970	1.0385	30
40	352	100	601	930	686	163	961	356	20
50	381	125	587	969	675	165	951	327	10
31° 00′	.5411	.5150	.8572	.6009	1.664	1.167	1.942	1.0297	59° 00′
10	440	175	557	048	653	169	932	268	50
20	469	200	542	088	643	171	923	239	40
30	.5498	.5225	.8526	.6128	1.632	1.173	1.914	1.0210	30
40	527	250	511	168	621	175	905	181	20
50	556	275	496	208	611	177	896	152	10
32° 00′	.5585	.5299	.8480	.6249	1.600	1.179	1.887	1.0123	58° 00′
10	614	324	465	289	590	181	878	094	50
20	643	348	450	330	580	184	870	065	40
30	.5672	.5373	.8434	.6371	1.570	1.186	1.861	1.0036	30
40	701	398	418	412	560	188	853	1.0007	20
50	730	422	403	453	550	190	844	977	10
33° 00′	.5760	.5446	.8387	.6494	1.540	1.192	1.836	.9948	57° 00′
10	789	471	371	536	530	195	828	919	50
20	818	495	355	577	520	197	820	890	40
30	.5847	.5519	.8339	.6619	1.511	1.199	1.812	.9861	30
40	876	544	323	661	501	202	804	832	20
50	905	568	307	703	1.492	204	796	803	10
34° 00′	.5934	.5592	.8290	.6745	1.483	1.206	1.788	.9774	56° 00′
10	963	616	274	787	473	209	781	745	50
20	992	640	258	830	464	211	773	716	40
30	.6021	.5664	.8241	.6873	1.455	1.213	1.766	.9687	30
40	050	688	225	916	446	216	758	657	20
50	080	712	208	959	437	218	751	628	10
35° 00′	.6109	.5736	.8192	.7002	1.428	1.221	1.743	.9599	55° 00′
10	138	760	175	046	419	223	736	570	50
20	167	783	158	089	411	226	729	541	40
30	.6196	.5807	.8141	.7133	1.402	1.228	1.722	.9512	30
40	225	831	124	177	393	231	715	483	20
50	254	854	107	221	385	233	708	454	10
36° 00′	.6283	.5878	.8090	.7265	1.376	1.236	1.701	.9425	54° 00′
		Cos	Sin	Cot	Tan	Csc	Sec	Radians	Degrees

Natural Trigonometric Functions (*Continued*)

Degrees	Radians	Sin	Cos	Tan	Cot	Sec	Csc		
36° 00′	.6283	.5878	.8090	.7265	1.376	1.236	1.701	.9425	54° 00′
10	312	901	073	310	368	239	695	396	50
20	341	925	056	355	360	241	688	367	40
30	.6370	.5948	.8039	.7400	1.351	1.244	1.681	.9338	30
40	400	972	021	445	343	247	675	308	20
50	429	995	004	490	335	249	668	279	10
37° 00′	.6458	.6018	.7986	.7536	1.327	1.252	1.662	.9250	53° 00′
10	487	041	969	581	319	255	655	221	50
20	516	065	951	627	311	258	649	192	40
30	.6545	.6088	.7934	.7673	1.303	1.260	1.643	.9163	30
40	574	111	916	720	295	263	636	134	20
50	603	134	898	766	288	266	630	105	10
38° 00′	.6632	.6157	.7880	.7813	1.280	1.269	1.624	.9076	52° 00′
10	661	180	862	860	272	272	618	047	50
20	690	202	844	907	265	275	612	.9018	40
30	.6720	.6225	.7826	.7954	1.257	1.278	1.606	.8988	30
40	749	248	808	.8002	250	281	601	959	20
50	778	271	790	050	242	284	595	930	10
39° 00′	.6807	.6293	.7771	.8098	1.235	1.287	1.589	.8901	51° 00′
10	836	316	753	146	228	290	583	872	50
20	865	338	735	195	220	293	578	843	40
30	.6894	.6361	.7716	.8243	1.213	1.296	1.572	.8814	30
40	923	383	698	292	206	299	567	785	20
50	952	406	679	342	199	302	561	756	10
40° 00′	.6981	.6428	.7660	.8391	1.192	1.305	1.556	.8727	50° 00′
10	.7010	450	642	441	185	309	550	698	50
20	039	472	623	491	178	312	545	668	40
30	7069	.6494	.7604	.8541	1.171	1.315	1.540	.8639	30
40	098	517	585	591	164	318	535	610	20
50	127	539	566	642	157	322	529	581	10
41° 00′	.7156	.6561	.7547	.8693	1.150	1.325	1.524	.8552	49° 00′
10	185	583	528	744	144	328	519	523	50
20	214	604	509	796	137	332	514	494	40
30	.7243	.6626	.7490	.8847	1.130	1.335	1.509	.8465	30
40	272	648	470	899	124	339	504	436	20
50	301	670	451	952	117	342	499	407	10
42° 00′	.7330	.6691	.7431	.9004	1.111	1.346	1.494	.8378	48° 00′
10	359	713	412	057	104	349	490	348	50
20	389	734	392	110	098	353	485	319	40
30	.7418	.6756	.7373	.9163	1.091	1.356	1.480	.8290	30
40	447	777	353	217	085	360	476	261	20
50	476	799	333	271	079	364	471	232	10
43° 00′	.7505	.6820	.7314	.9325	1.072	1.367	1.466	.8203	47° 00′
10	534	841	294	380	066	371	462	174	50
20	563	862	274	435	060	375	457	145	40
30	.7592	.6884	.7254	.9490	1.054	1.379	1.453	.8116	30
40	621	905	234	545	048	382	448	087	20
50	650	926	214	601	042	386	444	058	10
44° 00′	.7679	.6947	.7193	.9657	1.036	1.390	1.440	.8029	46° 00′
10	709	967	173	713	030	394	435	999	50
20	738	988	153	770	024	398	431	970	40
30	.7767	.7009	.7133	.9827	1.018	1.402	1.427	.7941	30
40	796	030	112	884	012	406	423	912	20
50	825	050	092	942	006	410	418	883	10
45° 00′	.7854	.7071	.7071	1.000	1.000	1.414	1.414	.7854	45° 00′
		Cos	Sin	Cot	Tan	Csc	Sec	Radians	Degrees

Punch Tonnage for Mild Steel

APPROXIMATE PRESSURES REQUIRED FOR PUNCHING ROUND HOLES IN MILD STEEL

$P = 3/1416 \times D \times T \times 25\ \text{ton/in}^2$

PRESSURE IN TONS

HOLE DIAMETER		1/8 .125	3/16 .1875	1/4 .250	3/8 .375	1/2 .500	5/8 .625	3/4 .750	7/8 .875	1 1.00	1¼ 1.25	1½ 1.50	1¾ 1.75	2 2.00	2½ 2.50	3 3.00	3½ 3.50	4 4.00	4½ 4.50
METAL GAUGE	THICK. INCHES																		
#28	.015	.1	.2	.3	.5	.6	.7	.9	1.0	1.2	1.5	1.8	2.1	2.4	2.9	3.5	4.1	4.7	5.3
#26	.018	.2	.3	.4	.5	.7	.9	1.1	1.2	1.4	1.8	2.1	2.5	2.8	3.5	4.2	4.9	5.7	6.4
#24	.024	.2	.4	.5	.7	.9	1.2	1.4	1.7	1.9	2.4	2.8	3.3	3.8	4.7	5.7	6.6	7.5	8.5
#22	.030	.3	.4	.6	.9	1.2	1.5	1.8	2.1	2.4	2.9	3.5	4.1	4.7	5.9	7.1	8.2	9.4	10
#20	.036	.4	.5	.7	1.1	1.4	1.8	2.1	2.5	2.8	3.5	4.2	4.9	5.7	7.1	8.5	9.9	11.3	13
#18	.048	.5	.7	.9	1.4	1.9	2.4	2.8	3.3	3.8	4.7	5.7	6.6	7.5	9.4	11.3	13.2	15.1	17
#16	.060	.6	.9	1.2	1.8	2.4	2.9	3.5	4.1	4.7	5.9	7.1	8.2	9.4	11.8	14.1	16.5	18.8	21
#14	.075	.7	1.1	1.5	2.2	2.9	3.7	4.4	5.2	5.9	7.4	8.8	10.3	11.8	14.7	17.7	20.6	23.6	27
#12	.105	1.0	1.5	2.1	3.1	4.1	5.2	6.2	7.2	8.2	10.3	12.4	14.4	16.5	20.6	24.7	28.9	32.9	37
#11	.120	1.2	1.8	2.4	3.5	4.7	5.9	7.1	8.2	9.4	11.8	14.1	16.5	18.8	23.6	28.3	33.0	37.7	42
#10	.135	1.3	2.0	2.7	4.0	5.3	6.6	8.0	9.3	10.6	13.3	15.9	18.6	21.2	26.5	31.8	37.1	42.4	48
5/32	.157	-	2.3	3.1	4.6	6.2	7.7	9.2	10.8	12.3	15.4	18.5	21.6	24.7	30.8	37.0	43.2	49.3	56
3/16	.188	-	2.8	3.7	5.5	7.4	9.2	11.1	12.9	14.8	18.5	22.1	25.8	29.5	36.9	44.3	51.7	59.1	66
1/4	.250	-	-	4.9	7.4	9.8	12.3	14.7	17.2	19.6	24.5	29.5	34.4	39.3	49.1	58.9	68.7	78.5	88
5/16	.313	-	-	-	9.2	12.3	15.4	18.4	21.5	24.6	30.7	36.9	43.0	49.2	61.5	73.8	86.0	98.3	111
3/8	.375	-	-	-	11.0	14.7	18.4	22.1	25.8	29.5	36.8	44.2	51.5	58.9	73.6	88.4	103.1	117.8	133
1/2	.500	-	-	-	-	19.6	24.5	29.5	35.8	39.3	49.1	58.9	68.7	78.5	98.2	117.8	137.4	157.1	177

25 ton/in² = 50,000 PSI = 35.16 kg/mm² (973)

Courtesy of U.S. Amada, Ltd.

Punch Tonnage for Mild Steel (*Continued*)

APPROXIMATE PRESSURES REQUIRED FOR PUNCHING SQUARE HOLE IN MILD STEEL

$P = 4 \times A \times T \times 25$ (ton/in²)

PRESSURE IN TONS

"A" DIM. → METAL GAUGE	THICK. INCHES	1/4 .25	1/2 .50	3/4 .75	1 1.00	1¼ 1.25	1½ 1.50	1¾ 1.75	2 2.00	2¼ 2.25	2½ 2.50	2¾ 2.75	3 3.00	3¼ 3.25	3½ 3.50	3¾ 3.75	4 4.000	4¼ 4.250	4½ 4.500
#28	.015	.4	.8	1.1	1.5	1.9	2.3	2.6	3.0	3.4	3.8	4.1	4.5	4.9	5.3	5.6	6.0	6.4	6.8
#26	.018	.5	.9	1.4	1.8	2.3	2.7	3.2	3.6	4.1	4.5	5.0	5.4	5.9	6.3	6.8	7.2	7.7	8.1
#24	.024	.6	1.2	1.8	2.4	3.0	3.6	4.2	4.8	5.4	6.0	6.6	7.2	7.8	8.4	9.0	9.6	10.2	10.8
#22	.030	.8	1.5	2.3	3.0	3.8	4.5	5.3	6.0	6.8	7.5	8.3	9.0	9.8	10.5	11.3	12.0	12.8	13.5
#20	.036	.9	1.8	2.7	3.6	4.5	5.4	6.3	7.2	8.1	9.0	9.9	10.8	11.7	12.6	13.5	14.4	15.3	16.2
#18	.048	1.2	2.4	3.6	4.8	6.0	7.2	8.4	9.6	10.8	12.0	13.2	14.4	15.6	16.8	18.0	19.2	20.4	21.6
#16	.060	1.5	3.0	4.5	6.0	7.5	9.0	10.5	12.0	13.5	15.0	16.5	18.0	19.5	21.0	22.5	24.0	25.5	27.0
#14	.075	1.9	3.8	5.6	7.5	9.4	11.3	13.1	15.0	16.9	18.8	20.6	22.5	24.4	26.3	28.1	30.0	31.9	33.8
#12	.105	2.6	5.3	7.9	10.5	13.1	15.8	18.4	21.0	23.6	26.3	28.9	31.5	34.1	36.8	39.4	42.0	44.6	47.3
#11	.120	3.0	6.0	9.0	12.0	15.0	18.0	21.0	24.0	27.0	30.0	33.0	36.0	39.0	42.0	45.0	48.0	51.0	54.0
#10	.135	3.4	6.8	10.1	13.5	16.9	20.3	23.6	27.0	30.4	33.8	37.1	40.5	43.9	47.3	50.6	54.0	57.4	60.8
5/32	.157	3.9	7.8	11.7	15.6	19.5	23.4	27.3	31.3	35.2	39.1	43.0	46.9	50.8	54.7	58.6	62.5	66.4	70.3
3/16	.188	4.7	9.4	14.1	18.8	23.4	28.1	32.8	37.5	42.2	46.9	51.6	56.3	60.9	65.6	70.3	75.0	79.7	84.4
1/4	.250	6.3	13	18.8	25.0	31.3	37.5	43.8	50.0	56.3	62.5	68.8	75.0	81.3	87.5	93.8	100.0	106.3	112.5
5/16	.313	-	16	23.4	31.3	39.1	46.9	54.7	62.5	70.3	78.1	85.9	93.8	102	109	117	125.0	132.8	140.6
3/8	.375	-	19	28.1	37.5	46.9	56.3	65.6	75.0	84.4	93.8	103	113	122	131	141	150.0	159.4	168.8
7/16	.438	-	22	32.8	43.8	54.7	65.6	76.6	87.5	98.4	109	120	131	142	153	164	175.0	185.9	196.9
1/2	.500	-	25	37.5	50.0	62.5	75.0	87.5	100	113	125	138	150	163	175	188	200.0	212.5	225.0

25 ton/in² = 35.16 kg/mm²

Courtesy of U.S. Amada, Ltd.

335

Air Bending Force Chart

If the material thickness and inside bending radius are known, the following can be obtained from the chart below:

(1) Pressure required for bending the material for 1 foot.
(2) Opening of the die to be used.
(3) Minimum bendable flange length.

- **t**   Material thickness (tensile strength: 56892-71115 lbs/in²)
- **F**   Pressure per 1 foot
- **Ir**   Inside bending radius
- **b**   Minimum flange length
- **v**   Die opening

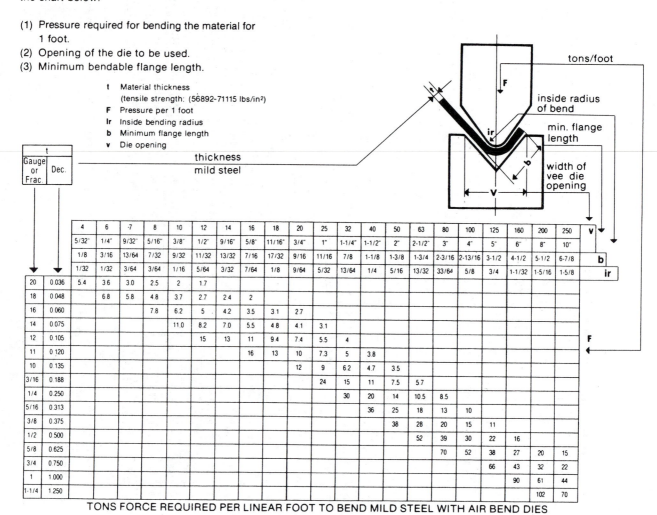

Gauge or Frac.	Dec.	4	6	7	8	10	12	14	16	18	20	25	32	40	50	63	80	100	125	160	200	250	
	v	5/32"	1/4"	9/32"	5/16"	3/8"	1/2"	9/16"	5/8"	11/16"	3/4"	1"	1-1/4"	1-1/2"	2"	2-1/2"	3"	4"	5"	6"	8"	10"	v
		1/8	3/16	13/64	7/32	9/32	11/32	13/32	7/16	17/32	9/16	11/16	7/8	1-1/8	1-3/8	1-3/4	2-3/16	2-13/16	3-1/2	4-1/2	5-1/2	6-7/8	b
		1/32	1/32	3/64	3/64	1/16	5/64	3/32	7/64	1/8	9/64	5/32	13/64	1/4	5/16	13/32	33/64	5/8	3/4	1-1/32	1-5/16	1-5/8	ir
20	0.036	5.4	3.6	3.0	2.5	2	1.7																
18	0.048		6.8	5.8	4.8	3.7	2.7	2.4	2														
16	0.060				7.8	6.2	5	4.2	3.5	3.1	2.7												
14	0.075					11.0	8.2	7.0	5.5	4.8	4.1	3.1											
12	0.105						15	13	11	9.4	7.4	5.5	4										F
11	0.120								16	13	10	7.3	5	3.8									
10	0.135										12	9	6.2	4.7	3.5								
3/16	0.188										24	15	11	7.5	5.7								
1/4	0.250												30	20	14	10.5	8.5						
5/16	0.313													36	25	18	13	10					
3/8	0.375														38	28	20	15	11				
1/2	0.500															52	39	30	22	16			
5/8	0.625																70	52	38	27	20	15	
3/4	0.750																	66	43	32	22		
1	1.000																			90	61	44	
1-1/4	1.250																				102	70	

TONS FORCE REQUIRED PER LINEAR FOOT TO BEND MILD STEEL WITH AIR BEND DIES

Courtesy of U.S. Amada, Ltd.

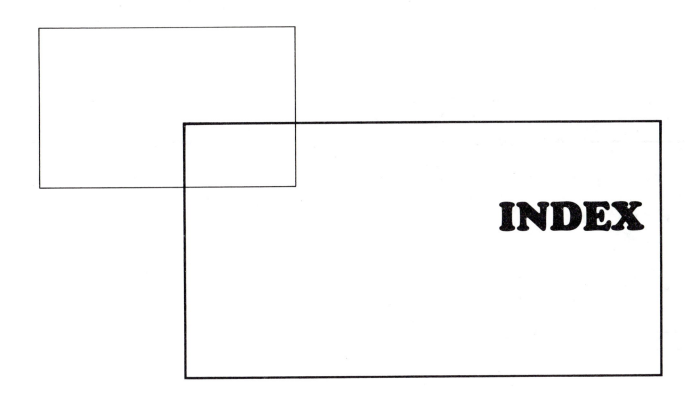

INDEX